THE INVESTOR'S GUIDE TO HEDGE FUNDS

THE INVESTOR'S GUIDE TO HEDGE FUNDS

SAM KIRSCHNER

ELDON MAYER

LEE KESSLER

WILEY

John Wiley & Sons, Inc.

Copyright © 2006 by Sam Kirschner, Eldon Mayer, Lee Kessler. All rights reserved.

Published by John Wiley & Sons, Inc., Hoboken, New Jersey.
Published simultaneously in Canada.

No part of this publication may be reproduced, stored in a retrieval system, or transmitted in any form or by any means, electronic, mechanical, photocopying, recording, scanning, or otherwise, except as permitted under Section 107 or 108 of the 1976 United States Copyright Act, without either the prior written permission of the Publisher, or authorization through payment of the appropriate per-copy fee to the Copyright Clearance Center, Inc., 222 Rosewood Drive, Danvers, MA 01923, (978) 750-8400, fax (978) 646-8600, or on the Web at www.copyright.com. Requests to the Publisher for permission should be addressed to the Permissions Department, John Wiley & Sons, Inc., 111 River Street, Hoboken, NJ 07030, (201) 748-6011, fax (201) 748-6008, or online at http://www.wiley.com/go/permissions.

Limit of Liability/Disclaimer of Warranty: While the publisher and author have used their best efforts in preparing this book, they make no representations or warranties with respect to the accuracy or completeness of the contents of this book and specifically disclaim any implied warranties of merchantability or fitness for a particular purpose. No warranty may be created or extended by sales representatives or written sales materials. The advice and strategies contained herein may not be suitable for your situation. You should consult with a professional where appropriate. Neither the publisher nor author shall be liable for any loss of profit or any other commercial damages, including but not limited to special, incidental, consequential, or other damages.

For general information on our other products and services or for technical support, please contact our Customer Care Department within the United States at (800) 762-2974, outside the United States at (317) 572-3993 or fax (317) 572-4002.

Wiley also publishes its books in a variety of electronic formats. Some content that appears in print may not be available in electronic books. For more information about Wiley products, visit our Web site at www.wiley.com.

Library of Congress Cataloging-in-Publication Data:

Kirschner, Sam, 1948–
    The investor's guide to hedge funds / Sam Kirschner, Eldon Mayer, Lee Kessler.
      p.   cm.
    Includes bibliographical references and index.
    ISBN-13: 978-0-471-71599-3 (cloth)
    ISBN-10: 0-471-71599-9
    1. Hedge funds. 2. Investments. I. Mayer, Eldon, 1935– II. Kessler, Lee, 1956– III. Title.
    HG4530.K57 2006
    332.64'524—dc22

                         2006003341

Printed in the United States of America.

10 9 8 7 6 5 4 3 2 1

To the giants

A. W. Jones, Julian Robertson,
George Soros, and Michael Steinhardt

upon whose shoulders we stand

CONTENTS

FOREWORD

IT TAKES NO GREAT PREDICTIVE GENIUS TO FORECAST THAT HEDGE FUNDS and funds of hedge funds will outperform the average mutual fund and stock portfolio during and after the next recession, whenever it occurs. That is what they have done for the past two recessions. Simply put, hedge funds outperform equities at such times because they do not suffer from extreme bear market volatility. As *The Investor's Guide to Hedge Funds* clearly shows, the majority of hedge fund strategies are designed to withstand market corrections. Their absolute return mandate means that their benchmark is zero. Investors have learned that there is small comfort in beating an equities index by 2 percent if that index is down 20 percent.

In the opening chapter of this book, you'll read that there are more than 8,000 funds globally managing well over $1 trillion and that assets under management are growing at double-digit rates. Why? *The most significant reason for this spectacular growth is investment returns.* If institutional and high-net-worth investors could get the same returns by simply investing in stocks, bonds, or mutual funds, would they instead choose hedge funds, which have higher fees, are harder to find and evaluate, and need more scrutiny? The answer is they would not. The demonstrably observable higher risk-adjusted returns make the effort worthwhile for the sophisticated investor.

Each chapter of this well-researched book details how these superior risk-adjusted returns can be obtained. Through careful analysis and by providing the data to support their views, the authors show which strategies do better in bear markets (funds of funds, market neutral) and those that prosper in bull markets (equity long/short, event driven). For each approach, the authors also present via candid interviews that disclose the thinking and insights of some of the most talented newer hedge fund managers. In short, they reveal the strengths and weaknesses of each strategy so that readers can select funds that are appropriate for their objectives and risk profiles.

Recent studies cited in this book and elsewhere document the clear growth in hedge fund and alternative investments among the most sophisticated market participants. Indeed, many ultralarge endowment and family office investment portfolios now have a larger exposure to alternative investments than they do to equities or bonds! The reason is simple and the authors demonstrate it clearly: Adding hedge funds to a portfolio of traditional assets lowers the resulting portfolio's volatility and increases its Sharpe ratio. Savvy investors should therefore try to position their portfolios in exactly the same way as their wealthier counterparts.

Critics typically claim that hedge funds are illiquid, highly leveraged, and subject to a variety of uncertain market and specific risks including fraud. I would readily agree with all those statements. But those statements also describe the residential real estate market. Additionally, homes are subject to termites, tornadoes, hurricanes, and floods. Those of us who live in Texas know that home values can go down as well as up. Yet no one would propose that the average U.S. citizen is not capable or smart enough to ascertain the risks of home ownership.

Hedge funds pose different types of risks and rewards than homes, mutual funds, and stocks. Thus investors wanting to invest in hedge funds should plan to spend ample time studying this book. *The Investor's Guide to Hedge Funds* shows exactly how top professionals assess potential risks, conduct due diligence, and monitor managers after they invest. In sum, the guide provides the tools you need to successfully add these exciting and profitable investment vehicles to your portfolio.

—John Mauldin

ACKNOWLEDGMENTS

THE AUTHORS THANK EACH OF OUR INTERVIEWEES, WHO WERE GENEROUS with their time and contributed invaluable insights to *The Investor's Guide to Hedge Funds*. We are grateful to Steve Winters and Rich Yakomin for their assistance with the Convertible Arbitrage chapter, as well as Scott Wittman and Armando Lacayo of Munder Capital Management for their helpful comments on equity market neutral. We express our gratitude to David Pugh and Stacey Farkas, our editors at John Wiley & Sons, for their confidence and patience throughout the process. We also thank our friend John Mauldin for writing the Foreword.

We are immensely grateful to our Mayer and Hoffman partners, Ron Panzier and Matthew Hoffman. Ron Panzier, CFA, FRM, is the firm's Chief Risk Officer. He co-authored the chapter on due diligence and turned it into an especially clear, useful, and, we hope, powerful tool for the reader. In addition, Ron's help with the research and data analysis, coupled with his smart and careful editing of the entire book, made the finished project far better than the original draft! Our partner and Chief Investment Officer, Matthew Hoffman, sourced talented managers to interview and encouraged them to participate in this project. Matt also provided invaluable feedback every step of the way. Our colleague Alex Boguslavsky gave us great insights on Direct Financing funds. We are also thankful for the support and encouragement we received from our talented colleagues Ken Ostrowski, Caren Dina, Sunny Tam, and May Wang; and for David Paulsson's help on the graphs; Chris Hansen's research; Josephine Quartano's being there and helping no matter what; and Sam Panzier's creative designs.

In addition, we want to thank our partner, Tacie Fox, for her support and belief in us and the project and her thoughtful suggestions all the way through. Jack Rigney, our attorney at Seward and Kissel, has been immensely helpful. Meredith Jones of PerTrac provided invaluable and timely research and data for the project. We are grateful to

Enrique Chang, James Patterson, and Bill and Sandy Fox for all of their encouragement and support.

Our co-author, Lee Kessler, spent many hours editing the transcribed interviews and added humor and color to the manuscript. Lee, known to his friends as Sam, thanks Tom Kerns, his first hedge fund teacher, and sends love to Sally, Alec, and Nell.

Dr. Sam Kirschner would like to acknowledge his wife, the author Dr. Diana Kirschner, for always being there with practical suggestions, editing help, and, most importantly, the steadfastness, love, and TLC that nourish him and make everything possible. He is grateful to his children, Concetta and Jason, and his sister, Belle Grubert, for their love and support. He would also like to thank Stan Richelson and Dr. Hildy Richelson, Vince DiBianca, Tom Daquanni, Tony Freedley, Don Arnoudse, Dr. Peter H. Blake, Jim Selman, Phil Wachs, Myron Bari, John Schaad, and Jenny Banner for their ongoing encouragement.

Eldon Mayer would like to thank first and foremost his loving wife, Betts, for her encouragement and support during the many midnight hours of the writing and editing process. He is grateful to his daughter, Sarah, and grandson, Ty, who would rather have cavorted on the beach with Grampa at a time when the final push kept him at his desk. He also thanks his daughter, Carey; son, Eldon III; and their children for their understanding and patience. Importantly, he pays respect to his late colleagues, John M. Hartwell, William G. Campbell, and Robert E. Mitchell, who collectively helped Eldon learn the tricks of the hedge fund trade early on. Full credit also goes to Tony Boeckh, Dennis P. Lynch, Gerry Manolovici, Mike Winton, and the late David L. Dodd for playing seminal roles in the development of his investment philosophy.

Sam Kirschner, Ph.D.
Eldon C. Mayer Jr.

March 2006
New York City

CHAPTER 1

The Case for Hedge Funds

OPEN A NEWSPAPER OR A FINANCIAL JOURNAL. IT'S TOUGH TO FIND A SINGLE day when some outlet of the financial press hasn't featured an article on hedge funds. They're everywhere—articles expressing opinions that run the whole spectrum from good to bad to ugly. Why all the attention? Because the hedge fund and funds of hedge funds (FOFs) sectors are experiencing explosive asset growth, maintaining an increase of more than 20 percent per annum over the past 15 years according to the Hedge Fund Research Institute.[1] In the past three years alone, assets under management (AUM) have doubled from an estimated $600 billion to between $1.14 trillion and $1.35 trillion.[2] As 2005 draws to a close, there are some 8,100 individual funds and more than 2,000 FOFs that report to at least one of the 12 major global databases.[3]

Figure 1.1 presents the number of single manager hedge funds and FOFs adjusted for clone funds, offshore/onshore versions, and currency share classes of a single fund. Figure 1.1 also includes data on the new funds (adjusted for clones and so on) that emerged in 2003, 2004, and 2005.[4]

Despite being the most controversial asset category (more on that later in the chapter) hedge funds have become a very important part of the asset management industry, growing much more rapidly than mutual funds or conventional unhedged separately managed accounts. They have also been responsible for innovating new investment strategies, redefining traditional asset allocation models, and developing more effective risk management techniques.

Perhaps most importantly, the robust hedge fund business model

FIGURE 1.1

The Global Hedge Fund Universe of 2006

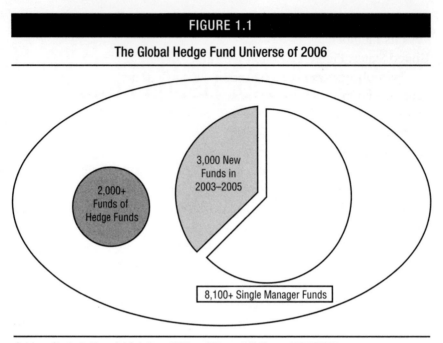

Sources: Strategic Financial Solutions, HFRI, and Mayer & Hoffman, 12/31/2005.

has been responsible for the brain drain away from academia, conventional asset management firms, mutual funds, investment banks, and even the legal and accounting professions. Any leading executive recruiter will bear witness to this phenomenon. What is luring them away? Simply, the compensation potential that exists as large management and incentive fees are divided among a few participants. This migration of talent has perhaps been more responsible than anything else for the sometimes stunning performance of successful hedge funds.

THE INVESTOR COMMUNITY

The early adopters of hedge funds and FOFs were high net worth investors and family offices. More than half the money invested came from "the smart money" as these investors are called even though their total assets lagged well behind those of institutions. As an example of this investor base, The Institute for Private Investors (IPI) annually surveys its members, who represent 300 of the wealthiest families in the United States. Figure 1.2 shows the results of their 2005 survey.[5]

Two observations can be made. First, the families have a 40 percent allocation to alternative investments, above the level given to equities. These investments are so named because they offer an alternative to the traditional asset classes of stocks and bonds and include hedge funds, FOFs, private equity, venture capital, and real estate. Second, despite general perceptions, wealthy families are not primarily invested in fixed-income securities. Allocations to hedge funds and FOFs were 23 percent, compared with just 17 percent in fixed-income securities. This finding suggests that sophisticated investors are viewing hedge funds as attractive alternatives to today's relatively low-yielding fixed-income securities. (See Figure 1.2.)

Most wealthy investors have hedge fund allocations that lag far behind the levels shown in Figure 1.2 or those recommended by asset allocation experts, many of whom urge investors to place 20–30 percent of their portfolios in alternative investments. We predict that wealthy

FIGURE 1.2

Asset Allocations of IPI Families in 2005

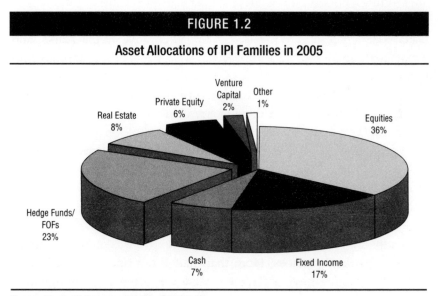

Source: Family Performance Tracking® 2005, IPI.

investors will likely continue to raise their investments in hedge funds in the years ahead.

While only a decade ago most hedge fund assets came via wealthy investors, that trend has changed. For example, university endowments have in recent years approximately doubled their allocations to hedge funds, bringing them to almost 17 percent of total assets according to the 2005 National Association of College and University Business Officers (NACUBO) Endowment Study.[6]

Corporate and public pension funds, however, have begun a more gradual move into hedge funds. The typical pattern seems to be an initial gingerly testing of the waters, followed annually by larger allocations. The California Public Employees Retirement System (CalPERS), the largest public pension fund in the country, announced in 2004 its intention to double its hedge fund allocation by funding emerging funds and FOFs with a $3 billion commitment.[7] Yet, overall pension fund allocations that currently stand at $90 billion are only about 1.6 percent of their total assets.[8]

Still, there were some early adopter plans that realized the return-generating and risk-reducing potential of hedge funds. Two examples are worth mentioning here. More than 15 years ago the pension managers at Weyerhaeuser Corporation made the controversial but in retrospect brilliant decision to invest 100 percent of Weyerhaeuser's pension assets in alternatives, and currently still have a 39 percent allocation to hedge funds.[9]

An even more impressive example of modern portfolio construction and the power of allocating to alternatives is the performance of Yale's $15 billion endowment. Led for the past 20 years by the brilliant David Swensen, Yale has outperformed all other U.S. endowments since 1985, averaging 16.1 percent per annum and 17.3 percent over the past 10 years. How, you wonder? Swensen has overweighted his portfolio with alternative investments, in particular relatively small and undiscovered hedge funds. As of the fiscal year ended June 30, 2005, Swensen had 70 percent of total assets in alternatives, with the largest allocation to any asset class being 25 percent to hedge funds.[10] Success stories such as these have played a role in the accelerating movement of institutional assets into hedge funds. Of course the large capital losses incurred in the stock market from 2000–2002 also stimulated many institutions to see if there was a more decline-resistant approach to constructing their portfolios.

More recently, while individual and wealthy family allocations have continued to grow, institutional asset flows into hedge funds have accelerated rapidly, becoming the dominant source of new capital. FOFs by far have been the biggest beneficiaries of these inflows. Depending on who's counting, AUM for FOFs range from $651 billion[11] to about $700 billion.[12] The reason given for FOF popularity is that most institutions do not have the in-house hedge fund research staff necessary to source, select, perform single manager due diligence, and ultimately monitor the funds postselection. As a result they have retained intermediaries such as consultants to assist them in the hiring of FOF managers and, less frequently, to help them invest directly. In this way, institutional investors and their advisers have come to rely upon FOFs as extensions of their own investment teams for their professional manager selection and due diligence capabilities.

Since 2002 the development of investable indices like the Morgan Stanley Capital International (MSCI) and S&P investable indices has also served to encourage institutional hedge fund investment. These products, which we describe in Chapter 12, offer capacity, better transparency, risk management, and liquidity features that appeal to many institutions.

Ironically, institutional investors may be exerting a significant conservative influence on hedge funds in two ways. First, some hedge funds have become so large that their size may be affecting their trading mobility and thus their performance. As of this writing in late 2005, there are more than 250 hedge funds globally with AUM exceeding $1 billion.[13]

Second, there may be a lessening of the risks hedge funds and FOFs are willing to take. In order to gather assets from these new and generally more conservative investors, many funds are deliberately lowering volatility. To a degree, then, institutions may be killing, or at least reducing the fecundity of, the geese that have been laying the golden eggs.

To be fair, institutional pressure is undoubtedly precipitating improvements in the risk controls and risk management procedures of many funds in which they invest. Furthermore, it is also increasing the transparency of hedge funds and removing their long-held shroud of secrecy. In addition, the Securities and Exchange Commission (SEC)'s registration requirements, which will have taken effect on February 1, 2006, will aid in improving the legitimacy of the industry. As a result of these influences, the hedge fund community is well along the path to gaining a seat at the table long reserved for its more traditional cousins.

Yet, despite the institutionalization of hedge funds and the torrent of money that has been flooding into the industry annually, hedge funds remain a controversial asset class. This chapter examines three major aspects of this ongoing and very public controversy: (1) hedge fund and FOF performance relative to other asset classes; (2) the benefits of diversification; and (3) the risks of investing in hedge funds, including a recap of the last few fund blow-ups. By the end of this chapter the reader should have a deeper understanding of the cases for and against hedge funds.

HEDGE FUND PERFORMANCE: REALITY OR MYTH?

Hedge Fund Performance

Far from being a Wall Street fad, hedge fund growth has been strictly performance driven. A departure from traditional equity and bond investments that generally require favorable markets to provide good returns, hedge funds offer a legitimate alternative. In fact, over long periods of time the case for investing in hedge funds is very compelling. Figure 1.3 shows the cumulative performance of the HFRI Fund-Weighted Composite Index, an equally weighted benchmark of all funds in the HFR database, versus equity and bond benchmarks over the period 1994–2005.[14] As the figure clearly shows, the HFRI has widely outperformed domestic and global equities as well as bonds over the 12-year period.

We further analyzed hedge fund performance from 1994–2005 in

FIGURE 1.3

Cumulative Performance of HFRI Fund-Weighted Composite Index versus Benchmarks

Growth of $1,000 USD, 1/1/1994–12/31/2005

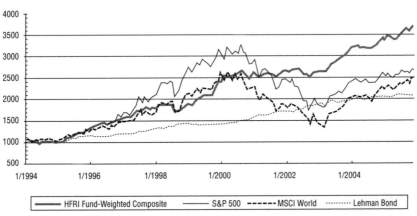

Sources: Mayer & Hoffman Capital Advisors, HFRI, and PerTrac.

order to see how various strategies held up over the full market cycle that this period of time represents. Table 1.1, which summarizes the results of our study, shows the annualized returns, standard deviation, Sharpe ratio, and correlations for most of the hedge fund strategies, the HFRI Fund-Weighted Composite Index, the S&P 500, the Lehman Gov/Credit Bond Index, and the MSCI The World Index for 1994–2005.[15] Before we review the results of this important table let's look at two key statistical terms. *Standard deviation* is the widely used measure for volatility of returns and simply measures the degree of dispersion of any data from the mean value. In measuring performance, the greater the standard deviation, the wider the dispersion from the mean and hence the more volatile or risky a fund is said to be.

TABLE 1.1

Hedge Fund Strategies, Performance, and Correlations to Stocks and Bonds, 1994–2005

Performance: Hedge Fund Strategies and Traditional Assets (1/1/1994–12/31/2005)

	Annual Return	Standard Deviation	Sharpe Ratio	Correlation with S&P 500	Correlation with Lehman Gov-Credit
HFRI Convertible Arbitrage Index	9.07%	3.70%	1.39	0.28	0.16
HFRI Distressed Securities Index	12.17%	5.40%	1.53	0.47	0.01
HFRI Equity Hedge Index	14.48%	8.97%	1.18	0.69	−0.01
HFRI Equity Market Neutral Index	7.99%	3.10%	1.31	0.15	0.19
HFRI Event-Driven Index	13.35%	6.42%	1.47	0.67	0.01
HFRI Fixed Income: Arbitrage Index	5.96%	3.86%	0.53	−0.12	−0.08
HFRI Fund-Weighted Composite Index	11.56%	7.05%	1.08	0.72	0.00
HFRI Fund of Funds Composite Index	7.46%	5.82%	0.61	0.53	0.06
HFRI Macro Index	10.14%	7.24%	0.86	0.39	0.32
HFRI Short Selling Index	0.99%	21.42%	−0.14	−0.69	0.05
CISDM CTA Asset-Weighted Index	8.01%	8.54%	0.48	−0.08	0.34
Lehman Government-Credit Bond Index	6.35%	4.50%	0.54	0.01	1.00
MSCI The World Index—Net	7.95%	13.83%	0.29	0.94	−0.05
S&P 500 Price Index	8.55%	14.73%	0.31	1.00	0.01

Sources: Mayer & Hoffman, HFRI, PerTrac, and CISDM.

The *Sharpe ratio* is a widely used measure of risk-adjusted return that was developed by the Nobel Prize winner Dr. William Sharpe. The Sharpe ratio is calculated by[16]

$$S(x) = (r_x - R_f)/\sigma(x)$$

where:

$S(x)$ = the Sharpe ratio of fund x

r_x = the return of fund x

R_f = the risk-free rate

σ = the standard deviation of fund x

This calculation measures both the upside and downside volatility of fund x and allows us to see if we are being rewarded for taking risks with an asset over and above a risk-free instrument like T-bills. The higher the Sharpe of a given asset, the higher we can say is its risk-adjusted return.

Now let's look closely at Table 1.1. On an absolute return basis, the Fund-Weighted Composite Index outperformed stocks and bonds by a substantial amount, returning 11.56 percent per year versus 8.55 percent for the S&P, 7.95 percent for the MSCI World, and 6.35 percent for bonds. The same Index also had a standard deviation of about 7 percent, half that of stocks but above that of bonds. The risk-free rate used for this period was calculated to be 3.93 percent.

As a result, the Sharpe ratio showed a distinct and highly significant advantage for hedge funds: 1.08 for hedge funds, which was three times higher than that for stocks and twice as high as the Sharpe for bonds. In terms of the *efficient frontier*,[17] that place on a chart that shows the portfolio or asset with the highest relative reward and the lowest relative risk, it is clear from the study that hedge funds occupy the cherished spot in the northwest quadrant. See the quantitative analysis section in Chapter 13 for additional discussion regarding other statistical tools used to measure hedge fund performance.

Table 1.1 also presents the correlations between the various strategies and the bond and equity indices. Note that no hedge fund strategy had a significant correlation with bonds, while several hedge fund strategies showed significant correlations with equity indices and others did not. That said, hedge funds overall do tend to perform better in positive equity environments, largely because the largest categories of hedge funds, Equity Long/Short and Event Driven, are more correlated with equity markets. Moreover, it is widely acknowledged that it is much easier over time to make money owning stocks than shorting them. One need only look at the past 12 years to see this phenomenon at work. Short-biased hedge funds have been the worst performing strategy averaging only 1 percent per annum.

So how have hedge funds performed more recently in comparison with equities? While the S&P declined 38 percent from its 2000 peak to its trough in 2002, hedge funds preserved capital. As Figure 1.4 shows, over the trailing five-year period ending 12/31/05, the S&P 500 is down slightly and the MSCI World Index is, in total, up about 10 percent. Meanwhile the average hedge fund has *gained* nearly 50 percent, and the average FOF is up more than 30 percent, making hedge funds a far better performing asset class in that period. In addition, the S&P has yet to return to its all-time high, reached earlier in 2000, while hedge fund indices continue to forge on to new all-time highs by a large margin.

We will examine this recent market cycle more closely in Table 1.3, but for now suffice it to say that it may be a long wait for stock market investors who hope to catch up with their hedge fund counterparts. Given today's historically low dividend yields, even prominent bulls like Jeremy Siegel are predicting that S&P total returns may average

FIGURE 1.4

HFRI Fund-Weighted and FOF Composite Indices and Equity Indices, Trailing Five Years

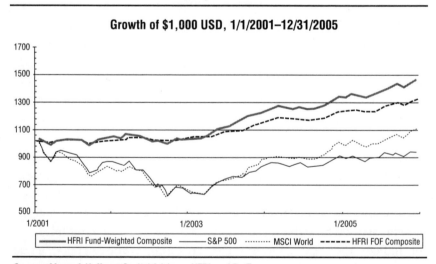

Growth of $1,000 USD, 1/1/2001–12/31/2005

Sources: Mayer & Hoffman Capital Advisors, HFRI, and PerTrac.

only 6–7 percent per year over the next decade. Value investors like the highly respected Jeremy Grantham are much less sanguine as they view the current market as still overvalued by historical standards.[18] Time will tell what future hedge fund returns will be, but if history is any guide, they are likely to do at least as well as stock returns under most scenarios. It is, of course, this sort of relative performance that has continued to attract investors to hedge fund investments. Should the stock market do poorly, the chances of favorable relative performance from hedge funds are probably as good as we saw in 2001–2002. In the event of a roaring bull stock market, hedge funds are highly likely to lag stocks as they did in 2003.

Survivor Bias, Attrition Rates, and Backfill Bias

Not everyone, of course, agrees that hedge funds have outperformed equities either on an absolute or even on a risk-adjusted basis. Three issues have been raised that cast doubt on the accuracy of hedge fund outperformance. They are *survivor bias*, *attrition rates*, and *backfill bias*. We review each of these issues and then draw tentative conclusions about the performance question only if those deductions have substantial academic weight behind them.

Survivor Bias.   In chastising the hedge fund industry for overstating performance results, Malkiel and Saha[19] concluded that hedge funds' performance may be overstated due to survivor bias. Survivor bias occurs when a database, for example, no longer includes the performance of funds that have stopped reporting or are defunct and incorporates only those that are still reporting. If we believe that the reason funds stop reporting is due to poor performance, then our hypothetical database has allowed poorer performers to disappear while retaining the stronger survivors in its sample. As a consequence, the historical return performance of the remaining sample is biased in an upward direction, and probably the risk/standard deviation is biased downward. Unless the databases include the performance records of the defunct funds in their indices, they may unwittingly be creating a survivor bias in their historical reporting. Thus are born inflated claims of outperformance.

Estimating the extent of survivor bias in hedge fund databases is more difficult than in mutual funds where the entire universe of funds is known. For example, Malkiel found that survivor bias in mutual funds from 1996–2003 was 1.23 percent per year.[20] Hedge funds, however, do not have to report to databases and may stop reporting for reasons other than poor performance. It is well-known that many large and highly successful funds that have reached their asset goals don't bother to report. Steve Cohen's SAC fund, among many others, comes to mind. Other funds like Jeff Vinik's and Michael Gordon's fund have closed down but not for reasons of poor performance. In fact, after generating enormous profits of about 50 percent per annum over four years, they returned all of their outside investors' capital and closed the fund in order to manage their own money. Because of these competing forces in survivor bias, that is, funds that close with poor performance and the opting out of top performers from databases, some studies have found that survivor bias had no impact on performance.[21]

Survivor bias especially colored reported hedge fund returns pre-1994. That's because many hedge funds simply didn't report to any database and when they became defunct, nobody knew. Thus, we may never know the real returns for funds prior to the emergence of the large databases. Even one of the largest and most reliable databases, HFRI, suffers from this problem. That database excluded defunct funds prior to 1994.[22] Starting in 1994, HFRI includes both defunct and active funds in its indices, and therefore its data presumably no longer suffers from survivor bias. *Therefore, we do not rely on pre-1994 HFRI data in this book.*

Attrition Rates.   Complicating the computation of survivor bias is confusion over failure rates for hedge funds. On the other hand, mutual fund failure rates have been widely studied. For example, for the period 1996–2003 mutual fund attrition rates ranged from 3.85 percent to 8.20 percent per annum.[23] For the years 2000–2003 in this Malkiel and Saha study, mutual funds suffered attrition rates around 8 percent. Knowing the attrition rate made it easier for Malkiel to arrive at a 1.23 percent survivorship bias for mutual funds. Estimates of hedge fund attrition, however, have depended on the period studied, the database used, and the type of hedge fund strategy investigated. These attrition estimates range from the 8.3 percent found by Liang[24] in the 1994–1998 sample period for the TASS database to more than 12 percent in a study of TASS from 1994 through 2003.[25] Other attrition studies have shown that about 30 percent of new hedge funds do not make it past three years,[26] while yet another study found that 40 percent of hedge funds do not make it past 48 months.[27]

In a recent and comprehensive review of the literature on the topic of hedge fund attrition, Getmansky, Lo, and Mei[28] found that a sample of 1,765 funds in the TASS database had an annual attrition rate of 8.8 percent over the period 1994–2004. This rate is very close to large earlier studies that found rates ranging from 8.3–8.6 percent depending on the database used and the time period studied. The authors also noted a wide dispersion of attrition rates among hedge fund strategies ranging from 5.2 percent in convertible arbitrage and 6.9 percent for fund of funds to 12.6 percent for global macro and 14.4 percent for managed futures.

What then is the impact of attrition on survivor bias and reported performance? While Ackermann et al. found no impact on survivor bias, a preponderance of post-2000 studies have concluded that survivor bias in hedge fund data has a 2–3 percent impact on annualized performance for the largest databases. For example, Liang, cited previously, estimated survivor bias at 2 percent,[29] while Fung and Hsieh[30] found a survivorship bias of 3 percent in the TASS database. Dr. Thomas Schneeweis and his colleagues at The Center for International Securities and Derivatives Markets (CISDM) in the University of Massachusetts's Eisenberg School of Management reviewed the literature on survivor bias and produced a series of studies on the topic.[31,32] They had four major conclusions:

1. Survivor bias ranges from 2–3 percent for various databases.
2. Survivor bias is due primarily to small hedge funds that close because of financial and/or operational problems.
3. Any database index that is equally weighted (like Hedgefund.net and HFRI) that includes very small funds may elevate the amount of survivor bias, since smaller managers have higher failure rates.

4. Like Ackermann, cited previously, offsetting the poor performance of funds that become defunct are the top performing funds that stop reporting because of self-selection. For example, Schneeweis's colleague Mackey found that a significant percentage of nonreporting funds had positive returns for the last 12, 9, and 3 months of their reporting periods.[33]

We may safely conclude, therefore, that survivor bias for hedge funds is somewhere between 2 percent and 3 percent, and that as time goes on and databases continue to improve, this number will trend downward. The difference between survivor bias in mutual funds and hedge funds is also not as great as previously thought because the attrition rate difference is also not substantial. Mutual fund attrition from 2000–2003 averaged 7.89 percent,[34] while hedge fund attrition averaged 8.8 percent in the large review study cited previously.

Backfill Bias.   A third critique of hedge fund performance is called *backfill bias* in databases. Backfill bias is a critique of databases that adds the performance of funds to their listings months or even years after inception. There are two problems with backfilled data: First is the issue of self-reporting where funds add themselves to a database a year or two after inception and report good numbers, whereas poorer performers presumably don't; and second is a more serious problem that we know has affected one of the largest and most respected databases, CSFB-Tremont, formerly CSFB-TASS.

The CSFB Index was established in 1999 after having acquired the TASS database. Researchers have pointed out the obvious "instant history bias"[35] that occurs when such a transaction takes place. CSFB had to select and backfill funds that were missing from the TASS database. As a result, pre-1999 data for CSFB-Tremont suffers from both survivor and backfill biases. Since then CSFB has maintained both defunct and surviving funds in the database so that it is more reliable as a source.

Now that we've covered three of the methodological issues facing hedge fund performance analysis let's turn our attention to a scathing article that appeared in Forbes.com, cleverly titled, "The Sleaziest Show on Earth."[36] The authors concluded that once survivor bias and other factors are considered, the actual return to hedge fund investors for the period 1996–2002 would be close to zero. What are we to make of these critiques?

The Forbes article relied solely on the unpublished paper of Posthuma and Van der Sluis.[37] Their findings, however, are at complete odds with the many studies and hedge fund indices that show annualized returns over the time period studied to be consistently in the 8–10 percent range. For example, HFRI's database showed annualized returns for hedge funds of about 8.5 percent[38] during 1996–2002 and, as we've shown previously has, *since 1994*, contained both active funds and those that are defunct; thus it has limited survivor bias.

Another major flaw was their reliance on one database, CSFB-TASS, for their conclusions. Of all the databases they could have selected, CSFB, as we've just shown, suffered from backfill and survivor bias for the period 1996–1998. Given that there are 12 major hedge fund databases globally, picking one as a proxy (especially one that was flawed) seems inadvisable.

Even so, the authors concluded that after accounting for biases, the CSFB-TASS database showed annualized returns of 6.3 percent. How did they get to zero as the Forbes article claimed? By projecting that the returns of funds in the month after they stopped reporting would drop by 50 percent. This claim has been shown to be highly inaccurate by others. For example, as we noted previously, Mackey found that a large percentage of nonreporters actually outperformed database survivors in the months prior to going silent. This is because successful funds that are closed to new investors no longer want to bother with databases. As Schneeweis and Kazemi (2005) recently noted, "The assumption that 50% of a fund's assets are lost in the month after they stop reporting has no basis in fact."[39] These methodological flaws seriously skewed the critics' conclusions on the impact of survivor bias.

Conclusions.   Researchers are finally getting their hands around the critical methodological issues that have plagued studies of hedge fund performance. Survivor bias, attrition rates, and backfill bias that only a decade ago were virtually unquantifiable have now been clearly benchmarked for the major databases. In terms of attrition and survivor bias, it is clear that differences between mutual funds and hedge funds are not as great as previously thought. Therefore, hedge fund outperformance of equities remains a valid phenomenon. Downward revisions of more recent hedge fund performance will not substantively alter the fact that the S&P 500 has been essentially flat (up 2 percent) since 12/31/1998 (the S&P 500 closed the year 1998 at 1,229 and closed 2005 at 1,248) while the HFRI Fund-Weighted Composite Index is up about 75 percent.

Another important conclusion that we take to heart in our own research is that it is unwise to use one hedge fund database to estimate the return potential or the historical returns for hedge funds or funds of funds. While very few hedge funds and FOFs report to more than 3 of the 12 major databases and most report only to 1,[40] for the purposes of this book, we use multiple databases to present performance. Furthermore, we use data only from 1990 to 1999 when it has been adjusted for survivor bias, as CISDM has done.

THE BENEFITS OF DIVERSIFICATION

Diversification is often referred to as the title of the first chapter in the book on investing. It is at the heart of Modern Portfolio Theory (MPT)[41] and drives contemporary portfolio construction and optimization. For institutional investors, adding carefully selected hedge funds or FOFs will lower the risk of their overall portfolio of stocks, bonds, and other alternatives like real estate and private equity. As Table 1.2 shows, Portfolio 1, which was invested 50/50 in the MSCI World and Lehman high-grade bond indices, significantly underperformed and had higher volatility over the 12-year period, 1994–2005, than Portfolio 2, which was invested 40/40/20 with the 20 percent invested in a composite of hedge funds. Portfolio 2, which included hedge funds, outperformed Portfolio 1 by 105 basis points per annum while enjoying lower volatility of about 0.50 percent per year through a complete market cycle. Note that the Sharpe ratio of Portfolio 2 is also higher

TABLE 1.2

Performance of Asset Classes and Portfolio Combinations, January 1994–December 2005

	Annualized Return	Annualized Standard Deviation	Sharpe Ratio
HFRI Fund-Weighted Composite Index	11.56%	7.05%	1.08
Lehman Government-Credit Bond Index	6.35%	4.50%	0.54
MSCI The World Index—Net	7.95%	13.83%	0.29
Portfolio 1 (Equities and Bonds)	7.18%	7.75%	0.42
Portfolio 2 (Equities, Bonds, and Hedge Funds)	8.23%	7.24%	0.59

Portfolio 1 = 50% MSCI The World Index/50% Lehman Government-Credit Bond Index
Portfolio 2 = 40% MSCI The World Index/40% Lehman/20% HFRI Fund-Weighted Composite Index
Source: Mayer & Hoffman Capital Advisors.

than that of Portfolio 1. The results of our study reflected in Tables 1.2 and 1.4, replicate the earlier findings of CISDM for the period 1990–2004.[42]

How then were the superior risk-adjusted returns depicted in Table 1.2 achieved? Let's digress for a moment and recall Sharpe's seminal paper on the capital asset pricing model (CAPM).[43] In it Sharpe described two fundamental risks of portfolios: market or *systematic risk*, the risk of holding the market portfolio; and, *specific* or idiosyncratic *risk*, the risk of selecting a specific asset. The Greek letter *beta* denotes the extent to which a portfolio or individual asset has market risk.

Returning to our portfolios of stocks and bonds, how can we lower their market risk? You need to add an asset class with a beta that is sufficiently low. If we use HFRI's Fund-Weighted Composite Index as a proxy, the correlation to the S&P 500 was 0.72 percent. Beta of the Hedge Fund Index is calculated by:

$$\rho(R_a, R_m) \times \sigma(a) \times \sigma(m)/\sigma^2(m)$$

where:

ρ = the correlation coefficient between the asset class returns
R_a = the return of the Hedge Index
R_m = the return of the market (the S&P 500)

times the σ (standard deviation) of each asset *all divided by* σ^2 (market).

In this case, beta of the Index =

$$[0.72 \times 7.05 \times 14.73]/14.73^2 = 0.34$$

The relatively low beta value of 0.34 demonstrates the proposition that by adding a hedge fund portfolio with those characteristics, we are contributing to the lowering of the portfolio's market risk.

As discussed in greater detail in Chapter 12, the full benefits of diversification from investing in hedge funds accrue to those who pay close attention to the pair correlations and the market correlations of the managers in their portfolio. A diversified multistrategy portfolio of hedge funds or FOFs will offer greater protection during market declines than, say, a homogeneous portfolio of equity long/short managers.

In particular, portfolios that have exposure to commodities or currencies through managed futures and certain global macro funds will have reduced correlations to the equity markets. Similarly, relative value arbitrage strategies that have low correlations to both bond and equity markets will likely help protect portfolios during market declines.

Another way in which hedge funds offer investors downside protection is by having the ability to sell short in both the equity and credit markets. This flexibility is a significant advantage and can help to preserve capital in bear markets. Witness 2001 and 2002: The S&P 500 was down 13 percent and then down more than 23 percent, respectively, while the average FOF was up 3 percent in 2001 and 1 percent in 2002.[44] Table 1.3 shows the performance of equities, bonds, hedge funds, and FOFs over the market cycle 2001–2005.[45]

Table 1.3 shows that every hedge fund strategy and FOFs outper-

TABLE 1.3

Hedge Fund Strategies, Performance, and Correlations to Stocks and Bonds, Trailing Five Years

Performance: Hedge Fund Strategies and Traditional Assets (1/1/2001–12/31/2005)

	Annual Return	Standard Deviation	Sharpe Ratio	Correlation with S&P 500	Correlation with Lehman Gov-Credit
HFRI Convertible Arbitrage Index	6.15%	3.48%	1.12	0.04	0.17
HFRI Distressed Securities Index	14.76%	4.48%	2.79	0.43	0.07
HFRI Equity Hedge Index	6.57%	6.48%	0.67	0.81	−0.21
HFRI Equity Market Neutral Index	4.09%	2.28%	0.80	−0.28	0.13
HFRI Event-Driven Index	10.68%	6.01%	1.40	0.71	−0.09
HFRI Fixed Income: Arbitrage Index	6.89%	1.97%	2.35	0.08	0.34
HFRI Fund-Weighted Composite Index	8.00%	5.20%	1.10	0.81	−0.13
HFRI Fund of Funds Composite Index	5.89%	3.30%	1.10	0.58	0.02
HFRI Macro Index	9.26%	5.03%	1.39	0.17	0.29
HFRI Short Selling Index	2.58%	15.24%	0.02	−0.91	0.34
CISDM CTA Asset-Weighted Index	7.72%	8.25%	0.66	−0.19	0.39
Lehman Government-Credit Bond Index	6.10%	4.86%	0.79	−0.33	1.00
MSCI The World Index—Net	2.18%	14.67%	−0.01	0.97	−0.29
S&P 500 Price Index	−1.11%	14.90%	−0.23	1.00	−0.33

Source: Mayer & Hoffman, HFRI, CISDM, and PerTrac.

formed equities on an absolute and risk-adjusted basis (the risk-free rate over the period studied was calculated as 2.26 percent) over the past five years. Bonds, while performing well over the period, were outperformed on a risk-adjusted basis by FOFs and every strategy except CTAs and Equity Hedge (HFRI's term for Equity Long/Short).

Table 1.4 shows that having part of their portfolios somewhat hedged shielded those investors who were astute enough to diversify in this way. Table 1.4 also illustrates that investors enjoyed a

TABLE 1.4

Performance of Asset Classes and Portfolio Combinations, January 2001–December 2005

	Annualized Return	Annualized Standard Deviation	Sharpe Ratio
HFRI Fund-Weighted Composite Index	8.00%	5.20%	1.10
Lehman Government-Credit Bond Index	6.10%	4.86%	0.79
MSCI The World Index—Net	2.18%	14.67%	–0.01
Portfolio 1 (Equities and Bonds)	3.86%	7.09%	0.23
Portfolio 2 (Equities, Bonds, and Hedge Funds)	4.96%	6.41%	0.42

Portfolio 1 = 50% MSCI The World Index/50% Lehman Government-Credit Bond Index
Portfolio 2 = 40% MSCI The World Index/40% Lehman/20% HFRI Fund-Weighted Composite Index
Source: Mayer & Hoffman Capital Advisors.

1.10 percent per year performance boost by adding hedge funds to their portfolios.

How exactly do the individual hedging strategies either enhance the returns or diversify the risk from stock and bond portfolios? As Tables 1.1 and 1.3 showed, some of the hedge fund strategies, like Equity Long/Short, were highly correlated with equities but not with bonds. Others, like Convertible Arbitrage, are modestly correlated with both asset classes. The results of our studies summarized in Tables 1.1 and 1.3 also confirm the findings of CISDM's longitudinal study (1990–2004) on hedge fund performance and correlations to stocks and bonds.[46] Their[47] conclusions as to the specific contributions that each hedge fund strategy makes to equity, high-grade, and high-yield bond portfolios are summarized in Table 1.5.

Table 1.5 shows that four of the primary strategies are risk diversifiers for stocks while the other four are primarily return enhancers. We discuss these benefits in greater detail in the chapters devoted to each individual strategy. In sum then, diversification into hedge funds offers the benefits of reduced portfolio volatility; improved absolute and risk-adjusted returns; and a measure of downside protection from negative stock and bond markets. See the quantitative analysis section in Chap-

TABLE 1.5

Portfolio Risk and Return Contribution

Hedge Fund Strategy	Stock Portfolio	High-Grade Bond Portfolio	High-Yield Bond Portfolio
Event Driven	Return Enhancer	Risk Diversifier	Return Enhancer
Equity Hedge	Return Enhancer	Risk Diversifier	Return Enhancer
Equity Market Neutral	Risk Diversifier	Return Enhancer	Risk Diversifier
Merger/Risk Arbitrage	Return Enhancer	Risk Diversifier	Return Enhancer
Distressed	Return Enhancer	Risk Diversifier	Return Enhancer
Fixed Income Arbitrage	Risk Diversifier	Risk Diversifier	Return Enhancer
Convertible Arbitrage	Risk Diversifier	Risk Diversifier	Return Enhancer
Global Macro	Risk Diversifier	Risk Diversifier	Risk Diversifier

Source: CISDM, 2005.

ter 13 for a discussion using value at risk (VaR) to quantify the benefits of diversification.

With strong academic support for diversifying traditional portfolios through allocating to hedge funds and FOFs and a long track record of attractive risk-adjusted returns, why have many institutional investors thus far avoided this asset class? There are four major reasons that investors cite.

1. Hedge funds and FOFs typically lack transparency, that is, investors do not have detailed knowledge of the underlying portfolios. For institutional investors, lack of transparency is anathema because it prevents them from being able to input the hedge funds' or FOFs' positions into their risk management software. As a result, their portfolio analyses as to leverage and market risk will be incomplete.
2. An even more compelling reason for hesitating to invest is that hedge fund strategies can be foreign and complex to the institutional investor who has been schooled primarily in the long-only world. Without a team of well-trained hedge fund analysts, pension plans in particular have moved cautiously into this unfamiliar territory.

3. Then there are the fees. Why pay "one and twenty" a (fixed management fee of 1 percent plus 20 percent of the profits) and be locked into an investment for a year or more when a stock index fund can be purchased for 25 basis points or less and have instant liquidity? Moreover, add the fees charged by FOFs, typically a 1–1.5 percent management fee and 10 percent of the profits, and the investor, it is claimed, has little chance to make attractive returns.

4. Finally, there are the "blow-ups." There have been a number of well-advertised instances of fraud and/or gross mismanagement in recent years, resulting in the loss of all or nearly all of investors' money. As shocking and upsetting as these blow-ups have been, the monies lost pale in comparison to the sums lost in mutual funds and brokerage accounts during the bursting of the Internet bubble, or the billions lost in the World Com, Global Crossing, Enron, Tyco, and other corporate scandals of recent years.

THE RISK OF INVESTING IN HEDGE FUNDS

The notion that hedge funds are highly risky grew out of the obscurity clouding funds of the previous era when they were open almost exclusively to secretive superwealthy investors. That idea received a big boost in 1998 when Long Term Capital Management lost investors billions and secured the fund's place in history as the poster child of an industry gone awry.[48] It also cemented, in the minds of many, the mistaken notion that the average hedge fund is perpetually on the brink of annihilation. Those responsible for the $1 trillion plus invested in hedge funds today obviously disagree with this conclusion.

But as with any other investment there are risks to hedge fund investors. They come from two sources: market exposure and fund management.

Market Exposure Risk

As we discussed in the previous section, any type of investment, conventional or alternative, faces market exposure risk or systematic risk as Sharpe named it. In many cases market exposure risks in hedge funds are substantially lower than conventional investments because managers have the ability to hedge away this risk from their portfolios. For example, Equity Long/Short managers can, through expert portfolio management, lower or even neutralize the beta of their portfolios. Chapter 2 details the techniques for accomplishing this goal.

Using similar tactics, many hedge fund managers have designed strategies, usually categorized as relative value arbitrage, whose primary objective is capital preservation plus some return over T-bills. Such funds tend to have very low volatility and relatively consistent, if modest, returns that are uncorrelated to the stock market.

Market exposure risk is generally expressed as the net long exposure. If a $100 million fund has invested 100 percent of its assets in various stocks and has used this collateral to sell short $50 million of stocks, the fund is said to be 50 percent net long. This is an indicator of risk, as it is more or less equivalent to being only 50 percent invested, but a rather imperfect one, since the stocks held long could decline in price while the stocks sold short could advance. This may seem unlikely, but one version of Murphy's Law is that anything that can happen in markets will happen, so it is not without precedent.

Another indicator of risk to watch is gross exposure, calculated by simply adding the long and short percentage exposures. In the preceding case, gross exposure would have been 150 percent.

Probably the most widely scrutinized indicator of market exposure risk is *leverage* (or, as they say across the pond, gearing), which we define as the amount of money borrowed for investing and trading activities (some use the term to refer to gross exposure). Leverage, as the name implies, magnifies the gains and losses occurring in a portfolio, not to mention causing the payment of margin interest. In a worst case scenario, leverage can bring about a margin call, necessitating the sale of positions at large losses.

Fund Management Risk

Specialized due diligence is required before investing in any hedge fund. Yet, despite that caveat, investors have given substantial amounts of money with apparently negligible up-front investigation to fraudulent hedge fund operators with little or no investment experience and who lie about their accounting firms, auditors, and administrators. In 2005, the SEC closed down the Bayou Group, a $450 million hedge fund firm and filed charges against Wood River, KL Financial, and a few others. Bayou's manager, Samuel Israel III, claimed to have been the head trader at the highly successful hedge fund, Omega Advisors. Yet, a simple phone call to Omega would have revealed that Mr. Israel had never been the head trader there. Similarly, the *Wall Street Journal*[49] pointed out that a quick call to the accounting firm Grant Thornton, touted as Bayou's auditors, would have yielded the fact that the firm had not audited Bayou's books for years. Also, a search of Lexis/Nexis would have revealed an unresolved claim of fraudulent activity filed by a former Bayou partner. This type of information routinely shows up in the operational and business due diligence best practices that we detail in Chapter 13.

But the reader may still ask, hasn't the risk of investing in hedge funds increased lately with more default rates and frauds? In our opinion, no. The SEC brought 20 cases to light in 2005 as compared with 19 in 2004.[50] From 1999–2004, the SEC filed 51 cases of fraud that cost investors a total of $1.1 billion.[51,52] In an industry with more than 8,000 funds (and more than double the number of funds extant in 1999) one would expect a sharply growing trend line of fraud. It hasn't happened. But even if the number of cases were to rise as we would expect statistically, the total numbers of dollars lost by hedge fund fraud according to the SEC study cited previously is dwarfed by the losses caused by the equity frauds of the recent past.

What can we expect going forward? Closer scrutiny by the SEC. The new SEC regulations that took effect in February 2006 have placed hedge fund managers under the microscope as never before. And as professional investors, the authors welcome this change. It can only help the industry flourish.

ABOUT THIS BOOK

This book arms investors with the knowledge needed to make more informed decisions regarding their hedge fund and FOF investments. We focus mostly on the U.S. market, the largest hedge fund spawning ground, although hedge funds are a decidedly global phenomenon. Hedge funds have sprung up all around the world in recent years, and the markets traded in are truly global. There are traders in Hong Kong trading on the New York Stock Exchange (NYSE) while traders in Boston are simultaneously trading on the Hang Seng. Financial information is instantly available to any portfolio manager in the world, regardless of whether he or she is sitting in a farmhouse in the British countryside or in "a hedge fund hotel" (a suite of offices dedicated to hedge funds) on New York's Park Avenue.

Unique in the growing library on the industry, this book takes you into the inner sanctum of the hedge fund manager. You'll meet top innovators and performers, see what makes them tick, learn how they evaluate their respective markets, and discover how they apply proprietary strategies to outperform in varying market environments. You'll also hear from two top due diligence experts as they walk you through the multistage process of evaluating managers.

Written by industry insiders primarily for the institutional and family office investor, this book lifts the veil of secrecy that has cloaked hedge funds. The authors clarify all terminology and supplement their professional insight into hedge fund strategies with in-depth interviews of successful managers from each major strategy. These managers give an unprecedented inside view that will enable investors to learn about the complexities of their strategies at both the macro and micro levels. In their own words, they give us the whole picture—the real picture.

The strategy chapters are grouped as follows by the S&P Hedge Fund Index Fund style matrix:[53]

- *Directional*—Equity Long/Short, Managed Futures, Global Macro.
- *Event Driven*—Event Driven (including Merger Arbitrage and Special Situations), Distressed Securities.

- *Arbitrage*—Equity Market Neutral, Convertible Arbitrage, Fixed-Income Arbitrage.

Each of the strategy chapters examines the advantages and disadvantages of the particular investment approach and presents performance charts for the strategy relative to other benchmarks. This will help the reader see how a particular strategy tends to perform in both bull and bear markets. While the past is not a predictor of future performance, it can certainly serve as a useful tool for understanding the risks and rewards associated with each strategy. Finally, each chapter closes with an interview primarily focusing on a newer manager specializing in the strategy.

This book does not cover pure short sellers and long-only non-hedged funds. It also does not break out sector funds like healthcare, biotech, precious metals, or energy funds, all of which are at best Equity Long/Short funds and at worst equivalent to long-only managers. Similarly, while Emerging Market funds have become the rage du jour in the industry, we have chosen not to highlight them in a separate chapter inasmuch as most of them fall into either the Equity Long/Short or Event Driven categories. The book does devote a full chapter to Managed Futures, a strategy that is often omitted even in the best hedge fund databases, like HFRI.

Subsequent chapters are devoted to:

- *Emerging Strategies*—An overview of today's newer investment opportunities including private financings for public companies.
- *The Search for Alpha*—An analysis of the research on alpha in hedge fund performance and the outperformance of newer managers relative to their older and bigger peers.
- *Funds of Hedge Funds*—A look at the relative merits of investing in FOFs.
- *Due Diligence Best Practices*—Two experts in due diligence teach investors the five stages of the due diligence process complete with sample questions and scorecards.

The hedge fund world is ever changing, adapting itself to the evolving landscape of the securities markets. Many hedge funds have sprung up in the past two or three years employing strategies that were not dreamt of five years ago. Hedge funds are like honey bees, forever searching for new market inefficiencies from which they might extract profit. Some of these new markets are growing by leaps and bounds. Some are also exceedingly complex and characterized by occasional large but fleeting pricing imperfections. Agile hedge funds, run by expert traders, are profiting handsomely by capitalizing on such anomalies. At the same time, other more traditional types of hedge funds are finding their markets overcrowded, and profit opportunities few and far between. Along with these dynamic changes have come new opportunities and challenges for the discerning investor. The way to capitalize on these opportunities is now more accessible than ever: You're holding it in your hands.

CHAPTER 2

The Directional Strategies: Equity Long/Short

INTRODUCTION

This chapter and Chapters 3 and 4 are devoted to the directional strategies, so named because equity long/short (ELS), managed futures, and global macro managers all make directional bets on their respective markets. As a group they are very popular among investors and account for more than 50 percent of all monies invested in hedge funds. They are also very different from one another in terms of correlation to the markets, volatility, role in a portfolio, and, finally, performance.

The ELS strategy is the progenitor of all hedge funds. In 1949, a New York attorney named Alfred Winslow Jones established the first hedge fund, A. W. Jones & Company. The principle was very simple. A portfolio of stocks (longs) would be hedged by a portfolio of shorts. Longs would be selected that were considered attractive, and shorts would be selected that were considered relatively unattractive. The idea was that in good markets the longs would increase in value more than the shorts, producing a profit. Conversely, in bad markets the longs would decline less than the shorts, again producing a profit. In sideways markets the hope was that profits would be realized on the longs as well as the shorts.

By the time co-author Eldon Mayer arrived on Wall Street in the early 1960s, the Jones hedge fund had spawned several others. Among the most prominent were City Associates and Fairfield Partners and, by 1969, the Quantum Fund. These managers were considered among the best and brightest, most well-informed investors of the day. The name of the game was making money, so they were not constrained as most hedge funds are today by feeling they had to stick to a particular strategy. As active traders in a buy and hold world, they were important commission generators. Thus they received excellent coverage from the Street's best brokers and analysts. They also received favored attention from syndicate departments, which allowed them to take down large allocations of new issues. One of them in fact got into such disfavor for "flipping" hot issues that a leading investment banking firm closed its account and refused to do business with them thereafter.

A. W. Jones continued to serve as a spawning ground for start-up hedge funds into the 1970s. It was not uncommon for a bright analyst to learn the tricks of the trade at Jones for a few years and then strike out on his own. Mayer was a hedge fund manager starting in 1968 and knew quite well most of the New York hedgie crowd, a number of whom had started their hedge fund careers at A. W. Jones. That was always considered a blue ribbon credential.

In 1968, Eldon Mayer, while at J. M. Hartwell & Co., designed, helped launch, and managed the first mutual fund hedge fund, the Hartwell and Campbell Leverage Fund. For the decade 1970–1980, this ELS fund placed in the top 20 in terms of annualized return for all equity mutual funds.[1]

Another feature of the early 1970s was the appearance of several "whisper groups," composed primarily of hedge fund managers who met for breakfast or lunch on a regular basis. The format was standard—each attendee was expected to give his best ideas and provide a brief rationale for each investment. The idea was to both tout one's own portfolio and to get fresh new ideas from other smart managers. Some brokers established their own versions of the whisper group, the difference being that the meal was free but that commissions were expected in return. The most well-known of these were the lunches hosted by the late Robert Brimberg, who was made famous by the author G. J. W. Goodman (aka Adam Smith) as Scarsdale Fats in his best selling book *Supermoney*.[2] At some point during the meal

Brimberg would rise and say, "Now it's time to pay for your lunch; Wilson, why don't you start out with your best ideas, then we'll go around the table."

During this era, hedge fund managers were considered by many to be the elite of the Wall Street world. They were generally very smart, focused, and well informed. They had their own informal fraternity, the gatherings of which generally didn't include long only managers. They received the best possible service from the brokerage community, ranging from having the best moneymaking brokers assigned to their account to having the best trading desk coverage to having instant access to the most senior research analysts. They typically were the first call whenever a brokerage firm had a new recommendation.

The performance of many ELS funds in these early days was often outstanding. They were aggressive, willing to take big positions and use leverage. Risky, yes, but they also had very quick triggers and typically made hasty exits from positions at the slightest sign of a shift in the wind. Annualized performance in excess of 20 percent was common among the better hedge funds during the 1970s and 1980s. Two hedge fund legends, Julian Robertson and Michael Steinhardt, produced consistently spectacular returns in this era.

During the 1980s some of these same funds began to invest globally, not only in stocks, but also in currencies. The most famous and probably the most successful of these pioneers was the Quantum Fund (renamed the Quantum Endowment Fund), managed by George Soros. Fifty percent was considered a good year for Soros, and he reached or exceeded that target a number of times. In the 35-year period of 1969–2004, the Quantum Fund had an average annual return of more than 30 percent.[3] Soros paid his investment staff generously and attracted a star-studded roster of analysts and portfolio managers. Soros's most famous conquest was his billion dollar profit in 1992 when his large short position in the British pound hit pay dirt.

Most ELS funds of that era were not confined by limits as to the types of investing or trading they might engage in. *Style drift* (when a fund purporting to manage its assets via a particular strategy begins trading using other strategies) was of no concern to them. The rule of thumb was if money could be made buying or selling anything, they would do it.

Today, the ELS manager is generally much more tightly disciplined. Of course there are exceptions, and these old school hedge funds are much less constrained in what they do in a number of respects. These funds tend to have much more variable returns, are much less diversified, often take larger positions, and commonly take a market view. They also may take an activist role in the management of the companies in which they invest in order to create even greater opportunities for their investors.

Emblematic of the ELS activist school is Norwalk, Connecticut-based Pirate Capital LLC, founded by Thomas and Gabrielle Hudson in 2002. Their first fund, Jolly Roger LP began trading in July of that year, while the offshore version started in January 2003. Jolly Roger LP's cumulative returns through 2005 were about 160 percent, placing it near the top of the performance rankings. These funds were up nearly 20 percent in 2005 and assets have topped the $1.2 billion level. Pirate Capital launched a fully dedicated activist hedge fund on January 1, 2006.[4]

The Jolly Roger funds are hybrid ELS and event-driven funds focused on value and activist investing and typically hold a portfolio of 60–70 percent longs and 10–20 percent shorts. Neither fund employs leverage. The funds' activist approach typically involves quiet accumulation of a large position in the shares of an underperforming company. When a 13-D filing becomes necessary (required of a holder of 5 percent or more of a company's shares), it usually signals management that Pirate is about to declare war. Accumulation of the stock continues as long as the shares remain depressed. The manager, Tom Hudson, does not mind building a large position, as much as 10 percent or more of the funds' net assets. Pressure is applied on management, first in friendly fashion, to do a better job of realizing shareholder value. Explicit suggestions of steps that might be taken in this regard are invariably offered. Pirate is unafraid of litigation and has pursued this course in at least half a dozen instances, including early in 2005 in a suit against Toys "R" Us.

Proxy solicitation is another activist tool often used by Pirate to shake up management. In August 2004, Pirate filed a 13-D that included a letter sent to the directors of Houston-based Cornell Companies (NYSE:CRN), a provider of adult and juvenile correctional, treatment, and educational services. CRN operates these services on behalf of federal, state, and local governmental agencies through 70 facilities. Over the next 10 months, Pirate accumulated more and more of CRN's shares and eventually became the largest shareholder at 15 percent. Pirate believed that the board was ineffectual and that the company would be more valuable if it were sold or taken private. As a way of seizing control, Hudson began a proxy solicitation of other shareholders urging them to vote for his slate of candidates. On May 18, 2005, CRN's board and management agreed to Pirate's demands and agreed to put Hudson and six of his nominees on the slate for the June 30 shareholder meeting along with only two board holdovers. In return, Pirate agreed to cease the proxy fight.[5] As we write this chapter it remains to be seen how, when, and to what degree Pirate will accomplish better value for CRN shareholders let alone for its two funds, which own some 2 million shares.

THE ELS TRADING AND INVESTMENT STRATEGIES

The modern ELS manager uses three strategies that distinguish him from his long-only peers: short sales, the purchase and sale of options, and the use of leverage. Short selling attempts to profit from declines in equity prices. Here's how it works: The ELS manager borrows the securities from a third party, usually a broker, so that he can sell them. Later, the manager will buy back the shares so that he can return them to the lender. If the price he pays is lower than the price at which the shares were sold short, the short seller will profit from the transaction. If the price goes up, the manager will lose money. The ELS manager also can make additional revenue on his shorts by collecting interest on the cash proceeds (the short interest rebate) usually at the T-bill rate. There also are costs associated with the transaction including fees paid to the broker for arranging the stock loan and reimbursement of any dividends due the lender.

There are a number of ways for ELS managers to execute their short selling strategy. One common way is through pairs trading. The manager goes long a stock in, say, the pharmaceutical industry while shorting a stock in the same industry he believes will be an underper-former. The manager is predicting that the former will outperform the latter in both up and down markets.

A newer approach is the one taken by Charlotte, Virginia-based Rivanna Partners. Characterizing his strategy, co-founder Craig Col-berg says, "We look at small-cap value on the long side and mostly large-cap on the short side." If this focus seems particularly narrow, consider the numbers. "Actually, we have quite a sizable universe of stocks to choose from on the short side," said Colberg. "And the market often gives us opportunities on the long side that we never anticipated. In our market cap range, there are roughly three and a half thousand different companies. And there always seems to be a sector that's way out of favor. We're basically looking for the gem within that sector." Colberg is our featured interviewee at the end of this chapter.

ELS managers also can buy and sell options on stocks and stock in-dices. When purchasing an option, either a put or a call, the risk in the transaction is limited to the cost of the option. For example, a manager might buy call options on a stock he believes has upside. In the event the share price declines prior to the expiration of the options, the man-ager may either continue to hold the position, risking that the options will expire worthless, or sell the options at a loss. Similarly, put options may be purchased on an anticipated decline of a stock.

Covered put and call writing are relatively conservative strategies that give the ELS manager substantial protection against adverse price moves in either long or short stock positions. Naked sales of put or call options are much riskier propositions inasmuch as they are unhedged speculations. For example, a value investor might sell for $2 naked puts at 20 on a stock trading at that price believing there is limited downside. If the share price declines to $19/share, the stock is put to him at $20 but this loss is more than offset by the $2 premium, in our example, that he has received. Should the stock decline below $18 be-fore the expiration of the put, substantial losses can occur. For exam-ple, if the stock goes to $10, the investor has lost $10/share all for the sake of collecting a $2 offsetting premium.

In addition to buying and selling individual stock options, ELS managers may short baskets of stocks or use stock index options to hedge against overall market risk. Theoretically, ELS managers can make money from both their longs and shorts; in reality, however, it is extremely difficult to make money on short positions in a rising market. Consequently, when markets are up there is usually a net cost associated with the short side of the ELS managers' books that offsets some of the gains on the long side of their portfolios.

Finally, ELS managers, unlike their long-only mutual fund peers, can use leverage to boost performance. Leveraging involves borrowing money to increase the fund's exposure on the long and/or short side of the portfolio. The ELS manager does this in the belief that the gains from leveraging will be greater than the costs of borrowing. Aggressive ELS managers use more leverage and take larger positions than more conservative ones so that overall gross and net market exposures vary greatly from manager to manager.

A typical ELS portfolio might look like this:

35–40 long positions, equally weighted at cost.

50–60 short positions, equally weighted at cost.

No long position will be allowed to exceed 5 percent at market.

No short position will be allowed to exceed 3 percent at market.

Gross long position will be between 75 and 150 percent.

Gross short position will be between 30 and 50 percent.

Maximum sector exposure 25 percent.

Maximum group exposure 15 percent.

Maximum gross exposure not to exceed 200 percent.

There are as many variations on the preceding example as there are funds, but the common thread today is that the ELS manager lays out in advance for investors the way the fund will invest. If he wants to change his investment parameters, he is expected to notify investors and offer them the opportunity to redeem. If he changes without notifying investors, he can expect redemptions.

After about 1990 venturesome ELS funds in the developed nations started investing in specific ranges of companies selected by market capitalization, specific industry sectors such as healthcare, real estate, precious metals, technology, energy, and biotech. Today, sector funds account for about $63 billion of hedge fund assets.[6]

Around the same time that sector funds emerged, ELS managers found opportunities in the emerging markets of Asia, Latin America, and, later, Eastern Europe and India. Emerging markets were the hottest area in terms of asset flows in 2005, not surprising since overall it was the best performing strategy over the 2004 and 2005 period. Emerging markets' AUM have doubled since 2003 and have topped the $125 billion mark.[7] Asset flows both lead to and follow good performance in emerging markets and typically continue until markets peak. Time will tell if and when their outsized gains will morph into losses; the current flood of capital could be viewed as an early storm warning.

ELS continues to be the biggest category in the hedge fund world, amounting to at least 40 percent of total hedge fund assets not including their share of the $125 billion in Emerging Markets that are primarily ELS funds.[8] Globally, it is estimated that in the three-year period of 2003–2005 around 3,000 new hedge funds commenced operations. Of these about half were ELS funds of various stripes.[9]

Why the glut of ELS funds? Simply put, many analysts and traders have been schooled in equity analysis and stock selection on either the *buy* or *sell side*, primarily at long-only firms. There is a prevalent idea (even if it is misguided) that such an education is sufficient for becoming an ELS manager.

It is quite easy then for these smart investment types to open up a prime brokerage account, take space in a hedge fund hotel, obtain boilerplate offering and subscription documents from a lawyer, raise some money from friends and family, and give it a whirl. This may sound like an advantage to the hedge fund manager and not to the investor, but it is this ease of entry that leads to the many hundreds of ELS start-ups each year. Yet, it is also from these minnows that some of the mightiest game fish in the hedge fund world have developed. It is hard to believe that many of the greatest managers of our time started out pretty much as just outlined. Were it not for the relative simplicity of the strategy and this ease of entry, a number of these greats would never have become hedge fund managers.

A final reason for the dominance of ELS funds in the hedge fund world is liquidity and ease of trading. In most cases, purchase or sale of a good-sized block of most mid- and large-cap stocks can be accomplished electronically with the click of a mouse. Other hedge fund strategies, especially those that deal in illiquid securities, require more complicated back offices and more sophisticated trade execution capabilities.

Performance

In our study of hedge fund performance from 1994–2005, we found that ELS widely outperformed domestic and global equities as well as bonds. As Figure 2.1 graphically shows, the HFRI Equity Hedge Index (the HFRI term for ELS) almost doubled the cumulative return achieved by equities.

FIGURE 2.1

Cumulative Performance of HFRI Equity Hedge Index versus Benchmarks

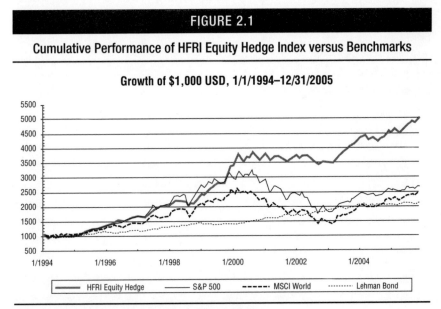

Sources: Mayer & Hoffman Capital Advisors, HFRI, and PerTrac.

For ease of comparison we have duplicated Table 1.1 here. Table 2.1 compares performance of the various hedge fund strategies and traditional assets from 1994–2005 on a number of key variables. ELS funds were the best performing strategy over the 12-year period, averaging more than 14 percent per annum and outperforming the S&P and world markets with significantly less volatility. Table 2.1 also shows the performance of each of the other major strategies tracked by HFRI.[10] Managed Futures, not covered by HFRI, are tracked by

TABLE 2.1

Hedge Fund Strategies, Performance, and Correlations to Stocks and Bonds, 1994–2005

Performance: Hedge Fund Strategies and Traditional Assets (1/1/1994–12/31/2005)

	Annual Return	Standard Deviation	Sharpe Ratio	Correlation with S&P 500	Correlation with Lehman Gov-Credit
HFRI Convertible Arbitrage Index	9.07%	3.70%	1.39	0.28	0.16
HFRI Distressed Securities Index	12.17%	5.40%	1.53	0.47	0.01
HFRI Equity Hedge Index	14.48%	8.97%	1.18	0.69	−0.01
HFRI Equity Market Neutral Index	7.99%	3.10%	1.31	0.15	0.19
HFRI Event-Driven Index	13.35%	6.42%	1.47	0.67	0.01
HFRI Fixed Income: Arbitrage Index	5.96%	3.86%	0.53	−0.12	−0.08
HFRI Fund-Weighted Composite Index	11.56%	7.05%	1.08	0.72	0.00
HFRI Fund of Funds Composite Index	7.46%	5.82%	0.61	0.53	0.06
HFRI Macro Index	10.14%	7.24%	0.86	0.39	0.32
HFRI Short Selling Index	0.99%	21.42%	−0.14	−0.69	0.05
CISDM CTA Asset-Weighted Index	8.01%	8.54%	0.48	−0.08	0.34
Lehman Government-Credit Bond Index	6.35%	4.50%	0.54	0.01	1.00
MSCI The World Index—Net	7.95%	13.83%	0.29	0.94	−0.05
S&P 500 Price Index	8.55%	14.73%	0.31	1.00	0.01

Source: Mayer & Hoffman, HFRI, PerTrac, and CISDM.

CISDM.[11] The CISDM CTA Asset-Weighted Index returned 8 percent per year, slightly less than the S&P 500 over the same time period and ahead of the MSCI World. All of the strategies and FOFs (except for the short sellers) had higher risk-adjusted returns than global and domestic equities, and most had higher risk-adjusted returns than bonds.

Table 2.1 also shows that ELS had the highest positive correlation, 0.72, to the S&P 500 of any strategy (the short sellers were –0.69 percent). This finding and its implications for investors and portfolio construction are discussed later in the chapter. In addition, ELS funds showed the highest standard deviation of all the strategies (except for short sellers). Nevertheless, ELS volatility was still significantly lower than that of the S&P 500, which was 14.73 percent. The combination of higher volatility and lower performance earned domestic equities a Sharpe ratio of 0.31 while ELS funds enjoyed a healthy Sharpe ratio almost four times higher.

But how have ELS funds done lately in the face of a wicked bear market that was followed by a recovery? They've far outperformed both domestic and global long-only indices. They have also outperformed bonds by a narrow margin over the most recent five-year span. As Figure 2.2 shows, domestic equities are slightly down over the period while ELS funds have gained about 40 percent, including a +10 percent performance in 2005 that was substantially higher than either bonds (Lehman up 2.4 percent) or equities (S&P 500 up 3 percent). In the bear market of 2000–2002, the average ELS fund was up 9.1 percent in 2000 and 0.4 percent in 2001, and was down 4.7 percent in 2002 while the S&P 500 over that period lost 38 percent.[12]

Advantages

There are four primary advantages of the ELS strategy:

1. First, since over the very long term global equity markets tend to go up, providing historical annualized total returns on the order of 10 percent, an investment vehicle that tends to benefit from that uptrend makes sense. Take the period 1994–2005 that we presented in

FIGURE 2.2

HFRI Equity Hedge versus Benchmarks, Trailing Five Years

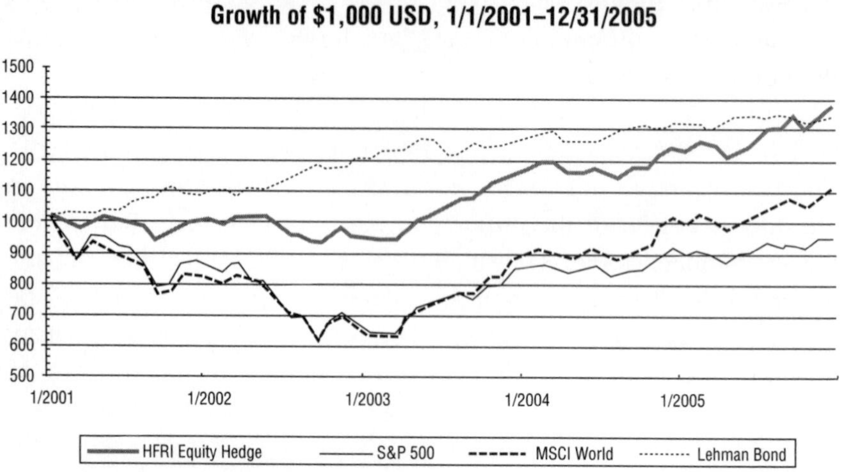

Growth of $1,000 USD, 1/1/2001–12/31/2005

Sources: Mayer & Hoffman Capital Advisors, HFRI, and PerTrac.

Table 2.1. The S&P 500, despite a horrendous drawdown of more than 45 percent from August 2000 to September 2002, still managed an 8.55 percent annualized return over the 12 years. Clearly, ELS funds with their significant correlation to world equity markets, 0.72 percent, captured a lot of the upside generated by equities while avoiding most of the downside.

2. Second, many of the best performing hedge funds have, over the years, inhabited the ELS space. Because of the ease of entry and limited amount of capital necessary, many talented stock pickers have been able to start funds. A lot of money has been made by identifying and investing with talented ELS managers.

3. A third advantage lies in the flexibility that can reside within this category. Investors can choose among large-cap, mid-cap or small-cap growth, value-oriented funds, sector funds, regional and country-specific funds, conservative or aggressive funds. In fact, it is difficult to find any two ELS funds that look alike.

4. A final advantage is the ability of an outside investor to understand the investment risks being taken, assuming the hedge fund provides good transparency re exposures, leverage, position sizes, and sector weightings. Many other hedge fund strategies are so complex that fully comprehending the risks, even with substantial transparency, is much more difficult.

Disadvantages

The ELS strategy has three disadvantages: (1) stock selection risk, (2) the short squeeze, and (3) its high correlations with equities and other hedge funds. ELS and equity market neutral are the strategies that rely heavily on stock selection. As such, they are both vulnerable to stock selection risk, or, in CAPM terms, specific risk.

Furthermore, both of these strategies use short selling of specific stocks on a regular basis. As a result they are vulnerable not only to stock selection risk but also to that rare bane of short sellers called "the short squeeze." The beginnings of a squeeze could occur when the aggregate number of shares of a specific stock sold short exceeds the number of shares that have been borrowed. Under these conditions, the brokerage firms carrying the shorts' accounts *buy in*, that is, they cover the number of shares needed to make up the gap. This buying in turn can propel the stock higher causing the ELS managers to scramble and cover their short positions in order to reduce them or close them out completely. As a result of this escalating demand, the price of the stock can skyrocket. Furthermore, a manager's broker may demand additional collateral to cover losses. If the manager can't provide cash or securities, the broker may cover additional short positions and turn paper losses into real ones and in the process bring even more buying into the market.

A dramatic illustration of the short squeeze risk occurred in the late 1970s to a hedge fund run by Robert Wilson, a well-known, well-respected, and colorful member of the New York hedge fund crowd. At one point he went to Indonesia and, as Eldon Mayer recalls, Wilson was out of touch much of the time. He was relaxed about his portfolio because he was well hedged. Even if things were to go against him while he was away, the affluent Wilson was not concerned. As it happened, he was short a number of casino stocks, being convinced of their deteriorating fundamentals. While he was gone, a short squeeze began, and the stocks moved up sharply. Wilson could not be reached. Day after day, as margin calls and buy-in notices went out to short sellers, covering took place, driving the shares nearly straight up. Had Wilson been reachable, he likely would have been able to produce additional collateral, but such was not the case. His prime broker, Neuberger & Berman, found it necessary to cover his shorts by buying large amounts of the thinly traded stocks again and again as prices skyrocketed, sometimes advancing five or more points in a trading day. Finally, most if not all of his short position was covered, at very large losses, the short squeeze was over, and the share prices gradually retraced their large advances.

Table 2.2 illustrates the third major disadvantage of this popular strategy and the source of its greatest strength: Most ELS funds correlate closely with equity markets, a statistically significant correlation of 0.69 percent to domestic equities and an equally significant correlation to the MSCI world at 0.72. While in theory ELS funds can make money in both up and down markets, they do much better in bull markets than they do in either bear or even sideways markets. As an example of performance in a bear market, take 2002 when the average ELS manager lost 4.7 percent and many did significantly worse than that. Analyzing the relationship between ELS and the MSCI a bit further, we calculate the *beta* of ELS over this 12-year period to be *0.47*, a fairly significant exposure to market risk.

We sound an additional caution here to fund of hedge fund investors. Because many funds of funds have ELS-dominated portfolios and therefore tend to have significant correlations with the equity markets, their investors might be in for disappointment when the next bear market rolls around.

Furthermore, as Table 2.2 also shows, ELS is highly correlated with other popular strategies like event driven, distressed, and global macro. Investors would therefore be well advised to ensure that their hedge fund and FOF portfolios are sufficiently diversified to include other and less correlated hedge fund strategies.

TABLE 2.2

Correlations between Strategies and Benchmarks, 1994–2005

	CISDM CTA Index	HFRI Convert Arb	HFRI Distressed	HFRI Equity Hedge	HFRI Equity MN	HFRI Event-Driven	HFRI FI Arb	HFRI Fund-Weighted Composite	HFRI Macro	Lehman Gov/ Credit Bond	MSCI The World Index	S&P 500 Price Index
CISDM CTA Index	1.00	−0.01	−0.08	0.01	0.15	−0.02	0.06	0.02	0.49	0.34	−0.06	−0.08
HFRI Convertible Arb Index	−0.01	1.00	0.57	0.45	0.28	0.54	0.18	0.51	0.39	0.16	0.26	0.28
HFRI Distressed Index	−0.08	0.57	1.00	0.64	0.20	0.81	0.31	0.75	0.50	0.01	0.52	0.47
HFRI Equity Hedge Index	0.01	0.45	0.64	1.00	0.35	0.81	0.03	0.95	0.61	−0.01	0.72	0.69
HFRI Equity Market Neutral	0.15	0.28	0.20	0.35	1.00	0.29	0.11	0.32	0.28	0.19	0.16	0.15
HFRI Event-Driven Index	−0.02	0.54	0.81	0.81	0.29	1.00	0.17	0.89	0.59	0.01	0.69	0.67
HFRI FI Arb Index	0.06	0.18	0.31	0.03	0.11	0.17	1.00	0.13	0.17	−0.08	−0.03	−0.12
HFRI Fund-Weighted Composite	0.02	0.51	0.75	0.95	0.32	0.89	0.13	1.00	0.67	0.00	0.75	0.72
HFRI Macro Index	0.49	0.39	0.50	0.61	0.28	0.59	0.17	0.67	1.00	0.32	0.41	0.39
Lehman Gov/Credit Bond Index	0.34	0.16	0.01	−0.01	0.19	0.01	−0.08	0.00	0.32	1.00	−0.05	0.01
MSCI The World Index—Net	−0.06	0.26	0.52	0.72	0.16	0.69	−0.03	0.75	0.41	−0.05	1.00	0.94
S&P 500 Price Index	−0.08	0.28	0.47	0.69	0.15	0.67	−0.12	0.72	0.39	0.01	0.94	1.00

Source: Mayer & Hoffman.

Craig Colberg

Co-Founder and Co-PM
Rivanna Partners, LP

RIVANNA PARTNERS, LP, IS A SMALL-CAP, VALUE-FOCUSED ELS FUND launched in January 2003 by Craig Colberg and Jack Sorensen, the founders of Rivanna Capital. Judging by the negative investor sentiment of that time, many would have questioned their judgment. Yet Rivanna finished its inaugural year up 45.6 percent and followed that in 2004 with a strong gain of 21.7 percent. Rivanna posted these numbers while correlating to the Russell 2000 Index at 0.41 percent. By year end 2005, Rivanna was managing $157 million in assets and was up 14.2 percent, well ahead of the HFRI Equity Hedge Index in 2005.

In an economy that separates the men from the boys, the guys at Rivanna are clearly doing something right. Sam Kirschner sat down with Craig Colberg to find out about Rivanna's edge.

SK: *Okay, for the record, I'm sitting with Craig Colberg, and he does not have a crystal ball with him at the table.*

CC: (Laughing). We keep that in the back office.

SK: *I believe it. Because with the numbers you're putting up in these tough markets, you've gotta have one, right?*

CC: Well, I wish it were that easy. The reality is somewhat more mundane. It's a lot of hard work.

SK: *Sure, but a lot of guys are working really hard these days and not putting up your numbers. So let's try to get a glimpse of what you're doing at Rivanna Capital. How do you describe your approach?*

CC: Our goal is positive absolute returns in all market environments with low portfolio volatility. We want to give our clients a 15 to 20 percent return with a focus on the preservation of capital. In our opinion, that's what a hedge fund is supposed to do. It's supposed to protect you on the down side, and even make some money in the down months.

SK: *So that shapes your portfolio.*

CC: Yes. We're pretty close to market neutral right now. Actually when you adjust for beta, we're slightly net short. It's been that way for quite a while. If you look back over the history of our fund, you'll note that the majority of the months we've been in existence, we've had a higher beta on the short side. We factor that in when we look at our net exposure and when doing so, we end up being slightly net short in the whole portfolio, in spite of showing a nominal net long position. Currently, that's about 5 percent.

I think we do best in a declining market at this point, given our slightly net short exposure. But I'd say the reason for this is, in a very general sense, we are long predictability and short unpredictability. And, when you have a market that's declining, we get a lot of help on the short side. We have had relatively significant absolute performance in down months for the market.

SK: *What practices would you say give you a competitive advantage?*

CC: We spend a lot of time on the financials and the filings. They're better determinants of what the company's actually doing than listening to what management is saying that it's doing. We will listen to company calls, and we meet about 50 percent of the management teams on the long side.

Another thing is a willingness to be contrarian. Now that requires being fearless sometimes and it requires making sure you don't get too greedy at other times. You can't make money in anything unless you're willing to be contrarian. I think that's a must in this business.

Finally, and critical to our success, have been the two dozen or so screens that we use to aid us in sourcing our names on both the long and the short side. These are proprietary. But I'll tell you, they're focused on free cash flow, on sequential quarterly improvements, on tangible book value, and recent price movements. On the shorts we're looking for overleveraged companies with little or no asset protection.

SK: *That's good. But really, it's not anything that other funds don't do, or try to do.*

CC: Right. But we look for other things, too. When we look at a long, we want a measure of predictability there. Not only from the cash flow, but we want to make sure that we have some inherent assets to support our longs as well. In other words, if there's a disappointment, what's going to support this stock? That's what we're always asking ourselves. And what form do the assets of this company take to keep it afloat? In some cases, it's cash; in other cases, it's real estate. In other cases, it's something far more subjective. It might be the long-life contracts that they have. For example, if you're a lottery operator, you might have contracts that last from 5 to 15 years. If you're a prison operator, you might have 5-year contracts with high renewal rates. You know, high barriers to entry don't show up as a tangible asset on your books necessarily, but to us, they're very important.

SK: *Predictability? Can you give us an example of how that has worked for you?*

CC: A good example is the Alderwoods Group. They are one of the largest operators of funeral homes and cemeteries in the United States. It's a company that we sourced from our screening process, by looking for free cash flow and asset values. We took a long position. And subjectively we look for high barriers to entry as well as a lot of other metrics. The funeral home industry had a very difficult time over the past number of years. There was a roll-up strategy that was followed by the industry and essentially a number of other companies overpaid for the mom-and-pop funeral homes and cemeteries that they bought. Being a low-growth industry, they couldn't grow their way out of the problem. So they were left with a lot of debt on their balance sheets.

In the case of Alderwoods, what initially attracted us was that we noticed it had a 14 percent free cash flow yield. And that was about the time when the stock was around $9 per share. We got interested; it was one of a hundred names that showed up on a screen for us. We also noticed that within that screen there were a couple of other funeral home companies, which really meant that the sector was under a lot of pressure. That would be evident if you simply popped up a chart of the past decade. You would see that all of those stocks had been significantly higher at one point. But essentially, we noticed it was an excellent deleveraging story.

So what we noticed about Alderwoods was that they not only had a very attractive nominal free cash flow yield, but that they were using the money to deleverage the balance sheet. They had about $900 million in debt on their books several years ago. When we first looked at it, a year ago, it was at a level of about $600 million. And they had stated that it was their policy to be reducing that debt.

SK: *A good sign, for you.*

CC: Definitely. When we model it out, which is looking about one year ahead, we could see that they were taking about $30 million per quarter off their debt load. In addition to that, they had an insurance subsidiary that they sold for about $80 million and they used the proceeds to reduce the debt. So basically over one year they brought their debt down from about $600 to $400 million. And that had a powerful effect on the bottom line, which is what we anticipated would happen. The stock has moved nicely from the 9 level. It's at 16 today. And they continue to pay down their debt. Today, it's about a $650 million market cap company.

SK: *Nice. How does the long-life contract come into play?*

CC: Generally speaking, we measure the health of a company in this sector by looking at the preneed sales. Basically, you're buying your funeral before you die. The accounting on it is quite conservative in the sense that the company writes off all of the marketing expenses right away, but they can't recognize any revenue until that person dies. And it's important because the preneed business accounts for about 70 percent of their ongoing trade. So in a sense, it's their backlog. So that's the long-life contract I'm talking about. Seventy percent of their ongoing business is not listed as an asset on the balance sheet, but to us, it sure is a strong asset.

SK: *Is that still a hold for you?*

CC: We still own it, but a smaller piece. It's part of our policy to always trim positions, stocks that do well for us, with no change in the metrics. We always trim back.

SK: *Why is that?*

CC: I think this is a real hallmark of the kind of things we do. After you've had a gain on a position, we think it's really important to cut your risk rather than increase it. When you're doing well in a holding . . . that's not the time to buy more. It's the time to cut back. It goes back to what I said before about not trying to get greedy.

SK: *How else do you manage risk?*

CC: Well, the first thing is we maintain a concentrated portfolio. At any given time we'll have between 15 and 30 long positions. It's about the same on the short side. So we're not tracking more than we can handle.

SK: *And you have limits on any single position, right?*

CC: Right. We limit our exposure on the long side to 8 percent per holding, and 4 percent on the shorts. We use ETFs [exchange-traded funds] to hedge industry and market cap exposure and we adjust gross exposure based on market conditions.

SK: *Do you have an automatic stop-loss in place for a given holding?*

CC: No, we don't use stop-losses. Remember, we have a concentrated portfolio. Right now we have 45 names altogether. And we have three sets of eyeballs watching those 45 names. So nothing is going to get away from us. And there's too much new information that comes out all the time. So we monitor our positions "by hand," as it were. We know our capital is pretty well preserved, so it's not market risk that we are greatly concerned about. We're more concerned about company-specific risk.*

---

*The second of Sharpe's risks described in Chapter 1.

SK: *Can you give us an example of that?*

CC: An example would be a company called Friedman's, a jewelry retailer, primarily in malls. And we'd actually owned it in 2003 and sold it. The stock went significantly higher after that. They did an equity offering, I think at about $16 per share. We noticed that the stock had backtracked quite a bit from that price so it showed up again on our screens as a company that had a high tangible book value. So we took an interest in the company again on the long side. It was a small position for us, partly because we owned nonvoting shares. The founder of the company owned the voting shares. So that's always a concern.

Well, within a couple of days after taking that position, the Department of Justice announced that they were filing a lawsuit against Friedman's and a number of other companies on a factoring dispute. If that wasn't bad enough, it then became evident that a 50 percent-owned subsidiary was nowhere near as healthy as the equity holders had been led to believe. The rubber-stamp board had been allowing the healthy parent to continue to feed the unhealthy subsidiary. And, since the balance of that subsidiary was owned by the founder and head of Friedman's, the conflict of interest was all too apparent. We got out of the stock at about $5 a share. It cost us a little more than one percentage point in our performance. Friedman's eventually went bankrupt.

It was ugly. So there's a glaring example of company-specific risk. A lot of it came down to corporate governance. You know, it turned out they had a rubber-stamp board and the equity holders had no say. That's why you need to size positions carefully, which we did.

SK: *There's a good war story. Did things change at your shop as a result of that trade?*

CC: Well, we're not interested in nonvoting shares anymore.

SK: *Well, thanks for being open enough to offer that story of a loss. Let's end it on a high note, though. Tell us about a good win you had. We know about Alderwoods. How about sharing a win on the short side?*

CC: Okay. I can talk about Lexmark. They make printers and supply ink. They had been making all of their money in the ink business, virtually giving away the printers, and they had cushy margins there for a very long time. And it certainly propped up the whole company. We'd been short the stock for quite a number of months and it had gone against us. Their margins were so attractive there that it was also attracting a lot of competition. It came from the private branded folks, such as Office Depot and Staples, as well as the resellers, the remanufactured cartridges you can get over the Internet.

Then in the first quarter of this year [2005], we saw the first crack. Their margins began to get squeezed by the competition. What helped us was that Lexmark was a much-loved company. A lot of people followed it, and there were a lot of buy recommendations. We were the contrarians thinking margins would come under pressure, which ultimately they did for the reasons we suspected. And once again, when our initial positions began to pay off, we trimmed back and cut our risk.

SK: *And obviously this kind of trade is more typical of your performance. Rivanna is again putting up good numbers (+14.2 percent in 2005) this time in a sideways U.S. equities market.*

CC: Yep. We're trying to keep it up.

CHAPTER 3

The Directional Strategies: Managed Futures

INTRODUCTION

The second of our directional strategies is managed futures, a term that refers to professional money managers known as Commodity Trading Advisors (CTAs). CTAs manage their clients' assets using commodities, futures, and options markets. Managed futures funds provide exposure to global markets in all asset classes with the ability to take both long and short positions in more than 100 different markets. While some of the better databases like HFRI do not include managed futures, it is clear that as a strategy it is an important and, some would argue, a necessary component of any hedge fund portfolio. According to The Barclay Group, a leading database for CTAs, AUM for this strategy have quadrupled in the past 8 years going from $33 billion to more than $130 billion in 2005.[1]

In addition to investing with individual funds, investors can place money in managed futures index funds like those offered by Mt. Lucas Management (MLM). Its MLM Index Fund, for example, invests in fixed income, commodities, and currencies through 22 different futures markets.

What then is the allure of this strategy? In a word, diversification. Managed futures have been shown to be relatively uncorrelated to most traditional asset classes and even to other hedge fund strategies. Thus, they provide diversification in an overall portfolio asset allocation schema and within a portfolio of hedge funds. CISDM found that over the 15-year period 1990–2004, an equally weighted portfolio of CTAs (the CISDM CTA Dollar Weighted Index) showed a negative correlation of –0.10 to the S&P 500, a correlation of only 0.29 to the U.S. bond market, and an even more modest correlation of 0.19 to CISDM's Hedge Fund Composite Index.[2] As in our study,[3] managed futures performed about equal to equities with lower volatility and showed an almost identical correlation of –0.08 to the S&P and 0.34 to bonds from 1994–2005.

In 1983, Professor John Lintner of Harvard published what would become a landmark study on the benefits of managed futures investing. While Lintner analyzed only 3 years of performance data, he nevertheless concluded that "the combined portfolios of stocks (or stocks and bonds) after including judicious investments in leveraged Managed Futures accounts show substantially less risk at every possible level of expected return than portfolios of stocks (or stocks and bonds) alone."[4] Since then, larger studies spanning 7 years[5] and 15 years[6] of performance that also include hedge funds in the analysis have replicated Lintner's results.

Table 3.1 shows the results of our 12-year analysis of various asset classes and portfolio combinations including stocks, bonds, hedge funds and managed futures.[7] When portfolios of stocks and bonds alone are compared with those containing even modest amounts of managed futures allocations, the latter portfolios show higher risk-adjusted returns. As Table 3.1 shows, the best performing portfolio in the study, Portfolio 3, both on an absolute and risk-adjusted basis was one composed of the following mix: 36 percent in the MSCI World stocks, 36 percent in the Lehman Gov/Credit bond Index, 18 percent in the HFRI Fund-Weighted Composite Index, and a 10 percent position in the CISDM CTA Asset-Weighted Index. Our study confirms the findings of CISDM in its 15-year study on managed futures.[8]

How is this increase in the risk/reward profile as measured by the lowered standard deviation and higher Sharpe ratio achieved? As we discussed in Chapter 1, MPT offers the simplest and most elegant explanation. Efficient investment portfolios are those that diversify among asset classes with low or even negative correlations to each other. In this

TABLE 3.1

Performance of Asset Classes and Portfolio Combinations, January 1994–December 2005

	Annualized Return	Annualized Standard Deviation	Sharpe Ratio
HFRI Fund-Weighted Composite Index	11.56%	7.05%	1.08
Lehman Government-Credit Bond Index	6.35%	4.50%	0.54
MSCI The World Index—Net	7.95%	13.83%	0.29
CISDM CTA Asset-Weighted Index	8.01%	8.54%	0.48
Portfolio 1 (Equities and Bonds)	7.18%	7.75%	0.42
Portfolio 2 (Equities, Bonds, and Hedge Funds)	8.23%	7.24%	0.59
Portfolio 3 (Equities, Bonds, Hedge Funds, and CTAs)	8.94%	5.49%	0.91

Portfolio 1 = 50% MSCI The World Index/50% Lehman Government-Credit Bond Index
Portfolio 2 = 40% MSCI The World Index/40% Lehman/20% HFRI Fund-Weighted Composite Index
Portfolio 3 = 36% MSCI The World Index/36% Lehman/18% HFRI Fund-Weighted Composite/10% CISDM CTA Asset-Weighted Index
Source: Mayer & Hoffman, CISDM, and PerTrac.

case, managed futures made the portfolios of stocks and bonds more efficient by having a negative correlation to the S&P 500 and a modest correlation (about 0.3) to the Lehman. In addition, managed futures showed only a modest correlation to other hedge fund strategies further diversifying the portfolio (more on this later). Professor Harry Kat of London's Cass Business School summed up his seven-year study of the same asset classes by emphasizing that "*investing in managed futures can improve the overall risk profile of a portfolio far beyond what can be achieved with hedge funds alone* [italics by Kat]."[9]

THE MANAGED FUTURES TRADING AND INVESTMENT STRATEGIES

Since managed futures historically have not been correlated to the stock, bond, and other major markets, they truly rely on the skill of the traders to produce returns. These traders in turn rely on complex trading models for making their buy and sell decisions. Traders fall into two general classifications: systematic and discretionary. Both groups will trade either short-term, medium-term, or long-term, or a combination of all three.

Systematic

The majority of CTAs are systematic traders. These managers use proprietary trading models that they have developed for a number of different financial markets. These models can be either trend-following, countertrend, or a combination of both. Most models are based on historical price data and/or fundamental economic inputs. "Black boxes," as these models are sometimes called, also feature pattern recognition algorithms that allow managers to pick up subtle price and volatility trends that may be early precursors of longer-term and, therefore, tradable trends.

Dr. Bill Dunn is a long-time strict systematic trader and the founder of Dunn Capital Management. Dunn Capital's World Monetary Assets (WMA) system is a systematic, large-volume, long-term trend-following program developed in 1984 by Dr. Dunn, a Ph.D. in theoretical physics from Northwestern. The WMA system is characterized by a signature reversal component. Dunn explains, "We take a position, either long or short. Then, when our system dictates that we close that position, we automatically open an opposing one. So if our long stops out, we immediately take a short position. That's the reversal; the theory being that the market is either going one way or the other. It means we're never out of the market. With WMA, we're never on the sidelines." The average length of a trade by the WMA system is three to four months not including contract rolling. WMA has an impressive long-term record; a compound annual rate of return of 15.4 percent from May 1989 to October 2005 versus 10.99 percent for the S&P 500, with a negative correlation coefficient of –0.1 to the S&P.

Dunn Capital also runs the Targets of Opportunity System (TOPS). "TOPS still looks for long-term trends, but it's not a reversal system," said Dunn. "When certain patterns occur that are statistically meaningful, significant price movements may be in the offing. We'll take a position on that basis. The TOPS program has lots of built-in risk controls. If a trade is wrong, it's knocked out relatively soon. And if it's right, it has a price target that it's looking for. If it reaches the target, it takes the profit and steps aside. For any given future, TOPS may typically be out of the market as much as 40 to 45 percent of the time, sitting on the sidelines looking for an opportunity. And so our two programs go at trading differently. But they end up having a long-term relatively high correlation in the vicinity of 0.8 between them." Over the period May 1989 to October 2005, TOPS has produced a compound annual return of 17.0 percent versus the S&P 500 of 10.99 percent and a negligible correlation coefficient of –0.06.

"Long-term trend following," Dunn continues, "has built into it various features of survivability. It refuses to allow you to argue with the markets. Our model won't let us buy low, then watch it go a whole lot lower. It forces us to switch sides. But, of course, there's no free lunch. Generally, we're going to buy after the bottom and sell after the top, so we're going to leave some money on the table. But that's the game. The trend is your friend. Only the major trends are going to benefit us significantly."[10]

Discretionary and Hybrid Traders

As the name implies, discretionary and hybrid traders do not blindly follow their models but reserve the discretionary right to go against what the model is forecasting. Discretionary traders, unlike their systematic peers, can rely on personal beliefs, trading experience, or intuitions to make entry and exit decisions.

"Well, it's not for me," smiles Dunn. "Certainly there are people that have that kind of skill. And they understand all the technical aspects of the market like we do. And they also have a real good feel for timing. A couple of really outstanding names come to mind: Bruce Kovner of Caxton and Paul Tudor Jones. They're both just magnificently successful, wonderful guys who've got the gift. And they certainly know everything about trend following and all sorts of other technical tools. They have them at their fingertips, but they meld it with some other art. And they do a marvelous job."

In addition to the straight systematic and discretionary styles, there is a hybrid of the two. Michael Dever, the founder of Brandywine Asset Management, is a systematic trader but also employs discretion in the selection of a strategy. Mike is our featured interviewee at the end of the chapter.

One of Brandywine's newest funds, the Financial Futures Program, has developed a specific model for trading most world currency markets. Figure 3.1 shows the downtrend in the Australian dollar that reached a short-term bottom on May 17, 2004. Brandywine's Basis Arbitrage strategy became long the Australian dollar and earned substantial profits later in May as well as in June 2004 as the currency rallied against the U.S. dollar. Why were they long a market where trend followers were so obviously short? The answer is that Dever's Basis Arbitrage strategy signaled that the cash price for the currency was predicting a higher futures price despite the downward trend line for the futures contract. Brandywine's research shows that over time

FIGURE 3.1

Australian Dollar versus the USD

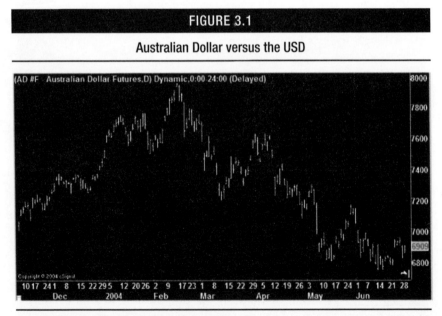

Sources: eSignal and Brandywine Asset Management.

FIGURE 3.2

Cumulative Performance of CISDM CTA Index versus Benchmarks

Growth of $1,000 USD, 1/1/1994–12/31/2005

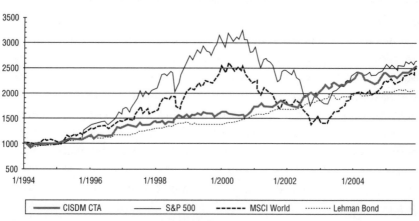

Sources: Mayer & Hoffman Capital Advisors, CISDM, and PerTrac.

the current cash price of a market is more predictive of the future cash price than is today's futures price.

Performance

Figure 3.2 shows the cumulative performance of the CISDM CTA Asset-Weighted Index from 1994–2005 versus several benchmarks. While managed futures absolute performance was slightly below domestic equities and slightly ahead of global equities, its Sharpe ratio was higher than both (0.48 versus 0.31 and 0.29, respectively) because of substantially lower volatility.[11]

How did managed futures fare during the most recent bear market? In our study of the most recent five years,* the CISDM Index widely outperformed bonds and equities on both an absolute and risk-adjusted

---

*See Table 1.3.

basis. The Index returned 7.72 percent per annum over the period 2001–2005 with a Sharpe ratio of 0.66 compared with negative Sharpes for both the S&P and the MSCI World. At the end of 2005, the S&P 500 had yet to return to its highs set in 2000 while the CISDM CTA Asset-Weighted Index had climbed to new all-time highs.[12] Figure 3.3 illustrates the performance of the CTA Index versus its benchmarks.

Another way to look at the performance of managed futures over the most recent market cycle is to measure their impact on portfolios of other asset classes. We studied the performance of bonds, equities, hedge funds, and managed futures as well as the performance of various portfolio combinations for the period January 1, 2001, to December 31, 2005.[13] Table 3.2 shows that diversified portfolios of stocks, bonds, hedge funds, and CTAs were the best performers through the bear market on both an absolute return and risk-adjusted basis (Portfolios 2 and 3). For example, Portfolio 3 contained a hypothetical mix of 36 percent S&P 500 stocks, 36 percent Lehman government and corporate

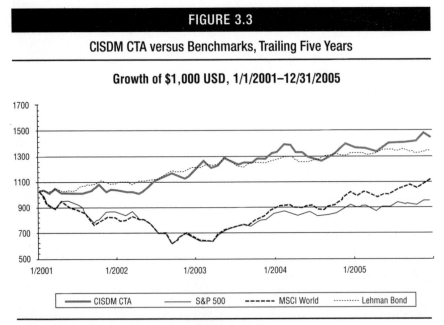

FIGURE 3.3

CISDM CTA versus Benchmarks, Trailing Five Years

Growth of $1,000 USD, 1/1/2001–12/31/2005

CISDM CTA   S&P 500   MSCI World   Lehman Bond

Sources: Mayer & Hoffman Capital Advisors, CISDM, and PerTrac.

TABLE 3.2

Performance of Asset Classes and Portfolio Combinations, January 2001–December 2005

	Annualized Return	Annualized Standard Deviation	Sharpe Ratio
HFRI Fund-Weighted Composite Index	8.00%	5.20%	1.10
Lehman Government-Credit Bond Index	6.10%	4.86%	0.79
MSCI The World Index—Net	2.18%	14.67%	−0.01
CISDM CTA Asset-Weighted Index	7.72%	8.25%	0.66
Portfolio 1 (Equities and Bonds)	3.86%	7.09%	0.23
Portfolio 2 (Equities, Bonds, and Hedge Funds)	4.96%	6.41%	0.42
Portfolio 3 (Equities, Bonds, Hedge Funds, and CTAs)	6.40%	4.53%	0.91

Portfolio 1 = 50% MSCI The World Index/50% Lehman Government-Credit Bond Index
Portfolio 2 = 40% MSCI The World Index/40% Lehman/20% HFRI Fund-Weighted Composite Index
Portfolio 3 = 36% MSCI The World Index/36% Lehman/18% HFRI Fund-Weighted Composite/10% CISDM CTA Asset-Weighted Index
Source: Mayer & Hoffman, HFRI, CISDM, and PerTrac.

bonds, 18 percent hedge funds, and a 10 percent position in the CTA Index.[14] Our study confirms the findings of CISDM for the period 2000–2004.

Advantages of Managed Futures

We have already looked at three of the major benefits of managed futures: ease of investing in global markets; diversification; and lower portfolio risk with the possibility of enhanced returns. We've also cited longitudinal studies showing that adding a CTA component to a portfolio containing stocks and bonds tends to improve the risk-adjusted return of the resulting portfolio. But there are two other benefits to investing in managed futures: as an insurance policy in case of disastrous macro events and as diversifiers to a portfolio of other hedge fund strategies.

Investing in CTAs could be considered an insurance policy in case of a major macro event. Take for example a massive disruption to the oil supply. Oil and gas prices would go even further through the roof, producing once-in-a-lifetime opportunities for commodity traders when many long-only and certain hedge fund strategies would be losing money. Another example is the flight-to-quality that occurred during and after 9/11 that sent world stock prices into a nosedive. Many commodity traders made fortunes on bond futures and options on futures.

Let's further examine what would happen if the U.S. dollar, the world's major reserve currency, goes into a major slide as the result of escalating trade deficits. A likely scenario is that interest rates would climb, stocks would get severely punished, gold prices would climb, and the economy would find itself in recession. Under such circumstances, many CTAs would profit. CTAs have a long history of outperforming the stock market during negative environments for equities. For example, the various CISDM Indices including both systematic and trend followers were *negatively* correlated to the S&P 500 during its 48 worst performing months over the 15-year period 1/1/1990–12/31/2004.[15] Like the Lehman Bond Index, which was also negatively correlated to equity indices during severe downturns, CTAs are a refuge from the periodic storms that assault global stock markets.*

Second, managed futures act as diversifiers to a portfolio of other hedge fund strategies. Table 1.3 showed that unlike the two major hedge fund strategies, ELS and Event Driven, CTAs, regardless of markets or style, showed a negative correlation to equities over the 2001–2005 period. How then do CTAs correlate to the other hedge fund strategies? The answer is very little. In Chapter 2 we presented a table† showing the correlations between all the major hedge fund strategies. Our study showed that the CISDM CTA Index had slightly negative, zero, or slightly positive correlations with the other strategies, including the HFRI Fund-Weighted Composite Index (0.02). The

---

*HFRI Event-Driven and Equity Hedge Indices were both negative in 2002.
†See Table 2.2.

only exception was its correlation with global macro of 0.49, which is not surprising since both strategies trade in similar global markets. These correlations help explain the results depicted earlier in Tables 3.1 and 3.2, that when added to portfolios containing both alternative and traditional assets, managed futures act as additional diversifiers lowering volatility and improving risk-adjusted performance.

Disadvantages

There are three primary risks associated with managed futures: margin calls, significant drawdowns, and herding. Margin to equity ratios generally range from 5 percent to 20 percent. Because so little money is typically supporting the trades, margin calls can come suddenly and very painfully when commodity markets take an unexpected turn.

Drawdowns can and do occur for most CTAs because trend followers sometimes are hit with long-lasting sideways markets with no clear direction. For example, as of this writing, Dunn Capital was weathering a 34-month drawdown. "That's longer than anything in the preceding 30 years," says Bill Dunn. Of course, Dunn Capital is not the only fund suffering through the stagnation. "When you're not doing well," he said, "people always ask, 'Have the markets changed?' Typically, we would say no, relative to our models. From the very beginning we were using dynamic algorithms that take their signals from the near-term past, not the long-term past. But on the other hand, obviously we wouldn't be having such a long drawdown if we didn't have a lack of major long-term trends. It's those trends that allow us to make money. And they have just not been around very much the past couple of years. In retrospect, maybe that is different. We've had dull periods before, but not as bothersome as this one."

A third major risk of managed futures has to do with the fact that so many of these funds end up following the same trend. Because so many CTAs use much of the same data, a herding effect can occur. For example, the factors that would suggest being long copper are pretty much the same to all commodity traders. If copper is in a major uptrend, most CTAs are going to be aboard, and many will have large positions. The problem occurs when the trend reverses and traders are all scrambling to sell or cover simultaneously. The heavy margin being used exacerbates the problem. It can get very bloody, very quickly. This happened to silver traders in 1980 when silver declined precipitously from $50/ounce down ultimately to $6/ounce.

Michael P. Dever

Founder and Chairman
Brandywine Diversified Futures Program

ENTHUSIASM FOR HIS WORK IS IMMEDIATELY EVIDENT WHEN MIKE DEVER sits down to talk shop. As Sam Kirschner observed, Dever is enthralled by the challenges of matching the market with the right blend of trading strategies. Twenty-five years of practice only seem to have increased his appetite for the game, much to the benefit of his investors. Dever formed the Brandywine Alliance Fund in June 1999. The Alliance Fund has had an annualized return of 12.49 percent since inception (through 11/30/05).

Brandywine has added an equity market neutral fund and several managed futures programs to its platform. Among the newest of these offerings is the Diversified Futures Program, which began in January 2004. Diversified Futures has had an annualized return since inception of 7.6 percent while a subset of this program, the top-decile performing Brandywine Financial Futures Program, is up about 21 percent annualized over the same time period. Diversified Futures trades a broadly diversified portfolio of financial and commodity futures using primarily fundamentally based yet systematic trading strategies. The Financial Futures Program trades in more than 50 of the most liquid financial futures contracts while targeting moderate volatility.

SK: *Mike, I'm anxious to talk about Brandywine and the strategies that have produced your exemplary track record. But before we dig into that, I'm curious about how you got started. I mean, there has got to be some aspect of your approach that lets you keep it fresh in a tough business.*

MD: It is a tough business. But I love it. I've always had a strong interest in math, science, and business. I got started in 1979 when the gold market started to bubble. I really wanted to get involved, so I sold my car, took a few thousand dollars, and started buying gold options.

SK: *You sold your wheels?*

MD: I guess I figured I could get where I wanted to go quicker riding gold options. So I started playing with it. And very quickly I realized that this combined math, science, and business is one great package. It's fascinating to me, even now after 25 years. Anyway, I started trading for myself. And slowly, through the 1980s, with a lot of fits and starts, I began developing different strategies; different market-specific systems. But at first I didn't really rely on the systems. I didn't trust them sufficiently, even though I could see that they were working.

It wasn't until the early 1990s that I really sat down to fully systematize an overall trading approach. By then, I was confident in my approach. So I launched a fully diversified, fully systematic futures program and began getting clients. In 1996 we started trading equities, too.

SK: *And that led to Brandywine?*

MD: Yes. We made the decision to combine everything into one product, which was our Brandywine Alliance Fund.

SK: *How do you describe the fund?*

MD: Opportunistic, multistrategy, systematic. The Brandywine Diversified Futures program, which is the futures-trading subset of that fund, is our most broadly diversified managed futures program. It trades in the most markets across the most strategies. The other managed futures programs that we offer are focused subsets of that. We might have some clients who are looking for a financial-only portfolio. So we simply carved out the financial markets that we're trading in Diversified

Futures and created the Financial Futures Program. Another option is the Aggressive Fund. That program uses three times the standard leverage. So it's really a cash-efficient product for institutional investors. Rather than putting money in a notionally funded managed account, they can get the same leverage in the fund.

But, you know, there are a lot of guys out there who are systematic, and certainly a lot who are opportunistic. With us though, the unique thing is multistrategy; the way we use multiple fundamental yet systematic strategies. We believe in this approach for many different reasons.

SK: *I really want to ask you about that, but before we go there, let me take a step back. How do you go about developing a strategy? I mean a single strategy? Then we can discuss the multiple approaches.*

MD: Very good. Essentially we're using the scientific method. So we start with a hypothesis. We can test it. We can quantify it and see if the strategy is effective across a variety of data sets.

Then, if it looks highly robust, we're ready for the prediction phase of the scientific method; which is running on a blind data set. Then we try it out in actual trading. At that point, we have spent a lot of time and research exploring and testing the theory, so we are confident that the original hypothesis is based on a sound logical premise, and it's been properly quantified. Then, we have a system, a strategy, and there is no ongoing human discretion to determine daily moves or choose parameters.

The only ongoing human discretion is in determining the validity of the strategy. And that's not generally something that changes day to day. That's something that may change over years or even a generation. Some of these strategies are highly persistent over long periods of time, where others are a bit more transient.

SK: *Can you give us an example? What is a persistent strategy? What is a transient one?*

MD: Okay, let's look at trend following, which is the primary systematic approach used by other futures managers. It's a good example of a systematic strategy that is highly persistent over long periods of time. That's because it's based on human nature; people jumping on trends when they emerge and perpetuating those trends. We're always going to have that.

More transient is a strategy that's looking at, for example, in today's market, the reaction of crude oil prices following the release of the weekly inventory reports. That's not a report that was that influential on the markets three years ago. Today it's highly influential. So a strategy that's based on that as a concept is much more transient.

Contrast that with another report-based strategy: the crop production reports for the citrus industry. That strategy is as effective today as it was 25 years ago when I started trading. The report has had a much more persistent influence on the market.

SK: *Great. Now let's talk multiple strategy. How many do you use?*

MD: We have more than three dozen independent strategies operating across about 100 different markets. So we may end up with anywhere between 400 and 500 market-strategy combinations, netting out to 100 or more distinct positions in the portfolio.

SK: *That's a lot.*

MD: It is, compared to many other managers. But if each strategy has a long-term positive return profile, diversification across all of them gives us coverage in any kind of market environment. Each strategy has an environment where it does well. We have some strategies that are based on fundamental cost of production data that take countertrend buy positions when markets are selling down to, or chopping around at, marginal cost of production levels. In an environment like that, trend following, for example, is unprofitable. We have other strategies that are looking for longer trends, or looking for narrowing relationships in cash and futures prices. Each individual strategy, though, is fully systematic. The only ongoing human discretion is in determining the validity of the strategy.

Then the main thing is controlling the risk with offsetting strategies. What you'll find with our approach is that, when we do incur losses, it's usually the interaction of a variety of different strategies that just isn't working. And a lot of our strategies, when they're losing, have a higher probability of future profit. So a downward trend in a given period, we feel, increases our opportunities in the coming periods. When a loss like that happens, we do bounce back pretty quickly from it.

SK: *And your record certainly bears that out. But before we get to that, I'm wondering: What kind of data are you looking at to make these strategic judgments? I'm not talking now about any single strategy, but overall, what is the pertinent information that you use?*

MD: Well, being fundamental traders, we first explore any opportunities that we feel meet our criteria, anything that's based on a sound, logical premise. The information can come from anywhere; our experience, our contacts, just reading the newspaper, or whatever.

Second, we look for a repeatable process. Something that's likely to persist for a reasonable period of time. And third, the trading approach must be able to be systematized, so it doesn't rely on human discretion. We don't get emotionally involved in a trade. And if we get up on the wrong side of the bed one morning, it doesn't make any difference really because the system is running based on the objective strategies that have already been tested and incorporated into it.

SK: *Right. It's like the car engine doesn't care how you feel when you turn the key. It's still going to start right up.*

MD: Exactly. And by having those three sorts of guidelines as our only constraints, it opens up the possibility of us looking at fundamental information, intermarket relationships, sentiment indicators, any number of factors that may drive market prices.

Now, as for that fundamental information—and I guess this is what you were asking a minute ago—of course, it varies by strategy. But essentially there are maybe 10 or 12 reports that are influential on various markets, such as the U.S. Bureau of Labor Statistics Employment Situation Summary. You've got crop reports for some of the commodity markets. Other raw fundamental information includes supply and demand indicators like the stock consumption ratios for the sugar market. Then there are the sentiment indicators like put/call ratios, as well as direct surveys of market participants. We also look at intermarket relationships. Certain markets influence or are indicators for others; like how gold serves as an indicator for the bond markets. So we're looking at a wide variety of different reports. We use each one to develop one or more cause-and-effect strategies.

SK: *You're frequently looking at physical markets, right? Give us an example, if you will, of one way that fact might affect a strategy.*

MD: Sure. Some of our fundamental strategies are looking at cost of production data on various commodity markets. Like you said, it's a physical market. It costs money to get your orange crop in. It costs money to deliver those pork bellies to the market. Day in, day out, those costs are going to be relatively stable. So there's a bottom to the market. Generally speaking, prices are not going to go down below the cost of production for very long. So when a market is trading way down near the cost of production, we've got countertrend strategies that rely on prices popping back up again. These strategies are based on sound underlying reasons. That's why we can anticipate an upward movement in that market within a reasonable period of time. It's not just based on some sort of statistical analysis. It's based on a fundamental understanding of the market.

SK: *Makes sense.*

MD: Of course, it doesn't always work out immediately. At times it will. The market will put in a sharp V-bottom on the graph. Where there's a steep decline, it hits a bottom point, and then there is a rapid price rise. It comes roaring out of there. And we're going to be there to quickly profit from that because we've been going long during the decline. But not every market behaves like that. Sometimes a market will ratchet downward over a long period of time and stay low for a year, or a couple of years. But as long as the strategy is buying only when the market is at low levels, it will profit during those periods by, essentially, range trading the market.

Once in a while, a market will drop to the marginal cost of production level and keep on dropping lower, month after month. In that case, you don't want to be standing around waiting for a bottom, which is what the cost of production strategy does. But that environment is great for producing profits from a trend following strategy. So we've got a lot of strategies—a lot of sockets for the wrench—that complement each other.

Our overall philosophy is that we can create a relatively hedged portfolio with our strategies. Not by buying hedges that might cost us a premium, but by incorporating multiple strategies in the portfolio that complement each other.

SK: *It sounds rock solid. But we know the real world is going to get rough once in a while, right?*

MD: It can happen at any time. When it does, the comment I make around the office is "Well, we're traders. And traders lose money once in a while."

SK: *Give us an example of that.*

MD: April 2004.

SK: *Ouch. That was a bad month for a lot of people.*

MD: Yes, but for us it was orange juice.

SK: *You got squeezed on orange juice?*

MD: Man, we got pulped. That was a case where we were long and the market just broke through. It sold down below the cost of production. Orange juice went from 75 cents to 54 cents. That's a 27-year low. Our strategy was consistently losing money, week after week. That started it. Then it just seemed like anything we touched on the commodity front just beat us up through that month.

The metals were crazy. One of our strategies evaluates the spread between futures prices and cash prices. It is what we refer to as a directional arbitrage strategy. Over time the forward or futures price will converge with the cash price. But in the short-term the prices can diverge substantially. In fact that is what creates the trading opportunity in the first place. Aluminum was one of the really tough markets where we held a position based on this strategy. We were long on aluminum and we had a 7 percent down day. During April 2004 we had a number of those arbitrage strategies that went against us. So there was a series of trades that just kept hitting us through that period.

I spent a lot of time at the end of that month explaining to investors what we did to lose money. But we lost it differently from other people, which is a funny argument to make. The reality was that some of our fundamentally based commodity strategies pulled us down. But the fundamentals were still correct. And we were able to show that over the following months. Straight through the summer, every month was profitable for us. A lot of people who had difficulty in April continued to struggle somewhat through the late spring and into the summer. And that turned out to be one of our strongest periods.

SK: *Good, let's talk about that turnaround. What went right for you?*

MD: Many things, but orange juice was a big contributor. It had a quick rally into the 70 cents range. And then it immediately sold off in a matter of days down to the low 60s again. And then the hurricanes came through and started hitting Florida. So what was nice about it, from our standpoint, is when the market rallied up to 70, we were able to take off some of the positions that we'd accumulated in the 50s. And when the market sold back down to 60, we put some positions back on again. And then when the hurricanes came and it rallied again, we took those positions off. That market paid off multiples on the initial risk we incurred in accumulating our position.

SK: *So the turnaround validated your strategy and helped you gain back the loss. How about a more recent example of a good trade? Let's look at the shiny side of the coin.*

MD: Okay. February 2005. We had been accumulating positions on the long side in the grain markets, based on some of our fundamental strategies. And sure enough, the grains broke out on the upside in February. So that provided a really strong base for our performance, both from a sector and a fundamentals standpoint. In addition to the grains, we had some arbitrage strategies in the meats that were working for us and an intermarket relationship that was working for us, too. On the interest rate side, we caught the sell-off in the interest rate contracts and the rise in rates just beautifully throughout the month.

SK: *Nice. Anything going on in energy at that time?*

MD: We were long natural gas and short crude oil. We've got some relative BTU strategies in place like that, and more fundamental spread strategies.

SK: *Interesting. Do you guys look at indices much?*

MD: Yes. We trade all the major global stock indices. They're actually excellent markets as there is a plethora of fundamental and sentiment data available to incorporate into trading strategies.

SK: *What do you see as the capacity of the Diversified Futures Program?*

MD: It's probably in the range of $500 million.

SK: *What does your crystal ball foresee, say, for this time next year?*

MD: Well, most of our strategies aren't looking out for a year from now. The time frame that we hold a position varies. Some of the strategies are looking at just a market reaction to a report. So that time frame may be a week to a month. We do have longer-term intermarket relationships affecting interest rate markets that could be on for a year or more. Our longer-term strategies right now are looking for higher rates. The main point for me to make though, is our belief in the dynamic nature of markets and therefore the need to take an active approach to both research and investment management. By incorporating multiple fundamental systematic strategies we are positioned to respond to whatever is occurring in each of the markets we trade.

SK: *Great. Let's close with your viewpoint of the managed futures space. You've been doing this a long time. How have things changed?*

MD: It's been interesting. Ten years ago, nobody conceived of a CTA being able to handle more than a couple of billion dollars. Today you've got CTAs with $10 billion. Capacity expectations have totally changed. Now CTAs have really become financial market traders. The commodities traders are a very small part of the whole CTA universe. And that's primarily because of the liquidity in the other markets that people are trading. Commodity markets by themselves can't support the very large CTAs.

Another thing that's been interesting is when I started trading, people tended to prefer discretionary traders. But as systematic traders, primarily trend following systematic traders, started to show more and more success, people started gravitating to them. That's where they started putting their money. They started realizing that, at least with the systematic traders, there was some long-term predictability of what re-turns to expect. And with the discretionary trader, they started seeing a kind of dependence on the trader essentially waking up on the right side of the bed every morning and having his mind-set in tune with the markets. That's difficult to sustain. The allocations started going to the systems guys. Now we're starting to see strong interest in our style of trading; fundamental approaches being systematized and incorporated into a multistrategy portfolio. This is a style that didn't even exist 10 years ago. I believe it takes a lot of the best attributes of what the dis-cretionary traders would do, but systematizes it through our multistrategy approach, so we can offer some predictability and reliable expectations going forward. Sometimes I wonder why more people don't do what we do. But you know, I'm not complaining.

CHAPTER 4

The Directional Strategies: Global Macro

INTRODUCTION

The third and final chapter devoted to the directional hedge fund strategies is on global macro. Macro investors are students of central government financial policies and of global economic trends and use this knowledge as the basis for investing. Accordingly, they participate in all major markets (equities, bonds, currencies, and commodities), though not always at the same time, and often use leverage and derivatives to amplify the impact of market moves. It is this use of leverage on directional bets, which often are not hedged, that has the greatest impact on the performance of macro funds and results in the high volatility that many macro funds experience.

Macro investing is perhaps the most publicized of hedge fund strategies, even though less than 10 percent of hedge funds are macro funds managing only about \$53 billion.[1] That's because macro hedge fund managers such as George Soros made headlines for making highly leveraged, high-stakes investments, often with great success. For example, in 1992, Soros bet \$10 billion, much of it borrowed, on the thesis that the British pound would be devalued. His Quantum Fund reaped a tidy \$1 billion profit. But these macro managers, including Soros, misfired in 1994, most notably when some placed huge, unhedged bets that European interest rates would decline, causing bonds to rise; instead, the Fed raised interest rates in the United States, causing European interest rates to rise in tandem and investors who had bet that European interest rates would fall, to lose money.

Not surprisingly, macro investing is perceived by many to be a high-risk, volatile investment strategy. This perception has been fueled and, indeed, exaggerated by the media, which seem to take great glee in reporting whenever a well-known hedge fund manager suffers a significant loss.

THE GLOBAL MACRO TRADING AND INVESTMENT STRATEGIES

There are probably as many approaches to identifying and capitalizing on macro trends as there are macro hedge fund managers. But all the players and their approaches have several things in common. First, as mentioned, macro players are willing to invest across multiple sectors and trading instruments. They move from opportunity to opportunity, trend to trend, and from strategy to strategy—whatever types of investments that expected shifts in economic policies, political climates, or interest rates make attractive.

Further, they all see the entire globe as their playing field and are well aware that events in countries or regions can have a domino effect across global markets. Witness how the problems that first surfaced in Thailand in the fall of 1997 spread to other Asian countries and economies and, subsequently, even to emerging markets as far away as Russia and Latin America. In July 1998, this downward spiral in emerging markets negatively impacted the European and U.S. equity markets and in a flight to safety and quality, drove bond prices higher. Felix Zulauf, a global macro thinker and founder of Zulauf Asset Management, had correctly anticipated these impending world market events. In August 1998 he started the Zulauf Europe Fund, an ELS fund with a macro overlay, and promptly shorted the European markets. Zulauf's fund has returned a compounded annualized return of 19.7 percent since inception while the MSCI Europe Index is basically flat (as of 12/31/2005).[2]

In contrast to Zulauf, Renee Haugerud, founder and chief investment officer of Galtere International Fund, uses an approach that is as organic as the grains she once traded for Cargill. True to her roots as a commodities trader, she established Galtere in 1999 as a commodities-based global macro fund. "We have a commodity view embedded in every trade we do," she explains, "even if the trade is a foreign exchange or fixed-income trade."[3] At any given time, 40–60 percent of her portfolio is in commodities. In this way, Galtere uses the physical markets as a lens to view the financial markets.

Asked how she characterizes her approach to running a fund, Haugerud leans forward with evident enthusiasm. "It's basically two-pronged," she begins. "Really, if you distill it down, there are only two ways that you can have an edge in investing. The first is through superior information or superior synthesis of information. It's getting more and more difficult to have superior information because there's so much information out there. But how do you sift the wheat from the chaff?"

Haugerud adds, "At Galtere we have information that's as good as anyone's. I've got 25 years of background in trading in four continents, in all asset classes and instruments. We've got a plethora of contacts across the board from the big names to the small shops. So from central bankers to journalists, we have great sources of information that can rival those of anyone."

"However," she continues, "it's in the second area of expertise where we really excel, that is, in the synthesis of information: pattern recognition, recognizing the importance of the periphery versus the center, finding wallflowers. And again, my experience and the experience of my staff come into play here, too. Basically we identify when we should be with the herd and when we shouldn't be. We're not purely contrarians, and we're not always lining up to follow every trend, either. But we're a good hybrid of the two."

So that's the first prong of her global macro pitchfork, the one that lets her define desirable trades. What about her model for timing the entry and exit of any given position? That's the second prong of the fork: Galtere's price analysis model.

"Our price analysis model," says Haugerud "is a proprietary, technical, and nondiscretionary model for entry and exit that I developed while I was still at Cargill. I've been using it since 1992. So our portfolio composition and direction come from synthesis of information. But let's face it," she says candidly. "We aren't always one-hundred percent right. Yet, we're in our seventh positive year with no down years in a very volatile market. I really believe that the fact we've never had a down year, despite sometimes being wrong, is due to our price analysis model controlling the entry, exit, and risk. We have very strict risk parameters," Haugerud emphasizes. "We never risk more than two percent of portfolio capital per trade and that's an absolute dollar stop. In addition, we scale into our positions."

When Galtere "scales in," it establishes positions at up to four different price points, in preidentified price value zones, buying in as the price goes down, for example, or selling out at four different points as the price goes up. In the portfolio, each of these price points functions as a "risk unit" in the price analysis model.

"Once we get to four risk units," she explains, "by policy, we wrap a protective risk collar around the position. So we use options, basically buying calls against a short position and simultaneously selling puts creating a zero cost collar. If something egregious happens overnight—say, a thousand-point rally in stocks—our options protect it. We've never had a situation where we've moved from the third risk unit to the stop-out overnight. That's not to say that it couldn't happen, but we've never had it. So our risk collars, the automatic stops, allow us to sleep through the night."

The full value of the risk collar policy was brought home to Haugerud the hard way, following what she has called "my worst series of trades." Before 9/11, Galtere used the risk collars only on an opportunistic basis, not as an all-encompassing practice.

"In 2001," Haugerud recalled, "we felt that we were basically starting the beginning of a commodity upswing: that commodities were coming out of their slumber. We felt that the economic slowdown (it brought short rates down to three percent) was ending. We had just come up with our theory of inverse stagflation: the weight of money seeking yield would keep interest rates stable to low, and we'd have commodity inflation. Equities would be sideways to down. Nominal interest rates would be sideways to down. When this happened, you'd have the mid-area of the curve outperform. This is all a commodity view."

"So we had a short equity basket, a long commodity basket, and then we were long in the mid-area of the curve: basically 10 years—relative to twos and threes. We felt that short rates down at three percent had come down far enough and that the economy was going to start taking off again. We were leveraged and confident. We didn't put the risk collars on. . . . and then 9/11 . . . derailed everything."

In reaction to 9/11 the Federal Reserve lowered the federal funds rate, and Galtere's positions took a beating. Yet the fund rebounded to finish 2001 up 6 percent, helped in large part by its equity short positions.

"But really, there was a silver lining," Haugerud said. "If you feel you always get everything right, it doesn't challenge you to improve. You might actually do better after a couple of bad trades because it recalibrates your thinking. Had we had the risk collars on we would have stopped out, and automatically reentered within two weeks, because many of those positions did come back. We realized later that if we had the risk collars on, we could have ended the year up 30 percent."

As an example of Haugerud using a commodities view to drive investment decision making, she cites oil. "Right now," she said, "if you look at our portfolio you won't see any oil or energy positions. You'd think we're not in it. But we do have positions in the Mexican peso. Mexico has significant oil reserves and they're valued under the market. So for us, the peso is a great way to be long oil at much cheaper levels." Galtere has posted positive returns every year since inception in 1999 and is up more than 200 percent on a cumulative basis. It ended 2005 up 8.96 percent, outperforming the HFRI Macro Index and the S&P 500.

Global Macro Sources of Return

So how does the newer generation of macro managers like Renee Haugerud and Peter Thiel of Clarium Capital (whose interview can be found at the end of this chapter) gain an edge when many industry pioneers like Soros have closed down their macro funds? Peter Ahl[4] says that macro funds can derive returns from three sources: behavioral biases, theoretical and academic research models, and/or asymmetric information.

Behavioral Biases.   Ahl believes that savvy futures traders who later become great macro managers (like Paul Tudor Jones, founder of the $10 billion Tudor funds) grow up observing and capitalizing on market psychology, specifically, fear, greed, and hysteria. The philosophy of these managers is to wait for periods of irrationality in any of the world's asset classes and then pounce on them. If oil is irrationally high as some think it is today, the macro trader would try to sell in anticipation of the bursting bubble and then buy in the beginning stage of a postcrash recovery. However, since timing is everything for global macro traders, knowing that oil is overbought in a hysterical market (as when Hurricane Katrina wiped out oil facilities and the city of New Orleans and the price of crude spiked to $70/barrel) is not the same as knowing when to short the commodity. As you read earlier, Renee Haugerud and others have developed sophisticated stop-loss techniques to minimize the impact of timing errors in their entry points for trades.

Theoretical Models and Academic Research.   A second approach used by global macro managers relies on theoretical models of several key economic variables including commodity price movements, currency and exchange rates, and trade imbalances and deficits. Soros was a pioneer in the study of currencies and as mentioned earlier was able to make billions on trades that exploited central bank and governmental mistakes in setting monetary policy in general and exchange rates in particular.

Today, the G8 central banks are less likely to make the types of errors that old school traders feasted on. As Ahl points out, the Federal Reserve, beginning with Alan Greenspan, shifted to a preemptive, forward looking mode in its attempts to avoid recession and control inflation. How? By using the best theoretical models, academic research, and micro level information available. Once these models become public, the opportunities they generate tend to dissipate.

Asymmetric Information.   Just as academic research helps traders gain an edge in their understanding of markets, so, too, do both macro and micro statistics that have not yet been fully or accurately scrutinized by the investing public. Ahl refers to this phenomenon as asymmetric information. Global macro traders in emerging markets, for example, who have local analysts gaining up-to-date information on housing starts, order backlogs, credit conditions, inventories, and other fundamental data can have a marked edge on competitors who trade in those or related markets. If a fund invests in Eastern Europe it better have people on the ground in Prague and Moscow because its competitors might.

Comparing Global Macro and Managed Futures

Investors are often struck by the similarities between global macro and managed futures. In fact, we've come across hedge funds that describe themselves as managed futures that we might categorize as global macro and vice versa. It is also common to see some FOFs, in their asset allocation charts, place the managed futures funds in which they invest under the heading of global macro.

To us, there are three principal differences between these two strategies:

1. Managed futures funds trade entirely in the futures markets, whereas global macro funds generally trade and invest a significant percentage of their assets in global stock and bond markets.
2. Global macro managers tend to be more fundamentally oriented, whereas most managed futures funds are more technically inclined, in that they identify and play trends and countertrends.

3. Most managed futures traders follow systematic approaches, whereas global macro managers are more inclined to practice discretionary decision making.[5]

In our study (see Table 1.1), global macro returned 10.14 percent per annum versus the CTA Index at 8.01 percent and had a much higher Sharpe ratio over the period 1994–2005. Global macro's volatility was also lower as its standard deviation was 7.24 percent compared with 8.54 percent for the CTA Index.

PERFORMANCE

From January 1994 through December 31, 2005, the HFRI Global Macro Index has averaged a 10.14 percent annualized return and has substantially outperformed both the S&P 500 Composite Index and the Lehman Government/Credit Bond Index.[6] Figure 4.1 shows the

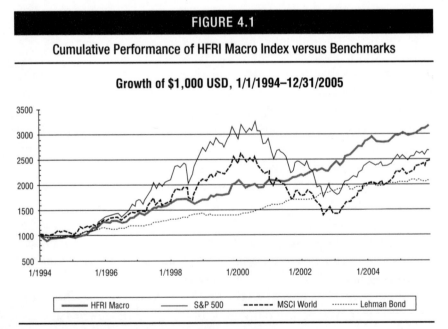

FIGURE 4.1

Cumulative Performance of HFRI Macro Index versus Benchmarks

Growth of $1,000 USD, 1/1/1994–12/31/2005

Sources: Mayer & Hoffman Capital Advisors, HFRI, and PerTrac.

FIGURE 4.2

HFRI Macro versus Benchmarks, Trailing Five Years

Growth of $1,000 USD, 1/1/2001–12/31/2005

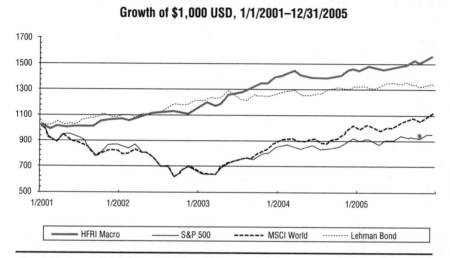

Source: Mayer & Hoffman Capital Advisors, HFRI, and PerTrac.

cumulative performance. In their study covering 1990–2004, CISDM found that global macro was the top performing hedge fund strategy producing about 17 percent annualized returns.[7]

Global macro strategies tend to be somewhat correlated with global equity markets (0.41 with the MSCI over the past 12 years*) and, therefore, their relative performance over the past five years has accentuated the advantages of this investment style. Figure 4.2 shows the HFRI Macro Index versus the same benchmarks and the HFRI Fund-Weighted Composite Index. Note that the Global Macro Index has outperformed the average hedge fund as measured by the HFRI Fund-Weighted Composite Index over the past five years. Not only did global macro investors weather the recent bear market but they have also been rewarded by a 60 percent cumulative return in the latest five-year time period.

---

*See Table 2.2.

Advantages of the Strategy

As shown in Figure 4.2 global macro investing can produce returns well above those normally attainable by long only as well as most other hedge fund strategies. These higher returns derive largely from the flexibility of having a greater array of asset classes in which to invest than most other strategies utilize. Stocks and bonds can be invested in but so can natural resources and currencies. In fact, currency trading is ordinarily an important component of this strategy. Not only do currencies not necessarily correlate with financial markets, they also can be exceptionally volatile, providing large profit opportunities for the astute trader. A global macro fund would not hesitate to be short the ruble against the euro or invest in Russian equities through a basket of stocks that represent the Russian stock market as opposed to getting involved in stock selection.

The flexibility afforded global macro managers often leads to interesting hedging opportunities. Using our Russian example, a manager might take a long position in that country's stock market (via a basket) hedged by a short position in the ruble. The thought process might be that the stock market there looks attractive unless the currency is devalued, in which case hopefully the profits on the currency hedge will offset the losses on the stock position.

A second strength of the strategy is that there are virtually always investment ideas for a global macro fund to pursue. Long or short positions can be taken in any market or any type or class of security. The primary limitations are generally self-imposed, either due to liquidity constraints or the desire to stick to what the manager knows best. Unlike other strategies that are dependent on volatility or other market-specific determinants, macro traders can leave a stagnant market behind in search of a more dynamic one. If, for example, you're a technology long-only specialist, and all the stocks in your screen are overvalued, then you have nowhere to go but cash.

A third advantage of the strategy is that macro has been shown to be relatively uncorrelated with both the equity and bond markets. Both the CISDM study[8] and ours found correlations over the long term to be around 0.4 percent with the S&P and MSCI World indices and around 0.3 percent with the Lehman Bond Index.[9] Unlike ELS and event-driven managers who tend to be highly correlated to the particular equity market(s) in which they trade, global macro managers generally are agnostic as to what market to trade in or whether they are long or short. As our interview with Peter Thiel will show, he is more interested in finding a good market opportunity regardless of where it is or in what asset class it is.

The fourth and final strength of the strategy is the quality of the managers who are attracted to the space. As the two managers interviewed in this chapter demonstrate, their ability to understand markets and the interrelationship between markets is very sophisticated. It takes a lot of brains, education, training, experience, and excellent information networks to cope profitably with the macro financial trends of the world. It is also grueling around-the-clock work answering questions like: Will the pound weaken? Will inflation subside in China? Will a particular banana republic default? Will there be war in the Middle East? And the most important question of all: How do my investors profit no matter what? A good batting average in such prognostications does not come from reading tea leaves, or even brokerage reports! Those who can put the above-mentioned resources together with "street smarts," good trading instincts, and excellent risk management can make outsized returns in this strategy. Finally, and most significantly, global macro, with its extraordinary pool of managers, has been, according to CISDM, the top performing hedge fund strategy since 1990.

Disadvantages of the Strategy

As measured by volatility, this strategy is considered to be riskier than some of the other less volatile hedge fund styles. In our study shown in Chapter 2, Table 2.1, macro had the third highest standard deviation at 7.24 percent, trailing only ELS and Managed Futures. Our study also showed that the volatility of global macro was about half that of the S&P 500.

The problem with equating risk with volatility is partly definitional. If risk is defined as volatility there is no argument. But volatility, like cholesterol, has two components: the good kind (upside) and the bad kind (downside). Over the 12-year period mentioned earlier, macro had tremendous upside volatility while shielding investors from most of the downside. The worst month suffered by the Macro Index was −6.40 percent.[10] Compare that with the −14.5 percent monthly hit suffered by the S&P in August 1998.

The major risk in global macro comes from its often directional nature and from the leverage that is used. The directional risk taken is a matter of risk management, conviction, and opportunism. Good risk management assesses the amount of loss likely if all but the most catastrophic external events were to occur, and the position is sized accordingly. It is not uncommon to hear managers say they size all positions so that no more than a 1 percent or 2 percent risk to the fund's net asset value is likely on any one position.

Conviction also plays a role in position size. It is only logical that a portfolio manager will want to own more of a security if he or she believes very strongly in its upside. Opportunism, sometimes a nice word for greed, is conviction's first cousin. If a manager sees an opportunity to make a lot of money in a hurry by having an outsized directional position, the best that can be said about this situation is that the manager's money is on the line, too.

Leverage is not simply a problem because its use exaggerates losses. The worst of all worlds can occur when in a leveraged hedged position both sides of the trade go against the manager.

Global macro hedge funds are as different from one another as M&Ms. One manager we know trades only U.S. government debt and the dollar, long and short. Others expand the mandate to all sovereign debt and all major currencies. For many managers there are few constraints. The investor must cross-index the perceived risk of the particular approach with the amount of leverage used, that is, one would rather see an inverse relationship (lower leverage being applied to riskier positions) but this is not always the case.

Perhaps the greatest risk in global macro is when managers have enormous conviction about their views. Anyone can be wrong at times.

Recently we asked a manager what it would take in order for him to begin to question his views. This is a fairly standard due diligence question, and there are several good answers to it. What one doesn't want to hear is arrogance. You guessed it—this manager's answer was that he couldn't come up with a scenario under which he would be wrong! Caveat emptor.

Peter Thiel

Founder and Portfolio Manager
Clarium Capital Management

PETER THIEL, LIKE RENEE HAUGERUD, IS ANOTHER OF THE GREAT NEW generation of macro traders with a spectacular record to date. Peter founded Clarium Capital Management in 2002 and began trading in October of that year. The fund is unusual in that unlike most other hedge funds it charges no management fee. Instead, Clarium charges a 25 percent incentive fee subject to a high-water mark.*

When Peter met with Sam Kirschner, the initial conversation touched on Thiel's investment philosophy. This general line of inquiry belies the fact that, strictly speaking, many fund managers don't really have a philosophy per se, just a set of market assessment techniques and an investment methodology. But Peter Thiel's methodology is actually philosophical: He really does have an investment philosophy.

SK: *What is the role of question asking at Clarium?*

PT: I like trying to figure out what's happening in the world. At Clarium, we try to formulate important questions. That's the first step, and it's quite a hard job by itself, like a physics or math problem, because

---

*A high-water mark provision conditions the payment of the incentive fee on exceeding the prior maximum share value.

you have to find questions that both lead to fundamental insights and that you believe are solvable. Many people eschew asking hard questions either because they believe that the questions cannot be solved or else because they pose questions that are unsolvable by their nature. When we research the answers to the questions we've carefully posed, we've consistently achieved insights that other people simply have not.

SK: *I guess your methodology didn't happen by chance. You earned a B.A. in philosophy from Stanford University, is that right?*

PT: Yes. Then I went on to earn a J.D. from Stanford Law School.

SK: *Give us, please, an overview of your career path from there.*

PT: I went to Wall Street as a securities lawyer for Sullivan & Cromwell. After that I became a derivatives trader for Credit Suisse Financial Products. I was based in New York and later in London. Then, late in 1996, I formed Thiel Capital Management (TCM) after scraping together a million dollars of friends and family money. TCM began with traditional trading and later branched out to venture capital deals. Gradually, over the next six years, TCM morphed into a fund with a heavy venture focus, given our macro perception of where the market's potential lay.

SK: *And you made a pretty good deal back then, right?*

PT: Yes, one deal in particular turned out pretty well. In December 1998 we made the initial investment in PayPal. I joined PayPal as what was then assumed to be the interim CEO. But I ended up staying on. By October 2002, a little bit under four years, PayPal had grown from four people to 900.

SK: *And, for our readers who don't recall, PayPal was sold to eBay for $1.5 billion.*

PT: That's about right. We backed the winning horse on that one.

SK: *And after that?*

PT: After that, Jack Selby (a founding member of PayPal and now a managing director at Clarium) and I opened up Clarium Capital Management and began trading as a global macro fund in the fourth quarter of 2002.

SK: *How would you describe Clarium?*

PT: We conceived of Clarium as a pure global macro hedge fund. We focus on opportunistic, directional investments with an emphasis on liquid instruments.

SK: *Why did you choose the global macro space?*

PT: Partly because there aren't many people doing global macro the way we are.

SK: *And that is?*

PT: Here's what I mean: Many funds in the global macro space actually focus on relative value arbitrage. Yes, those funds look at broad or global trends, but I believe very few attempt detailed fundamental analysis of the sort we do. Instead, those funds use relatively simplistic rationales to justify what are essentially trend-following strategies. We see a large number of traders all trying to dynamically hedge in nearly the same way, at nearly the same time. This overcorrelates the price movements of most major markets and asset classes, when referenced with economic reality, as we perceive it.

SK: *This convergence is certainly happening today.*

PT: So some people in the industry will say to you, "Global macro is a very popular strategy" but we say it's really relative value arbitrage that is very popular. And the popularity of this strategy is its own worst enemy, because it forces relative value managers to assume more leverage and more risk as the relative values of the arbitraged securities converge. That's what we have in the post-bubble era: too much money chasing too few good ideas. We think overinvestment during the 1990s bubble destroyed profitability and overcommitted capital to the pool of available ideas. The result is low returns across many asset classes.

SK: *But Clarium is different.*

PT: We are. We do rigorous proprietary research to develop absolute value trading themes across a true global macro spectrum. We want to generate returns that are uncorrelated with other global macro funds, and, in fact, our correlation with other global macro funds is close to zero. When you really look at it, I think true global macro is probably the one sector that is actually undercapitalized.

SK: *I see. So this would be a good example of investors really needing to understand an individual fund, not just relying on a style bucket, or some generalized label.*

PT: Absolutely.

SK: *So what are Clarium's trading themes today?*

PT: As of September 30 our portfolio looks like this: We have about 39 percent in currencies, about 40 percent in interest rates, about 9 percent in commodities and around 12 percent in equities. At any one time we typically have between 10 and 20 open positions. Of course, our goal is to enter trades before a trend develops and take profits when the risk/reward balance becomes unfavorable.

SK: *I'm looking at your numbers here, and it looks like you reached your goal in 2003 performance. You posted an increase at year-end of better than 65 percent!*

PT: Right, 65 percent net to investors. And compare that with the Tremont Global Macro Index, which ended 2003 up about 18 percent.

SK: *Nice job. 2004 was a bit tougher.*

PT: It was indeed. We weathered six months of drawdowns that year. Ugly.

SK: *Yet you still ended the year up, right? By more than 5½ percent.*

PT: True.

SK: *And, just to fill out the picture, your 2005 numbers as of this conversation are up more than 44 percent.* Cumulative performance since inception in Q4 2002 (exactly three years) is up by an astounding 227 percent.*

PT: That sounds about right.

---

*Clarium finished 2005 up more than 57 percent net to investors.

SK: *Let's talk about your 2003 performance for a minute. What drove those good numbers?*

PT: In a word, it was JGBs, our play in Japanese government bonds. Maybe one of the best trades we've ever made. Our research showed that Japan's deflation was not a liquidity trap. Rather, it was the result of government policies that compel Japanese consumers to save. That created a pool of investment capital. It also resulted in a $65 billion trade surplus with the United States, which strengthened the yen. So, to check this, Japan bought large quantities of U.S. Treasuries. With lower U.S. yields, JGB yields also needed to fall in order to maintain reasonable interest rate differentials with the United States. That was to prevent yen/dollar forward rates from becoming too attractive, which, of course, would force the yen back up. To achieve this, the government instructed pension funds to liquidate stocks and buy JGBs. By May 2003, this had forced the Nikkei down 80 percent from its 1989 peak and 10-year JGB yields down to an incredible 43 basis points.

SK: *So you saw this coming?*

PT: We were asking the right questions. So we shorted JGBs while hedging with a long position on the Nikkei. In this case, our timing was phenomenal. Within six weeks we made an enormous amount of money.

SK: *So you cruised into 2004 under full sail.*

PT: I'll tell you this can be a humbling business. At the start of 2004, we looked at some of the Fannie Mae convexity hedging. From that, we figured out that there was a high likelihood of a bond market sell-off in early 2004. And so we went short bonds. But in early March came the release of employment figures, which were much, much weaker than anticipated. Bonds rallied on that news and we were stopped out of our positions.

Wouldn't you know it, a few weeks later the bond sell-off we had predicted in fact finally occurred? But there's no joy in being right in theory if your trade timing is wrong.

SK: *You hear it from every manager: It happens to the best of them.*

PT: True enough. It helps to have long-term outlooks to overcome short-term setbacks, to keep the big picture in mind. One of our beliefs is that we live in a world of retail sanity and wholesale madness. People have bought into the efficient market ideology on a big scale. But quite to the contrary, we say the markets on a big scale are extremely inefficient; perhaps as inefficient as they've been in a long time. And besides if markets are in fact efficient, there's really nothing for us to do. But we think there are things to do. We think there are some comparably large distortions taking place.

SK: *Such as?*

PT: Take China, for example. Everyone's looking there. Is China in a long-term, secular bull market that, in 20 years, will make it into an economy larger than the United States? A lot of people think so. We debated it back and forth for a year, looking for the key question to ask on China. We decided it was this: What are the implied short-term interest rates in China? And it turned out that, as of the end of 2004 the answer was: minus two percent! That's an absolutely extraordinary fact. It's the first time in history that an emerging market economy had negative implied nominal interest rates.

SK: *How did that happen?*

PT: We see it as an artifact of two things: the peg of the Chinese renminbi with the U.S. dollar, and the expectation that the peg will be revalued upward. You know, you can't actually go to a bank in China and borrow a million renminbi and pay back 980,000 a year later. But in effect, the entire economy is functioning as though you could. People's investment decisions are driven as though you could do that. We think this fuels the real estate boom and makes investment capital assets readily available, both to artificial levels.

The basic advice I give people is, even if you believe the 20-year secular growth story on China, you should wait until the interest rates look normal before jumping in. We think China is the single market in the world that one should stay away from today. And if China really is the long-term growth story it has been made out to be, does it really matter if you get in now as opposed to next year? No, not really.

SK: *Great. Let's talk a bit about some of your fund parameters like the risk profile, the leverage profile, size of the portfolio, things like that.*

PT: Our way of doing business begins with our approach to research. We rely on qualitative information. It's not something you can program a computer to do. Similarly, our risk policy avoids needlessly complex formulas. We stress-test the portfolio by assuming that everything moves against us in a way that's perfectly correlated. We adjust exposure to ensure that even if a three-sigma event occurs—that is, the extreme event that occurs about a quarter of a percent of the time—and affects all of our positions simultaneously, that total portfolio losses would be about 10–15 percent, and no more than 20 percent. So from a risk perspective, we behave as if the entire portfolio is just one position.

SK: *I see. But you must also have a per trade limit, right?*

PT: Yes. We set an absolute stop to prevent any position from losing more than 4 percent of the fund's NAV [net asset value].

As for the leverage ratio, we typically go between three-to-one and six-to-one. But, you know, looking at the leverage ratio alone can be misleading. A lot depends on what the underlying instruments are, right? So for example, being three-to-one leveraged on equities is probably risky, whereas if you're six-to-one leveraged on one-year Eurodollars, that's actually not very risky at all. Our three-sigma risk controls provide inherent limitations to leverage in a way that's more economically sensible than a simple limit on leverage.

SK: *That makes sense. How about the fund size?*

PT: We currently have about $1 billion under management* (about $700 million came in to the fund in 2005 alone). About $50 million of that is our money, contributed by the fund principals. Ultimately, we'll take the fund up to several billion.

SK: *Thanks. Well in closing, Peter, what do you see as the challenges of running a fund today?*

PT: One of the challenges is to find investors with a long-term view. Many investors have a very short-term focus. I chafed against this a bit

---

*AUM as of 9/30/2005.

when I was the CEO of PayPal. You've got to meet your number every quarter. That skews a lot of decision making to the short term and precludes many people from making certain kinds of longer-term investments. U.S. public companies are, I think, at a real disadvantage globally because of this. And for me, running a global macro fund, if investors take a longer-term view, everyone benefits. You don't have to live and die with every spike or swoon in the market.

CHAPTER 5

The Event-Driven Strategies: Merger Arbitrage, Special Situations

INTRODUCTION

This is the first of two chapters devoted to the event-driven strategies. Not too long ago, event-driven funds were broken up into three distinct subcategories including Merger Arbitrage,* Distressed, and Special Situations. The S&P Hedge Fund Index still uses those three subcategories while HFRI, purveyor of one of the largest and best databases, has separate indices for Merger Arbitrage, Distressed, and Event-Driven. However, on close examination of hundreds of event-driven managers, we believe that only two truly separate classifications remain: Event-Driven and Distressed. Event-Driven includes Merger Arbitrage and the catchall Special Situations and is the subject of this chapter. The Distressed group is highlighted in Chapter 6.

What do all these event-driven strategies have in common? They invest in securities of companies that are undergoing or are expected to undergo significant events or transformations. A corporate event can be almost anything material and includes bankruptcies, the conclusion of bankruptcies, restructurings, mergers, acquisitions, 13-D filings, and

---

*Sometimes called Risk Arbitrage.

spin-offs. Activist hedge fund managers, who act as catalysts for corporate change and in the process aim to bring about gains for investors, are also often placed in this category.

The ebb and flow of the various corporate events just listed depend in part on the stage of the business cycle. Mergers, for example, tend to occur with greater frequency in good times when business confidence is high and financing readily available. Bankruptcies, however, are plentiful in tough times and during recessionary periods. Distressed investors love recessions because opportunities abound.

Manager experience is the most important factor in successful event-driven investing, as uncertainty is the common denominator in all such situations. Numerous questions fill the air around these transformative events: Will the announced event occur? Will it occur on the terms announced? How long will it take? What effect will it have on the securities prices of the company or companies involved? How long will it take for these newer prices to be realized?

In addition, an understanding of complex legal issues is often required, which explains the influx of bankruptcy attorneys into the space. Knowing bankruptcy laws, sitting on creditors' committees, and understanding how to emerge from Chapter 11 proceedings are all part of the event-driven manager's skill set.

Event-driven has been among the best performing hedge fund strategies, especially in the past five years. As a result, asset flows have increased into the space and numerous new funds have opened around the globe, many focusing on an emerging market or specific developed nation. According to the Barclay Group's asset flow survey,[1] Event-Driven managers manage about $128 billion not including Distressed. As a group, these managers account for about 12 percent of all hedge fund assets and if we add in the Distressed category, for more than 18 percent of the total.

Mickey Harley, president and CEO of Mellon HBV Alternative Strategies, LLC, and who is our featured interviewee at the end of this chapter, runs his three Event-Driven Funds with a broad mandate. His U.S. Event-Driven Fund, for example, invests in both equity and debt securities of public U.S. and Canadian companies involved in mergers and acquisitions, announced corporate restructurings, spin-offs, and stub transactions. More recently, Harley has moved in the direction of becoming an activist. Once upon a time such a flexible investment mandate would have been considered "style drift," a discovery that would have caused most professionals conducting due diligence to grimace. Today, even the highly regarded multibillion dollar merger arbitrage funds run by John Paulson have expanded the definition of merger arb to include other event-driven strategies.[2]

How are we to understand the changes that have occurred in the event-driven space and specifically to merger arb? Mickey Harley takes us on a brief historical tour of the space and then explains two dynamic changes that have leveled the playing field.[3]

"Historically," Harley says, "successful managers were able to generate *alpha* because they had an 'information superiority' edge. Alpha is the excess investment return that a fund generates that is above and beyond the risk-free rate and the fund's *beta* to the market. This excess return is credited either to the manager's skill, luck, or other random factor. We explore alpha in greater detail in Chapter 11. For example, in risk arbitrage and/or distressed investing, a hedge fund manager would use a network of contacts (lawyers, bankers, and so on) who could supply superior information (legal documents and merger agreements) more quickly and completely than competitors could get this information. Today, information about most merger transactions is readily available to everyone at the same time, in a variety of formats, from multiple electronic sources. This technological change is permanent. The establishment of an 'information edge' in this space will have to be created by other analytical means."

A second change that has affected both merger and convertible arb (see Chapter 8) is the flood of institutional money that has poured into specific strategies. Harley laments that "as more institutional investors and money enter into these areas of investing, these areas are becoming more 'mainstream.' This has resulted in making the market more efficient, and, therefore, it's more difficult to produce the desired outsized returns. As these areas of the markets become mainstream, they begin to look and behave more like traditional, relative value investment markets and are less like the fringes of the markets in which hedge fund managers have been able to create their 'edge.'"

THE EVENT-DRIVEN TRADING AND INVESTMENT STRATEGIES

Merger Arbitrage

Merger arbitrage profit opportunities hinge on the amount of merger and acquisition activity and the "spreads" available in the market after a deal is announced. Let us give an example of what looks like an attractive spread. Company A announces a cash offer for all of the shares of Company B at $40. The shares of Company B, which had been trading at $30, immediately start trading at $35. Shares of B can be purchased at $35 for a $5 profit if the deal goes through, a profit of about 14 percent allowing for commissions. If the deal is consummated in four months, the annualized return is 42 percent. Does this sound too good to be true? It is, because there is never a "free lunch" in these deals. There is always a reason, or several reasons, why the spread is this wide. The most likely is that there is a significant possibility that the deal will not go through, perhaps for regulatory reasons or because Company B has adopted a set of *poison pill* amendments* to prevent unwelcome offers. It is the job of the risk arbitrageur to assess the probabilities of any one deal being consummated and the amount of the spread, and determine whether the rewards and risks warrant the investment.

More often in the situation just described the shares of B will open very close to $40, a miniscule spread, or even above the offer price. A bad deal, right? Maybe not. The market is wise, and it is saying that a higher offer is likely, either from A or another company.

Merger and acquisition offers are often made for stock or part cash/part stock. Now the assessment is complicated by the fact that the stock of the acquiring company may decline, or even advance, before

---

*A maneuver by a company designed to make it less vulnerable to a hostile takeover.

the deal closes. Merger arb managers typically short the stock of the acquirer against a long position in the company being acquired, to hedge the risk that the stock of the suitor may decline, carrying the share prices of both companies down. The idea is to "lock in" the spread. The risk in such a position is that the deal might be called off, causing the acquirer's shares to rise and the shares of the acquired company to decline, a double whammy losing proposition.

Let's look at what happened in one of the largest proposed mergers of recent years. In December 2004, Johnson & Johnson (JNJ), the medical products giant, agreed to buy Guidant (GDT), a leading maker of implantable heart devices such as defibrillators and pacemakers, for $76/share or $25.4 billion. Guidant's share price jumped up to $74/share and the spread on the deal hovered in the $2 range for the next six months. In May 2005 problems with GDT's defibrillators surfaced and the Food and Drug Administration (FDA) stepped in and forced a recall of tens of thousands of the devices. Predictably, GDT's stock fell into the 60s and the spread widened to about $12/share. When the two companies were unable to renegotiate a revised price, JNJ announced that it would not continue the deal under the original terms.[4] As October came to a close, event-driven funds that had been banking on the merger saw their long position in GDT decline sharply. According to HFRI, the Merger Arb Index had its worst month of 2005 in October with the average fund losing 1.61 percent.[5] As we finalized this chapter, a new suitor (Boston Scientific) made a higher bid than JNJ, and GDT stock, which had plummeted into the mid-50s/share, went back up to $67/share.

In addition to being influenced by the odds of a deal being called off, or of bids being increased, spreads are also a function of the level of interest rates in the market. Borrowed money is often used for risk arbitrage, so high borrowing costs lead to higher spreads and vice versa. Spreads are also a function of the amount of money involved in risk arbitrage, which is conditioned by many factors. The greater the amount of capital in the game, the narrower are the spreads.

Merger arbitrageurs also participate in liquidations. This involves assessing the value of a company's assets and purchasing stock if a worthwhile spread exists between such an appraised value and the company's share price. If some of a company's assets are stocks, these may be sold short as a hedge. It is not uncommon for liquidations to take longer than anticipated, which, of course, tends to reduce the arbitrageur's annualized returns. However, it is not at all uncommon for asset sales to fetch proceeds well above street estimates.

Special Situations

The second subcategory of Event-Driven trading is the catchall Special Situations. Here, hedge fund managers try to profit from special corporate events such as asset sales or sales of a division or subsidiary, spin-offs, large share repurchase programs, 13-D filings, proxy filings, and shareholder class actions against management or the Board. The latter three events have become the focal point in the activities of activist hedge funds. As we saw in Chapter 2, Pirate Capital began its assault on Cornell with a series of 13-D filings that culminated 10 months later with the hedge fund taking over the Board.

Perhaps most emblematic of the activist type of special situations hedge fund is Greenwich, Connecticut-based ESL Investments, founded by Eddie Lampert. Lampert began the fund in 1988 managing $28 million; today AUM stands at roughly $9 billion. Racking up annualized returns of about 29 percent per annum, Lampert has made a name for himself that stands in the august company of George Soros and Warren Buffett. Indeed, Lampert studied Buffett closely. The year after founding ESL Investments, he flew to Nebraska to confer with the Oracle of Omaha for a reported 90 minutes. The words spoken in that room will forever be the subject of conjecture. However, it does not stretch the imagination to believe they talked about Berkshire Hathaway and how Buffett acquired the failing textile company, turned it around, and used excess cash generated by the business to invest in other businesses.

In 2002, Eddie Lampert found his Berkshire Hathaway when Kmart filed for Chapter 11 protection. Seeing his opportunity, Lampert acquired 53 percent of Kmart's outstanding debt, thereby gaining a measure of control over the bankruptcy proceedings.[6] For less than a $1 billion investment, he gained control of the $23 billion retailer and became chairman in the spring of 2003. In a well-documented series of moves, Lampert reversed the fortunes of the chain, sold off more than 70 stores to realize their enormous real estate value (about $1 billion), cut costs, and began building a multibillion dollar war chest for acquisitions. Meanwhile, Kmart, whose stock had been languishing around $15/share, emerged from bankruptcy and moved up to $120/share by November 2004. Then Lampert struck again. Using his now valuable Kmart stock, he engineered a merger with its much larger rival Sears, a company whose stock had fallen and was suffering through hard times. The merger was completed in March 2005 and Kmart Holding became Sears Holdings.[7]

The pundits are all straining themselves to predict whether Lampert will succeed in turning around the ailing Sears. Meanwhile, to the surprise of many observers, Lampert has installed himself as the chief marketer and retailer at Sears. Some say that this is simply a transitional move and that Lampert will just sell off the retailers as he has done with prior investments when the price is right. As of this writing, the smart money, that is, other giant hedge funds like Perry Partners, SAC Capital Management, and Citadel have invested substantial dollars buying into the proposition that their fellow manager Lampert can run both an event-driven hedge fund and a retail conglomerate. In the most recent filing (September 30, 2005) 9 of the top 25 largest holders of Sears' stock were hedge funds.[8]

PERFORMANCE

In our study, the event-driven strategy was among the best performers in the 12-year period 1994–2005. The strategy showed the second highest average annual returns of 13.3 percent, about 1 percent per year lower than ELS but with a much lower standard deviation. Next to their cousins in Distressed, Event-Driven had the second highest risk-adjusted return among all asset classes (slightly below Distressed) with a Sharpe ratio of 1.47, five times as high as the MSCI World Index and two and a half times higher than the Lehman Government/Credit Bond Index.[9] Figure 5.1 shows the cumulative return of the HFRI

FIGURE 5.1

Cumulative Performance of HFRI Event-Driven Index versus Benchmarks

Growth of $1,000 USD, 1/1/1994–12/31/2005

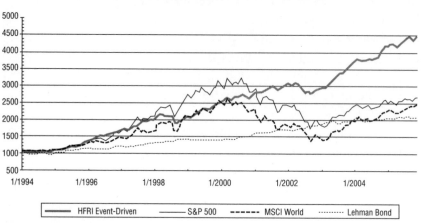

Sources: Mayer & Hoffman Capital Advisors, HFRI, and PerTrac.

Event-Driven Index versus its benchmarks. The cumulative return for this strategy is 80 percent higher than equities and more than double that of bonds.

In addition, event-driven managers for the most part avoided the bear market of 2000–2002. The HFRI Event-Driven Index was up 6.7 percent in 2000, more than 12 percent in 2001 and down about 4.3 percent in 2002 while the S&P and other global equity markets were in freefall. In our study of the trailing five years to 12/31/2005, the HFRI Event-Driven Index was the second best performing strategy next to Distressed averaging 10.7 percent per annum with a Sharpe ratio of 1.4.* Figure 5.2 shows the five years from 1/1/2001 through 12/31/2005. Again note that while world equity markets are finally back to square

---

*See Table 1.3.

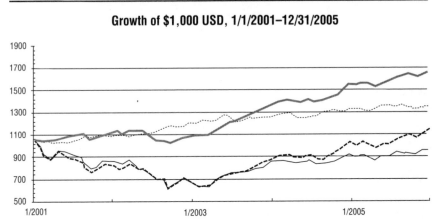

FIGURE 5.2

HFRI Event-Driven versus Benchmarks, Trailing Five Years

Growth of $1,000 USD, 1/1/2001–12/31/2005

Sources: Mayer & Hoffman Capital Advisors, HFRI, and PerTrac.

one for this long period, event-driven investors are cumulatively up 65 percent. In fact, event-driven managers have been among the best performing hedge fund strategies from 2003 through 2005.

ADVANTAGES

There are two major advantages to event-driven investing: performance consistency and the tenacity and deal-making skills of the managers. The Event-Driven strategy can be thought of as relatively dependable. From 1996 through 2005 it never ranked last among the various hedge fund strategies (according to HFRI), whereas the most popular strategy, ELS, did rank last in the bear market years of 2001 and 2002.[10] Figure 5.3 illustrates how well the strategy has done through the difficult period of the past five years versus the

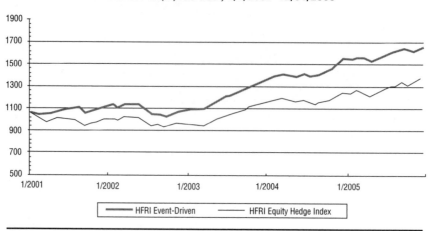

FIGURE 5.3

HFRI Event-Driven versus Equity Hedge Indices, Trailing Five Years

Growth of $1,000 USD, 1/1/2001–12/31/2005

Sources: Mayer & Hoffman Capital Advisors, HFRI, and PerTrac.

HFRI Equity Hedge Index. Note the significant cumulative outperformance of Event-Driven.

A second major advantage comes from being invested with managers who are tenacious deal makers. To be sure, not all event-driven managers rely on this quality, but some of the most successful have, again and again. Being a rougher, tougher player than your opponent can be used to great advantage, especially in activist situations. Perhaps the most notorious is the legendary Carl Icahn, who essentially authored the activist's bible and invented actions like "greenmail" over more than 20 years of shareholder actions. While a newcomer to hedge funds, in the past year Icahn forced Mylan to drop its acquisition of King Pharmaceuticals despite the support of another event-driven fund, Perry Partners.[11] And in tandem with the fund JANA Partners, Icahn forced Kerr McGee, with the threat of a serious proxy fight, to separate its chemical business and to institute a

$4 billion share buyback program with borrowed money to increase shareholder value.[12] To combat Carl as an adversary on a deal has been described as akin to being in the middle of a terrifying night-mare. Icahn has often been heard to say, "If you want a friend, get a dog."[13]

DISADVANTAGES

There are two disadvantages to the strategy: correlation with world eq-uity markets and deal-related or event risks. Event Driven has relatively high correlations with world equity markets (about 0.7) from 1994 through 2005. In addition, Event Driven showed a significant correla-tion of 0.8 to the Equity Hedge Index. While the HFRI Event-Driven In-dex suffered its worst year in 2002, down 4.3 percent, it hardly fared as poorly as equities in the recently concluded bear market. How are we, then, to understand this relative outperformance?

The answer is that while its correlation to equities was on the high side, because of a low standard deviation Event Driven had a modest beta of *0.32* to the MSCI World and an even lower beta of *0.29* to the S&P. Both values were substantially lower than those for ELS funds over the same time period. In short, Event Driven had less market risk than ELS. It's also fair to say that certain event-driven managers, ac-tivists in particular, are relatively immune to stock market cycles be-cause they themselves are the catalysts for the corporate changes that in turn create their profits.

A second disadvantage is event risk and especially where it di-rectly affects the merger arb part of an event-driven portfolio. For ex-ample, Merger Arbitrage can be a money loser when mergers or acquisitions fail to consummate. These failures occur for at least four major reasons: (1) When corporate profits are under pressure gener-ally, earnings disappointments at either company can derail discus-sions; (2) In negative stock market environments, a decline in the share price of the acquirer can have the same result; (3) Interest rate risk, especially when rates jump dramatically. Rising interest rates can jeopardize deal financings and the acquirer's ability to service the debt; (4) Unforeseen misfortunes that can derail any deal because a material event has befallen either company. Look at our example of JNJ and GDT. Device malfunctions followed by FDA recalls damaged GDT's prospects even though most of the defibrillators were back on the market within months. These events ultimately led to very sharp price declines in the share price of GDT, thus leaving the arbitrageurs who were long GDT with significant losses.

Mickey Harley

President and CEO
Mellon HBV Alternative Strategies, LLC

MICKEY HARLEY IS FOUNDER, PRESIDENT AND CHIEF EXECUTIVE OFFICER of Mellon HBV Alternative Strategies, LLC, and oversees the portfolio managers of Mellon's three event-driven funds and the three distressed funds. Before forming the company in 1999, Harley was the head of research at Milton Partners. At Milton, he concentrated on analyzing investment opportunities, developing new investment strategies and managing the overall direction of the risk arbitrage portfolio. At the same time, he managed a proprietary event-driven distressed fund for Milton. Prior to that position, Mickey was a vice president and director at Allen & Company. At Allen, Harley was responsible for the day-to-day management and investment strategies of the arbitrage department, which had AUM in excess of $150 million. While at Allen, he also had investment banking responsibilities and co-managed proprietary funds focusing on turnarounds and banking.

Mr. Harley graduated with a master's in public and private management from Yale University's School of Management in 1990 after receiving a Bachelor of Science degree in chemical engineering and a Bachelor of Arts degree in economics from Yale in 1986. The firm became a wholly owned subsidiary of Mellon Financial Corporation in 2002 and has offices in New York and London and a research team based in Hong Kong. Assets under management are $1.2 billion.

SK: *Mickey, as a manager of several domestic and global event-driven funds, obviously corporate restructuring events of all kinds are what you look for. And these events can occur in an up market as well as a down, right?*

MH: Yes. Theoretically, we should be indifferent to the market. That's one of the underlying principles at our shop. We do well when the economy suddenly becomes very high growth. It creates a lot of merger and acquisition and restructuring activity, lots of opportunity for us. An economy that's decelerating creates a lot of bankruptcies and other restructuring activity. That activity is what we need. A steady-state market is the worst for us.

SK: *Like this current market?*

MH: Yeah, like this one. The low volatility has caused risk premiums to contract. As a result, good ideas can become indistinguishable from bad ones.

SK: *That's interesting, but let's come back to that a little bit later. For context, tell us a little bit about your funds.*

MH: Sure. In our U.S. fund, we're looking for consistent risk-adjusted returns doing event-driven investments in the United States and Canada. Then we also have a Europe fund and a newly launched Asia fund. In all our funds, we tend to focus on mid- to small-cap situations.

SK: *What's your target capacity?*

MH: Well, that varies with our regional focus. The Asian event-driven fund, maybe $200 or $300 million is the target we're thinking about right now. So there are always capacity issues. That being said, I think one of the trends you see in general, and it's a trend we're following, is that there are occasional opportunities to deploy a lot of capital in a larger situation.

So what we're creating is this *side pocket* investment business where we have a core group of investors that are well-known to us who are willing to have less liquidity in exchange for higher returns. And so we find a situation like the one we had with Denny's. It was a big win for us, but we limited our exposure to protect our core portfolio. If we had this side pocket group at that time, we could have given those investors greater exposure. And a lot of them wanted that. And from a tactical perspective we could have driven an even better bargain with Denny's than we did at the time. I think if you look at other large event-driven funds, a big part, if not the majority, of their assets sits in these one-off side pocket deals that have controlled liquidity provisions. So that's how you expand the scalability of your fund as a business.

SK: *How big is the company right now?*

MH: We have about 50 people, 40 of whom are investment professionals. So we're a little people heavy for our assets. But we're looking to scale the business larger. And that's the way we've always run, historically. Build it first, and then let the assets come in if we can get it right on the return side.

SK: *How many investments are there in your portfolio today?*

MH: In our global fund, our multistrategy fund tends to carry 60 to 100 investments. Each regional subfund like the U.S. Event Driven is designed to carry 20 to 25. And what I tell those sub portfolio managers is: I want your best ideas. If you don't have a best idea, don't put it in the fund. And that's addressing an internal issue we had. We had evolved into a situation where we always felt we needed to be fully diversified. So we were putting a lot of ideas into these portfolios that were mediocre at best. Our portfolios were ballooning with positions in order to accommodate this diversification objective; we were invested in up to 100 positions in any single portfolio—and up to a few hundred in our multistrategy portfolio. As we've analyzed our performance over the past several years, we concluded that overdiversification negatively affected our performance. In order to improve upon our historical analytical edge, we have concentrated our investments in a fewer number of positions and performed deeper research and analysis in each of these positions. In order to offset the potential increase in risk that concentrating in fewer investment positions may introduce, we have reduced the amount of leverage that we are using in our investments.

SK: *So what's your role with the funds at this point?*

MH: Each of the regional funds has its own portfolio manager and research team. I'm at the global level with a trader and a researcher. Theoretically, no core position should be going into any regional fund that isn't also in the global fund. It's not always automatic. The regional managers talk to me on a daily basis. When they've got a position that's appropriate, it's also going into the global fund.

SK: *What would you then say are the pros and cons of investing directly into your global event fund as opposed to one of the regional funds?*

MH: Well the pros of investing in the global fund are diversification, obviously, and buying our skill set. On the regional side, because there's less diversification, there's more risk and perhaps more potential to the upside. But you get that regional concentration. So if you are a big bull on Asia right now, the Mellon HBV Asia Event-Driven Fund gives you the ability to participate in that. But if you want more diversification, the global fund will give you that. And that has been less volatile than the regional funds, definitely.

SK: *Well, that brings us to one of the less comfortable points in our interview. This is where we ask each manager to tell a story of a trade that really left you black and blue. And it happens to the best of them, right?*

MH: Yeah, no one is immune from that. For us it has to be U-Haul. We got hauled but good on that one.

SK: *How did it happen?*

MH: Well, let's see, it was in 2003. U-Haul was a family-run company that seemed to have high disregard for shareholders. And they seemed to have very opaque financial statements; seemed to do a lot of things with moving assets. It was almost a shell game with their assets. We looked at the fundamentals of the business and also what was going on in the bigger picture. That is, companies like this were getting punished by the financial markets. We predicted this company was going to file for Chapter 11.

The stock was trading at $10 or $15 a share. We were very confident it was gonna go down. So we shorted the equity. Sure enough, the company filed for Chapter 11. But the stock didn't go down to a dollar. It only went to three or five dollars a share and we thought that was ridiculous. You know, it should have been zero! So we added more shorts. And really, that broke one of our own tenets: When the event occurs, you get out of your position. Win, lose, or draw, you get out. But we were just so confident that this was going to zero. We were dumbfounded that it didn't go down there.

Now there were a lot of technical maneuvers that the other side was taking to make sure this stock didn't go down to zero. Because the family's net worth was tied up in the equity. And the family ended up winning that game. And we ended up getting really, really burned. Not only the short squeeze, but also we were outmaneuvered tactically by a very smart guy who was running U-Haul. And it cost us a lot of money.

SK: *You were holding on to the bitter end?*

MH: No, we started covering when it really started kicking us in the ass. But it cost us dearly. I think at the end of the day it probably cost us overall 400 or 500 basis points in performance. And this is in funds where we're trying to do 10 to 15 percent. That's a big hit. So, that's probably the single worst trade we've ever had. It really fooled us. And that position was held by multiple funds, where we have a lot of people working on one idea. We tend to do our best work in those situations. Not this time.

So that led to a reevaluation of our investment processes. We had to say, okay, what went wrong in this situation? And how could we have prevented it? One of those things is to stay true to what we say we're doing. And that is when an event occurs, you exit. The other is, when we short stocks, we've got to buy core protection. Also, in that case, I think we were relying too much on a lot of junior guys in the firm to do a lot of the analysis and decision making. And we had a lot of senior guys sitting around listening to them. And that's not a slight on people who are less experienced.

SK: *Alright, thank you. Now let's look at the other side of the coin. Obviously, this side is the more common occurrence: a trade that went well. You mentioned Denny's before.*

MH: Let's talk about Denny's, the restaurant chain. I guess it was two years ago that Denny's was just beginning its fundamental turnaround. They had brought in a new management team. And they had finally set it going forward. But the company still had a very overleveraged balance sheet and very high cost debt. So the bonds were trading in the 50 cents range. The stock was sitting at something like 30 cents a share.

We liked the franchise. We felt that the most likely next step here was a debt for equity swap. We bought bonds as a cheaper way to ultimately own the equity of a company that looked like it was going in the right direction and financially was going to be restructured. Lo and behold, the fundamental turnaround really started to accelerate during the early holding period of our bonds. And what we felt was the better value-enhancing alternative here, instead of a debt for equity swap, would be new investment, a new money deal, on whose back you can then refinance the balance sheet with lower cost debt.

And so we bought shares. We approached management. They were initially not too interested in talking to us. The bond holders of course didn't want a new money deal. They would have preferred to own the equity. We sold our bonds and bought more stock. And we took the approach that we're going to be the antagonist here. And we're gonna fight for what we think is the right plan for this company. After some 13-D filings and discussions with management, I think they finally saw it our way. I think it was apparent to everybody that, you know, hey, if you don't do this we're willing to take the next step and that would be a proxy fight to replace the board. And as a result everyone came together.

So we did a $90 million PIPE* (private investment in public equity) on whose back management did a new bank deal. And also a new bond deal that has basically saved the company $25 to $35 million a year in interest payments. So that was really only half the story. The real story was the job the management team had been doing to reposition and turn around this company. And it's just been a tremendous investment. It's worked very well.

---

*See Chapter 10 for complete description.

SK: *So the stock went from 30 cents to . . . ?*

MH: It's probably four and a half, four and three quarters, in that range.

SK: *To close, where should today's event-driven investor look for opportunities?*

MH: In the world today, the single biggest thing that's out there is globalization. There's a decline in the importance of the United States on the world economic scene. We're being matched by other economies. China is the hottest thing right now. India is hot on its tail. Brazil and the rest of Latin America seem to be gaining more and more prominence on the world economic stage. I think it would be a very natural phenomenon over the next 50 years to see that trend continue. It's partly a result of democracy becoming increasingly held in different shapes and forms across the world. With democracy comes capitalism. And with capitalism comes changing economic opportunity. Now you take that theme and you ask: Where do I put my capital? I think the answer is obvious. Because the U.S. hedge fund market has attracted a large flow of money and managers, more opportunities for event-driven hedge fund managers exist in Europe, Latin America, and Asia. For example, in Europe, buyers of companies are increasingly negotiating with the risk arbitrage investment community in addition to the shareholders of the takeover targets. As a result, the risk arbitrageurs are assuming what we would characterize as an activist role similar to those taken by debt holders in distressed situations in the United States in order to influence the outcome of a merger deal. Investors also want to be careful about dollar denominated U.S.-centric investments. You need to have global diversification because it's going to be volatile all over the place.

SK: *How about a final tip to the reader about selecting individual managers?*

MH: As for picking hedge funds, you need to know your manager. And that is really, really important. You need to know him all the time because managers grow and they do change. You need to really stay in touch with them. You know, has the guy become extremely wealthy and taken on three new girlfriends? Has his lifestyle suddenly changed and now he's taking his eye off the ball? If so, you're likely to lose money.

My investors know I have a wife and kids who are growing up. We live in the same town on Long Island where I grew up. Most of the guys I hang out with tend to be relatively modest. We know that it can be gone in a day. You know, you're as good as your last trade, as they say. And just like any other volatile industry, if you make too many mistakes you can be gone very quickly. I think as long as you recognize that, you won't get too big a head.

CHAPTER 6

The Event-Driven Strategies: Distressed Securities

INTRODUCTION

The second subcategory of Event Driven investing is Distressed. A distressed opportunity generally arises under three conditions: when a company's financial condition deteriorates significantly, bringing about debt ratings downgrades and possibly default; when a company, unable to meet all its debts, files for Chapter 11 (reorganization); and, finally, under the worst circumstances, when it files for Chapter 7 (liquidation) bankruptcy. Dion Friedland, chairman of Magnum Funds, says, "Chapter 7 involves shutting a company's doors and parceling out its assets to creditors. Chapter 11 gives the company legal protection to continue operating while working out a repayment plan, known as a plan for reorganization, with a committee of its major creditors. These creditors can be banks who've made loans, utilities, and other vendors owed for their goods and services, and bondholders.

"Stockholders are also among the constituents, though when it comes to dividing the assets of the company they are paid back last and usually very little, if anything. If, in a bankruptcy, a company does not have sufficient assets to repay all claims, the stockholders will get wiped out as they are last in line to receive any of the proceeds from the liquidation or reorganization. So a distressed-securities investor focuses mostly on the bank debt, the trade claims (claims held by suppliers owed for goods or services by the company), and the bonds (which can vary in terms of their place on the bankruptcy-claim totem pole, with senior bonds paid ahead of junior) when they are looking for bargain-priced securities." (See www.magnum.com.)

THE DISTRESSED TRADING AND INVESTMENT STRATEGIES

Entering the world of distressed securities is a little bit like stepping through the looking glass. All of a sudden, what's good is bad and what's bad is good—if not exceedingly good. "2002 was an extremely bad year,"[1] says Marc Lasry, founder and managing partner of Avenue Capital Group, the $8.5 billion asset management firm. But he's smiling when he says it. "The worst of times for everybody else," said Lasry, "is the best of times for us."

Distressed managers (the managers may occasionally be distressed but their securities always are) often find themselves looking into underresearched securities. By definition, the opportunity for mispricings can be great in such circumstances. Also, they commonly analyze highly complex investments requiring keen legal analysis and a willingness to dig into arcane documents. Here, too, because few analysts are experienced in this sort of investigation, or are willing to do the painstaking work, worthwhile profit opportunities exist in distressed securities. Those distressed practitioners who have gained superior knowledge through research and due diligence attempt to limit their downside by effectively buying a dollar at a deep discount. As a result, this particular strategy has yielded consistent and outsized returns over the past 12 years.

Bankruptcies and liquidations are only two examples of the equity-restructuring events that a distressed manager looks for in identifying investment opportunities. Others include companies in forced restructurings as a result of litigation, fraud, tax liens, or senior management changes. Often, events like these result in a company's securities being undervalued. Financial complexities or legal issues can scare away investors, especially those who live and die by quarterly results. In their wake lies opportunity.

Distressed investing is viewed by many as the dirty work of the investment world; thus, the majority of professional investors do not want to travel on this low road. The underpinning of successful contrarian investing requires that an investor be in a minority position, and if most don't want to go on the road less traveled, then distressed analysts automatically have the advantage of being in the minority.

Nevertheless it takes nerves of steel to succeed. The best investors are those who are happiest when there is blood in the streets, the news is terrible, and other investors are panicking. At such times, distressed managers have a natural edge, buying from those who purchased the securities when they were considered investment grade and now may have little if any ability to evaluate them. That's when those who have done their homework and know exactly what price they will pay for specific distressed securities pounce on the opportunities.

Analysts in this strategy will not only know everything about the company and its financials but will have studied the creditors involved in the reorganization as well. They analyze creditors' claims, their willingness to compromise, the complexity of their claims (which may indicate how long the reorganization will last), what the asset distributions might be, and whether the expected returns are worth the wait. The investor seeking to best capitalize on his investment may even go so far as to buy up enough of the company's debt or trade claims so as to earn a seat on the creditor committee and have an influence in the reorganization process. Remember Eddie Lampert and Kmart? In theory, the creditor committee decides on a plan of reorganization, which often includes the issuance of new equity to reduce the liabilities of the company—so that when the company ultimately exits Chapter 11, it emerges with a significantly stronger balance sheet, often with a greater equity-to-debt ratio than even its most viable competitors.

In the end, the best distressed securities investors develop patience and a longer-term investment horizon like farmers who know that their trees will ultimately bear fruit but only with a combination of time, good cultivation practices, and a little luck. Indeed, the long-term view affords managers like Lasry the luxury of taking a broad view of market anomalies like the conditions he perceives in the current environment. "You have an economy that's doing well," he marvels, "but interest rates are rising, oil is at an all time high, you have a huge deficit, and you have a low dollar!" If these are textbook conditions for a good economy, then it's some kind of textbook that hasn't been written yet.

Yet, because the economy is doing well and because a lot of money has flooded into U.S.-focused distressed funds, there is a growing concern that the strategy's future returns will be compromised. Asked his view of domestic deal flow, Lasry said, "There's still a large amount of supply here, but it is difficult to find value. In the United States, returns in the sector are challenging, as there are only so many situations that you can purchase in that range of 70 or 80 cents on the dollar. On the other hand, in Europe right now there's a huge supply of attractive investment opportunities and we can generate better returns. Germany, for example, has close to $250 billion of loans that it needs to get rid of."

Why the opportunity abroad? Lasry explains that there's been a profound evolution in U.S. bankruptcy processing. "In the 1990s," he says, "the United States had the first big wave of bankruptcies. The frontiers of the high-yield market drove a 10 percent default rate; Manville and other large companies filed for bankruptcy. But the judiciary just didn't have prior exposure to the unprecedented amount of megabankruptcies. So many of the issues were cases of first impressions for the courts. Consequently, the process could take as long as five years. First, you'd have a hearing to determine lender liability. Then, you'd have a valuation hearing to determine exactly what a company was worth and whether equity should get paid or not. That could take a year by itself. The length of these proceedings was such that counterparties could use it to their advantage."

Today, it's different in the United States. There have been so many bankruptcies in the past 10 or 15 years that it's no longer a case of first impressions for the court. Valuation hearings now get done in 30 days. There is precedent now, and you have a much better sense of how a judge is going to rule on issues. Some corporate bankruptcies now can get done in one or two years.

European and Asian Distressed

The European Union (EU), in contrast with the United States, has no universally accepted codes for bankruptcy protection. As a result, when a company is failing it can't easily obtain emergency relief because the financing is impeded by potential legal constraints. Mickey Harley, featured in Chapter 5, adds that "when a company files for bankruptcy the insolvency codes of most European nations do not provide for emergency financing or debtor in possession financing in which new money can be lent, senior to all existing debt of a company, to allow the company to operate and preserve value while it sorts out its balance sheet. The lack of this short-term, or bridge financing that is necessary for a reorganization, typically results in a liquidation of the company's assets, usually at a fraction of the value of the ongoing business."[2]

To address this situation, distressed hedge funds along with large banks and workout firms have stepped into the breach. Hedge funds are investing in the existing securities of the bankrupt company, its trade claims, or, even more boldly, by injecting new capital into the company.

There is no doubt that these investments are more risky than those in the United States, but most observers believe that very soon the EU will adopt more uniform bankruptcy codes and the bankruptcy process will become smoother. Until that happens, however, there will be numerous opportunities for outsized returns in the European Distressed market.

Another place that is seeing an explosion of distressed debt is Asia. For that reason, we are featuring Rob Petty, founder and portfolio manager of Clearwater Capital Partners, the Asia Distressed debt fund, at the end of this chapter. One place where he may go to look for opportunities is China where the largest settlement of nonperforming loans (NPLs) the world has ever seen is about to occur. According to Mickey Harley, who also runs three Distressed funds, "the driver behind this huge settlement of NPLs is the requirement for China to open up its banking system to foreign banks and adhere to global banking standards as a condition of admittance into the World Trade Organization

(WTO) that was agreed upon two years ago. The central government of China negotiated a five-year grace period with the WTO to reform its banking sector. One of the primary challenges facing such reform is the mountain of bad loans that state commercial banks still face despite their strenuous efforts to reduce them over the past several years. To help facilitate this process, the four largest banks in China have set up allied asset management companies into which they have been transferring, in rapid fashion, the bulk of the loans deemed to be nonperforming. In turn, the allied asset management companies have been selling these loans to third-party investors who believe that such loans can be settled at a value that is greater than the price at which they have purchased them."

Clearly, making a profit on these loans will require investors to understand Chinese foreclosure laws, local culture and politics, the status of the original borrower in the community, and the terms and conditions by which these loans were purchased from the allied asset management companies.

Back in the United States, Avenue foresees a coming increase in the supply of distressed opportunities, and for the better. "What's troubling me," said Lasry, before catching himself. "Well, it's not really troubling *me*. But we see huge opportunity ahead for us because there's too much liquidity in the market today. A lot of deals are getting done that probably shouldn't be; meaning that many companies with inadequate balance sheets are borrowing money on terms that don't require them to make principal payments for two or three years. We say it's a triple C market, using the old grade-school scale: A is the best, B is good, C is average."

Lasry is confident that a significant percentage of those deals will end up under the scrutiny of his distressed fund's research and analysis teams. "But the biggest fear that we have," says Lasry, growing serious, "is an exogenous event occurring." He may well have said *another* exogenous event, as catastrophes seem to be arriving with grim regularity: the devastation of 9/11; the tsunami at the end of 2004; and the recordbreaking and disastrous hurricane season of 2005.

"It could be," Lasry says, "that we're seeing the evolution of a new paradigm in market cycles. It used to be every 10 years you'd have two cycles of things getting ugly. But now, it is happening every five years, or every three. I think we're seeing the interval growing shorter. However, it's still only a question of when, not if," he concludes.

PERFORMANCE

Distressed investors have been amply rewarded for their investing acumen. From 1994–2005, Distressed was the third best performing hedge fund strategy (behind ELS and Event-Driven), returning 12.2 percent per annum with a low standard deviation of about 5.4 percent in our study.[3] Distressed also had the highest Sharpe ratio among all strategies at 1.53, about five times higher than either the S&P or the MSCI World and about three times higher than the Lehman Bond Index. Figure 6.1 shows the cumulative performance versus the equity and bond benchmarks.

Distressed has had only one down year in the past 12 and that was in 1998 when the HFRI Distressed Index was down 4.2 percent. That

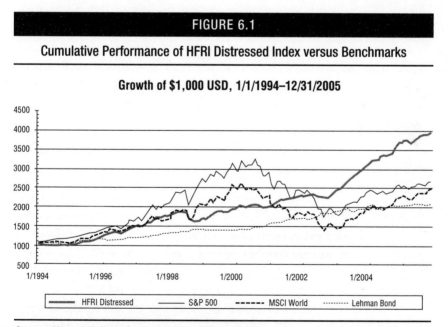

FIGURE 6.1

Cumulative Performance of HFRI Distressed Index versus Benchmarks

Growth of $1,000 USD, 1/1/1994–12/31/2005

Sources: Mayer & Hoffman Capital Advisors, HFRI, and PerTrac.

year world markets were rattled by the collapse of Asian and Eastern European markets (and Long Term Capital) which in turn set off a liquidity crisis that brought down U.S. and European equity markets in the second half of the year. How susceptible then is this strategy to general market risk? To answer that, we once again compute the beta value for Distressed relative to the S&P and MSCI World Indices for the period 1994–2005. The HFRI Distressed Index had a correlation of 0.47 to the S&P 500 and 0.52 to the MSCI World.[4] The beta values for Distressed are *0.17* to the S&P and *0.20* to the MSCI World. These rather low betas indicate that the strategy is not that susceptible to general market risk unless there is a major market event that temporarily shocks the entire financial system.

This hypothesis has been borne out over the past five years during which time global equities went through a major correction. The bond market has been a solid performer with the Lehman Index up over 40 percent. As good as that return has been, Figure 6.2 shows that over

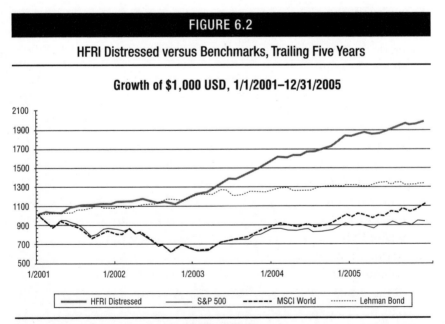

FIGURE 6.2

HFRI Distressed versus Benchmarks, Trailing Five Years

Growth of $1,000 USD, 1/1/2001–12/31/2005

Sources: Mayer & Hoffman Capital Advisors, HFRI, and PerTrac.

that same five-year period, the HFRI Distressed Index has doubled with an annualized return of 14.8 percent.[5] In fact, Distressed has been the top performer over the past five years both on an absolute return and risk-adjusted basis with an outstanding Sharpe of 2.79.[6] In 2005, Distressed was again among the top performing hedge fund strategies; the HFRI Distressed Index finished up 8.3 percent, more than 500 basis points ahead of the S&P 500 and nearly 600 basis points ahead of the Lehman. We conclude, therefore, that distressed funds seem to offer safe harbor for their investors through general market cycles, including bear markets, but are susceptible to the impacts of extreme financial crises.

ADVANTAGES OF DISTRESSED INVESTING

Distressed managers offer three distinct advantages:

1. They invest in an area of limited competition because many classes of investors are not allowed to hold debt with ratings below certain preestablished levels or to hold bonds that are in default. It is not uncommon for such investors to get left holding the bag when credit is downgraded, with the result that they must sell without delay. At times like this the distressed community makes bids at deeply discounted levels. Each airline bankruptcy in recent years has produced repeat performances of this phenomenon, with the distressed crowd gobbling up large amounts of equipment trust certificates based on their strong collateral.

   A variation on this theme occurs when banks decide to disgorge problematic paper, often just before year-end in order to take write-offs and improve their nonperforming loan ratios. Here too, distressed managers provide the needed liquidity but at a price where they can usually turn a tidy profit.

2. Another advantage that some distressed managers capitalize on is a willingness to do grunt work. An example of this comes from one of the deans of distressed managers, who tells the story of the great play he made by sending his people out into a bankrupt company's

warehouses to inventory the goods, only to find that somehow there were a lot more goods there than had appeared in the financial statements. Armed with this proprietary knowledge, this investor was able to purchase nearly an entire class of the company's debt securities at bargain basement prices and obtain par value for them at the end of the bankruptcy proceedings.[7]

3. Finally, Distressed managers can do well when more conventional approaches are faltering. Their opportunities tend to increase when interest rates are rising or when the economy is sputtering, both cyclically difficult times for many stock and bond investors, including ELS hedge funds.

It is often said that risk is all a matter of price. In fact, there is an old trader's expression, "I'll see a monkey's (expletive deleted) at the right price." Years ago one of the authors[8] happened to be in the Bear Stearns trading room when the great Sy Lewis, a notoriously brash and gutsy trader, was asked to bid on a large block of a deeply distressed stock. There were, as the saying goes, "wall-to-wall sellers" and the specialist was having difficulty opening the stock. When asked if he was prepared to file a 13-D if he bought the block, Lewis's guttural response as he stood towering over the trading desk was, "At 12 bucks I'll buy the whole G-D company!" As it turned out, of course, only the large block was purchased. By the end of the day, the stock was trading actively at $16. The point of the Sy Lewis story is that while distressed securities could be said to be inherently risky, they are not so risky when the right price is paid for them.

DISADVANTAGES OF DISTRESSED INVESTING

There are three major disadvantages associated with distressed investing:[9]

1. First and foremost is liquidity risk. Once the position is taken, even at a deeply discounted price, the distressed fund is in turn exposed to liquidity risk, which can prove costly if for any reason

the fund must thereafter sell relatively illiquid positions. As we noted before, when markets experience liquidity crises as they did in 1998 and again very briefly toward the end of 2000, distressed investors can be severely punished. The reason is that buyers disappear and those who remain offer low bids and usually only for small lots. Distressed managers who are sellers at those times will sustain significant losses and the positions they continue to hold will also be subject to the valuation risk of mark-to-market losses. While most hedge fund strategies (and long-only strategies, for that matter) have some degree of liquidity risk, it is greater for distressed funds.

2. The distressed investor is also exposed to corporate risk, the risk that the issuer will get into deeper financial distress than contemplated by the investor. This can happen if the restructuring or bankruptcy process gets slowed down. The longer a weakened company is stuck in the process, the worse its competitive position can become, reducing the value of the outcome.

3. Finally, settlement and legal risk come into play in the case of distressed bank debt, for settling some of these trades can be quite complex and can take a long time. Then of course there is legal risk. It is not uncommon for distressed companies to be subject to lawsuits that can materially threaten their financial position. Regardless of the amount of legal homework a manager does, he can still be hurt by an unexpected legal ruling. The laundry list of risks goes on and on, but many of these risks are common to most other modes of investing including event risk, credit risk, interest rate risk, general market risk, and foreign currency risk.[10]

It is obvious that the primary key to successful distressed investing is experience. There really is no substitute for having "walked the walk and talked the talk" of distressed investing. As one savvy hedge fund investor told the senior authors, "you make your most money going from terrible to bad."[11] The other side of the looking glass is a very different world from the rest of Wall Street.

INTERVIEW

Rob Petty

Founder and Portfolio Manager
Clearwater Capital Partners Opportunities Fund

SAM KIRSCHNER SAT DOWN WITH ROB PETTY, MANAGING PARTNER OF Clearwater Capital Partners Opportunities Fund, the dedicated Asia special situations debt hedge fund. After graduating from Brown University, Petty worked for Lehman Brothers Holdings from 1984 to 1996 in various capital commitment capacities of increasing responsibility. He was a corporate bond trader in Tokyo, risk manager for a $1 billion balance sheet in Medium Term Notes, and head of the Private Placement department. Following that, he moved to Peregrine Fixed Income Ltd. as head of syndication and high-yield trading. Prior to founding Clearwater, Petty was a managing director at Amroc Investments.

SK: *Rob, even a quick glance at your firm's performance and marketing materials shows us that Clearwater is not your typical distressed shop.*

RP: (Smiling) Well, we certainly think so. But exactly what are you referring to?

SK: *The thing that first leaps off the page is your corporate structure. You know, the image persists of a hedge fund manager being a gunslinger, experienced in his particular market niche, calling all the shots, tapping* *the prime broker for maximum leverage, and hedging his positions to guard against unfavorable movements. He's got a small support staff to help out with the nuts and bolts of fund managing.*

RP: No, that isn't the way we do things at all. Compared to that image, our fund is more like a division of a major investment bank. We're infrastructure-intensive, team-centric, and, in a word, big. This is not armchair investing. You need the ability to execute multiple deals in multiple countries simultaneously. It's a difficult business model.

SK: *How did that model evolve?*

RP: Well, given my background, I knew I wanted to focus on Asia. We built our business around the opportunity we saw there. You know, most people don't realize Asia represents 33 percent of the world's gross domestic product. It's roughly the same as the United States. We're building a business there for precisely that reason. It has as big an arena as the United States and yet there are one-third as many players, one-third as many investors looking for opportunities.

Of course, there are reasons the region does not attract more managers. This continues to be a harder and harder business to do. To execute deals in local law, in local language in multiple countries at the same time you need a lot of people. It's a resource intensive, roll-up-your-sleeves business that takes a team of 30 or more.

Another thing is that many of the deals we undertake are comparatively smaller than in the U.S. distressed market. That means we have to do more of them, and we must also be able to respond quickly to the opportunities we do identify. In industry segments where we have already conducted due diligence, we can turn around a deal in as little as two weeks. We're set up for a quick strike. We very consciously built an on-the-ground presence that gives us the ability to execute locally. That's the real differentiating factor for our firm. We can execute and we get a look at deals that others may not see. That's probably what is most distinctive about our approach.

SK: *With a large team like that, is it a challenge for you guys to stay on the same page? You have your headquarters in New York and offices in Seoul, Singapore, Hong Kong, and Mumbai.*

RP: That hasn't been an issue for us. The three partners make up the firm's investment committee. By making decisions together and speaking formally and informally on a weekly basis about investment opportunities and the portfolio, we are able to stay on the same page. My partner Amit Gupta lives in Hong Kong and focuses primarily on credit research, due diligence, and analysis. Our third partner, Bruno Beuque, lives in Singapore and focuses on asset management, restructurings, and credit negotiations. It's a very cohesive group.

SK: *Strategically, what kind of plays are you looking for?*

RP: We've created a portfolio of long-dated, cash generative amortization schedules. We look for noncorrelating instruments that provide natural exits and are sourced from low entry levels. To date, the average dollar cost of our portfolio is something like 60 cents on the dollar. As far as diversity in the portfolio, we can have as many as 40 different cash events, interest and principal, coming back to us every single month. This is what drives our return: credit investments that have exits from the cash flows of the company. Broadly speaking, that is our strategy. We can also perform a debt for equity swap when we want to participate in the equity upside of a company's rebound from a restructuring.

SK: *Is the potential upside of an investment a key consideration for you?*

RP: (Nodding) First and foremost, we want to empower management to run their company. That's in our mutual best interest. We've seen it firsthand: Debt restructuring can be tremendously time-consuming and draining to a company. We want to bring them to financial closure and let management get back to what they do best, not fixing the balance sheet, but running the company.

Also, we like to buy into amortizing bank loans. The bank loan business in Asia represents 75 percent of total debt in the region. If you're investing in credit in Asia, in our view, you need to be investing in the bank loan market as well.

SK: *Clearly your team engages in intensive credit research. That's the only way you can exist in the Distressed space. But even the best efforts* *can't eliminate risk completely. It's not an exact science. Can you give us an example of a deal that turned out to be sour?*

RP (Sighs): Yeah, we've been burned. A key factor in our due diligence is assessing management's willingness and ability to repay the debt after taking the loan. But, like you said, it's not an exact science.

We invested in a glass company in Indonesia. That was not our finest investment. We bought in following an initial restructuring of the family-owned company, so we were not the lead investor. However, the company stopped making payments after nine months and initiated a second restructuring. Looking back, we believe we underestimated their capital expenditure needs. You know, making glass in a sophisticated plant is more capital intensive and needed a higher capacity utilization rate to break even than we had been led to believe. Finally, we got out with a loss of almost $1.5 million. But that only represented about 1 percent of our portfolio at the time. What are you going to do? It happens to the best.

SK: *How is that company doing today?*

RP: I think they're muddling along, making some repayment to their creditors, but we're convinced that walking away was the best move.

SK: *Did you ever consider a legal proceeding against the company?*

RP: Generally speaking, we don't choose the litigation route even where the laws allow it. You have to make the wisest economic decision for the portfolio. We have to ask if it is really worth our time and effort. Often, it isn't. Especially in Indonesia, which is not a creditor-friendly country. Despite having good laws on the books, in practice, there's virtually no creditor-friendly judgment you can cite coming out of the Indonesian judiciary. Taking the legal route to a resolution there is, in our view, not very practical.

SK: *So Indonesia can be tough. In contrast, is there another country where you see better opportunities?*

RP: India. We share the excitement that India is generating in the investment community today. In the debt space, India is less mature than in its public equity or private equity spaces. With our team of six people on the ground, we think we're at the cutting edge of the deals that are getting done there. We're excited about India's ability to compete on a global basis in a range of different businesses.

SK: *Tell us about one of your recent plays there.*

RP: Okay, Calcutta Electric. They are the monopoly private sector supplier and distributor of electricity to the city of Calcutta. Their sponsors are a solid business group in India and had a willingness to pay. The company defaulted because the local government had interfered with a regulated rate increase and Calcutta Electric had a high pilferage of power. We had studied the industry extensively and knew a large power deficit was projected. We thought there might be a quick restructuring because of the NPL [nonperforming loan] implications for the Indian lenders. Also, the courts were reviewing the company's appeal on the rate increase and a decision was imminent. Plus the penalties for stealing power had become much harsher.

Meanwhile, the company was trading at just 2 × EBITDA. It took us quite a while to accumulate a meaningful position in the various debt securities. By working with the company and a financial adviser, we became a key anchor lender and were able to shape the success of the restructuring. There were multiple layers of lenders and a lot of detailed negotiations. We have doubled our money on half of our investment, and the remaining portion should be at least that much. It was lots of hard work on a complicated situation with a big payoff.

SK: *Great. Well, you've been very forthcoming about a trade that did not go well for you, the glass company. On the other side of the coin, why don't you tell us about one that was a home run?*

RP: Well, you know, we've had 'em. I guess we wouldn't be in business if we didn't have our successes.

SK: *Such as?*

RP: Well, really we don't like to rest on our laurels.

SK: *Understood.*

RP: In this business, you're only as good as your last trade.

SK: *(Waiting) Sure.*

RP: Well, I guess we could talk about Ital Thai Development. That position has now been fully exited from our portfolio. Ital Thai is a Thailand based developer of major building projects. They built the Bangkok Airport. They put in a fairly complex series of options to creditors, clearly trying to get them to take a cash resolution. They also offered a debt instrument over some, shall we say, very weak collateral. And they were offering equity, knowing that banks don't like to take it. But we don't mind taking equity. And, because it was undervalued, we did a 100 percent debt-for-equities swap. Ultimately, when the company was publicly listed, the share price surpassed our buy-in price and we delivered by a multiple of 3.1 ×. That's the kind of returns we like to make. That was a pretty nice equity kicker.

But, day in and day out, our equity ups are selective. Our largest return component continues to come from the amortization schedule and the cash payments. We feel good about being able to look our investors in the eye and say that we believe we can make 15 to 20 percent net IRR [internal rate of return] over the intermediate and long-term before leverage. That's where we are. We're absolute return guys.

SK: *I understand that Clearwater requires a two-year lockup on all investor contributions. That's a longer time than most hedge funds. What's your thinking there?*

RP: In a word, long-term. We encourage investors to come in with an intermediate-term horizon. If you think about the assets we're investing in, the duration of our portfolio is something like two years. So if we buy a four-year amortizing loan at 50 cents on the dollar, to illustrate with a simple case, it pays back our cost in two years. And then everything after that is profit.

SK: *Let's give the readers a snapshot of the Clearwater funds.*

RP: Sure. Clearwater manages $700+ million in three funds invested in the same deals, domiciled in the Cayman Islands. We follow a long-only strategy. As for hedging, we only do it to offset currency fluctuations. Over 90 percent of the portfolio is floating-rate or liqui-dations. As of this discussion, there are over 50 investments in each portfolio.

We feel good about our footprint today. Clearly China is a place where we may want to expand, to go from just a Hong Kong presence to more of an in-country presence. And honestly as we look at it, we have to recognize that Europe is a place where we've done about 10 percent of our business. But also it's a more natural place from which to work with Asia. We see London really as the hub of international in-vesting. So we conceive of a London presence and a China presence as we look out two to five years.

SK: *How about leverage?*

RP: Yeah, we use it, but it is limited to a one-to-one ratio in all our funds. We think we're in an appropriate asset class to leverage selec-tively. If you think about it: A diversified portfolio of cash-generative senior secured instruments, why shouldn't you leverage those?

SK: *It makes sense. Rob, in what markets do you do well?*

RP: Generally speaking, our performance is inverse to the markets. We do pretty darn well in an up market, but probably not as well as your good equity long/short guys. And conversely, we continue to do quite well in a down market.

Keep in mind the Asia Distressed space is really new, that it began as of January 1998. That's when the Asia currency crisis happened. Prior to that, there was no distressed or workout business in Asia. Af-ter the crisis, it took a good two or three years to have the benchmark transactions take place, to have the bankruptcy codes put in place, and to have the actual practice of restructuring occur across the re-gion. The space has been created only in the past five to seven years. We expect it to be fruitful for many years to come as the overall credit culture and financial markets continue to develop across 30 percent of the world's GDP.

SK: *Thanks, Rob. This has been great. But you know you've really done some damage to the popular image of the high-living hedge funds manager, buzzing around from party to party in his Ferrari.*

RP: (Smiles) Sorry. I have a Toyota Sienna. I'm married and have three kids. Whatever partying we do is sort of restricted to Friday nights 'cause it's the only time Asia isn't open. You know our money is right there next to our investors' money. So that's how we live—and this is an expensive business to run efficiently. You're not going to find me out buzzing around in a Ferrari. Instead, I'll be on an airplane flying to somewhere in Asia.

CHAPTER 7

The Relative Value Arbitrage Strategies: Equity Market Neutral

INTRODUCTION

This is the first of three chapters devoted to the relative value arbitrage strategies: Equity Market Neutral, Convertible Arbitrage, and Fixed-Income Arbitrage. This group of funds makes bets on the pricing relationship between two related securities, one believed to be overpriced and the other underpriced, hence the designation relative value arbitrage. The strategies are designed to shield investors from the vagaries of equity and bond markets and from a beta perspective to be market neutral and therefore they are often called market-neutral funds. In many ways, therefore, the relative value arbitrage trading methods are the most conceptually appealing of all hedge fund styles. What could be better than investment approaches that have been shown over and over again to be relatively uncorrelated with global equity markets?

Well, as is often the case in the world of investments, the more one learns about relative value strategies, the more complex they seem. One of your authors invested in a relative value fund of funds that in turn put money with funds representing all three major types of relative value arbitrage trading. To make a long story short, after a couple of years of clicking along with monthly returns of 1 percent, the fund of fund's returns in 1994 were wiped out by the collapse of one of its low volatility managers, a fund managed by Askin Capital Management.

David Askin's investments in mortgage-backed securities arbitrage (a subset of Fixed-Income Arb that we discuss in Chapter 9) were supposedly immune to interest rate fluctuations but this turned out to be very far from the case. You can imagine the investors' shock as they learned that their sure 12 percent per annum was not at all guaranteed.

Nearly a decade later a modest check came in the mail, the result of a lawsuit filed on behalf of the fund of funds' investors. While amounting to but a small percentage of the losses sustained as a result of the Askin blow-up, it was a not so gentle reminder of the possible risks in supposedly low-risk strategies.

According to the Barclay Group's latest asset flow survey, the three relative value strategies are the smallest of our three groups with about 11 percent of total hedge fund assets, roughly $138 billion between them.[1] Of that total, $58 billion is managed in Fixed Income Arb, $42 billion is held by Equity Market Neutral funds, and $38 billion by Convertible Arb managers. None of these AUM figures includes leverage.

THE EQUITY MARKET NEUTRAL TRADING AND INVESTMENT STRATEGIES

Pairs Trading and Statistical Arbitrage

Equity market neutral managers sometimes use pairs trading like their peers in equity long/short and another method called statistical arbitrage as ways of balancing the long and short positions in their portfolios. Pairs trading is a fundamentally driven approach to equity investing in which undervalued companies or those with accelerating earnings or the like are bought and then are matched with companies (often in the same industry) that are viewed as overvalued, undergoing negative changes, and so on, that are then sold short.

Statistical Arbitrage or Stat Arb, on the other hand, is a quantitatively based trading technique that identifies relative mispricings between pairs of stocks based on the expected fair value of those equities. For example, pairs of equities whose prices have tended to move in tandem (like those of companies in the same industry) are flagged by the manager's computational models if their historical price ratios are violated. The manager will then put on a long-short trade in the expectation that the stocks will return to their expected values. Stat Arb tends to be a more short-term trading strategy while the more fundamentally driven pairs trading method has a longer-term investment horizon.

Equity market neutral managers will use both of these techniques to create their long and short books. But unlike their ELS cousins, they will also ensure that their portfolios are beta neutral. As you recall, ELS managers are usually either net long or short depending on their market views and typically have high correlations to the market (around 0.6 percent long-term). As a result, ELS funds always have a certain degree of systematic risk that is partially reflected in their betas.

Equity market neutral traders, however, select hundreds of stocks to minimize specific risk while neutralizing their portfolio's beta to the market. Using proprietary statistical models and keen portfolio risk management to constantly size and resize their positions, these traders balance their high beta stocks on the long side, those equities that have a high correlation to the market and therefore rise and fall with it, with other high beta stocks on the short side. The resulting portfolio is said to be beta neutral because it should be fairly insulated from market swings.

In addition, equity market neutral managers shield their portfolios from market risk using four other techniques: (1) balancing the market value of their longs and shorts so the portfolio is cash neutral; (2) minimizing sector risk by balancing the longs and shorts in a given industry; (3) truing up the market capitalizations of the underlying stocks so they are not strongly weighted in any particular cap range; and (4) if investing in foreign equities, by also hedging away currency risk. The goal of this multilayered balancing act is to generate returns without taking the directional bets that ELS managers wager daily.

Nevertheless, both pairs trading and stat arb have several recurring problems associated with them that we discuss at length in the Disadvantages section. For now, we mention only one, the aptly named value trap. Value trap is a term used by portfolio managers to describe a long position that is deemed to be undervalued yet remains so or goes lower still. Sometimes a stock is cheap for a good reason, causing it to stay at a relatively low price and yet the reason may not be knowable by the manager. The opposite but just as nasty a problem is that the apparently overvalued stock is overvalued for a good reason, causing it to remain at a rich price or become even more so. Here, too, the reason may not be knowable by the manager. It might be revealed by an earnings surprise to the upside (which would be classified as event risk), resulting in an immediately widening loss to the short position.

Portfolio Optimization

An inside look at how equity market neutral portfolios are optimized is provided by Dr. John Schmitz, portfolio manager of SciVest Market Neutral Equity Fund, a Toronto-based hedge fund he founded in May 2001. Dr. Schmitz is also our featured interviewee at the end of this chapter. In his investment process, a universe of more than 10,000 stocks is first screened by his quantitative models. Stocks are then analyzed based on a multifactor proprietary model that includes models for expected returns, expected risk, expected correlations with every other stock, expected beta for each stock, and expected transaction costs for every stock. The risk model and its data are totally independent of the expected return model and its data, reducing the danger of what is known as *model risk.**

The next step in the investment process is defining the parameters and constraints of the portfolio so that the model can create an optimized portfolio of longs and shorts. These parameters include cash neutrality, forecasted beta equal to zero, sector and industry neutrality, no large net investment style exposure like large- versus small-cap, and no other large net systematic risk exposures (like foreign exchange risk).

Schmitz also risk controls his maximum and minimum position

---

*Model risk describes the risk that a manager's selection analytics, that is, his models that have worked consistently over the long term, simply stop working. This risk is detailed in the Disadvantages section.

sizes based on inputs that are not covered by either his stock-selection model, statistical risk model, or the aforementioned parameters. For example, he won't go long analysts' sell-rated stocks or stocks of companies with high probabilities of going bankrupt. On the short side he will minimize his position in a stock if analysts have given it strong buy ratings. These and other qualitative manager judgments ultimately put the finishing touches on an optimized portfolio that contains anywhere from 200–800 names.

SOURCES OF RETURNS

How then do equity market neutral managers make money? There are three sources of profits in this strategy: the long portion of the portfolio, the short portion, and the T-bill rate. At the heart of successful equity market neutral investing is the manager's stock-picking ability. Having eliminated the free ride that comes with beta-driven investing, the equity market neutral manager is forced to make money through sophisticated analysis of companies, ultimately deciding on what is a long candidate and what is a short. If the longs in the portfolio don't go up more or down less than the shorts, the portfolio won't make much more than the risk-free rate of T-bills (discussed next).

The second source of possible returns is the short book. Stocks are shorted for two reasons, either to profit from an anticipated fall in their prices because of weakness and/or as a hedge against securities held long. If the market goes down, the basket of short stocks will likely create a profit for the fund and offset some of the losses incurred by the long book. If the market goes up, there should be more than enough profits in the longs due to superior stock selection to offset the likely losses in the shorts that have served as insurance.

Finally, there is a third source of return, that of the proceeds from the short sales. As a reminder, the stocks that are sold short are borrowed from the broker. When they are sold, the cash that is raised is usually invested in a risk-free instrument like T-bills. That money goes to the manager less the broker's fees, expenses, and any owed dividends. This third component of return is commonly

TABLE 7.1

Three Markets and Their Impact on an Equity Market Neutral Portfolio

Expected Market Neutral Return	Rising Market +10%	Declining Market −10%	Sideways Market 0%
(a) Long Portfolio	16% (alpha = 6%)	−4% (alpha = 6%)	6% (alpha = 6%)
(b) Short Portfolio	−4% (alpha = 6%)	16% (alpha = 6%)	6% (alpha = 6%)
Equity Return = (a) + (b)	12%	12%	12%
Return on Cash Holdings	T-bills	T-bills	T-bills
Total Expected Return	T-bills + 12%	T-bills + 12%	T-bills + 12%

Sources: SciVest and Dr. John Schmitz.

known as the short interest rebate but more colorfully as the "monkey return" because it's the only piece of the return equation that requires no skill.

Let's examine this process in greater detail by using an example supplied by Dr. Schmitz. Table 7.1 illustrates three possible market outcomes with a look at how the Equity Market Neutral portfolio generates returns from all three sources described previously. As Schmitz notes, all of the positive results above the risk-free rate of T-bills (minus the broker's fees and expenses) are totally dependent on the manager's skill and the power of his quantitative models in selecting the right stocks to go long and the ones to sell short. Without that edge, there will be no alpha.* In this case, Table 7.1 shows alpha to be equal to 6 percent on the long side and 6 percent on the short. This outperformance is produced in rising, declining, and sideways markets and is dependent on manager skill. If the manager manifests those skills, his investors will be rewarded with positive returns regardless of market conditions. If he doesn't and the fund loses money, then investors will have substituted specific risk for market risk, in this case, the manager's selection of specific stocks.[2]

---

*Used here to connote outperformance.

PERFORMANCE

In view of the seemingly obvious advantages of Equity Market Neutral, one wonders how it is that global AUM for this strategy is less than 4 percent of all hedge fund assets. The answer is absolute performance. Unlike most other hedge fund strategies, Equity Market Neutral failed to outperform the S&P over the period 1994–2005 although it did outperform the MSCI World and the Lehman.[3] Figure 7.1 shows the cumulative performance of the various indices. In fact, over the past 12 years, three out of the four worst performing strategies are relative value arbitrage strategies.

But that's only part of the story. Equity Market Neutral also had the lowest volatility of any asset class with a standard deviation of 3.1 percent. The strategy had about two-thirds of the volatility of the Lehman Bond Index, and about one-fifth the volatility of the S&P 500. On a risk/reward basis, then, Equity Market Neutral had a

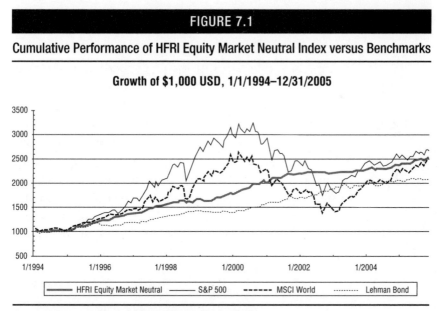

FIGURE 7.1

Cumulative Performance of HFRI Equity Market Neutral Index versus Benchmarks

Growth of $1,000 USD, 1/1/1994–12/31/2005

Sources: Mayer & Hoffman Capital Advisors, HFRI, and PerTrac.

respectable Sharpe ratio of 1.31 as compared with the 0.31 Sharpe achieved by domestic equities and the 0.54 Sharpe of the Lehman Bond Index.[4]

Over the past five years, however, Equity Market Neutral has substantially outperformed equities but not bonds. Figure 7.2 shows the results. Look at this figure closely. Observe that in 2001 and 2002, while the S&P was plunging dramatically, the HFRI Equity Market Neutral Index was actually up both years: in 2001, 6.71 percent and in 2002, a modest 0.98 percent. Over the latest five-year period, the S&P has languished while the HFRI Equity Market Neutral Index is up about 25 percent. This relative performance advantage is partly attributable to having a negative correlation with the market.

Yet, despite the risk-adjusted returns the marketplace has shunned Equity Market Neutral in favor of other strategies that have produced higher returns. Part of the problem has been that the strategy's double

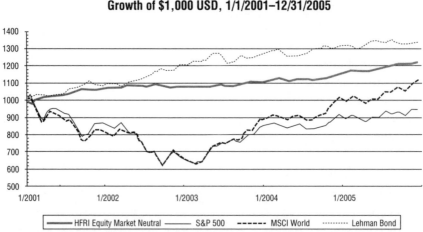

FIGURE 7.2

HFRI Equity Market Neutral versus Benchmarks, Trailing Five Years

Growth of $1,000 USD, 1/1/2001–12/31/2005

HFRI Equity Market Neutral ——— S&P 500 ------ MSCI World ·········· Lehman Bond

Sources: Mayer & Hoffman Capital Advisors, HFRI, and PerTrac.

digit returns of the 1990s have become a thing of the past. Returns in Equity Market Neutral have been steadily declining.

What has gone wrong?

There are two main explanations for the strategy's performance decline: the inflow of capital and the decline in short-term interest rates. Perhaps the more important of the two problems has been the amount of money that has flooded into hedge funds in general and into ELS in particular. This inflow of capital, in turn, has led to three significant issues for Equity Market Neutral traders: the relative scarcity of shares available for loan, the increased costs associated with borrowing those shares, and the competition among hedge funds for stocks to purchase or sell short.

1. On the short side, stock has become harder to borrow with the increase in demand for stock to sell short, making it more difficult for funds to capture attractive short sale opportunities. This is especially true with "investment grade shorts," shares of companies in such clear states of fundamental decline that hedge fund demand for borrowed shares outstrips the supply of shares available for lending.
2. Since demand for borrowed shares has outstripped supply, costs for short selling have risen. Fees levied by brokerage firms have increased, thus lowering the profits from the short side.
3. Competition among hedge funds to capitalize on good trading opportunities has become fierce. For example, if a stock moves down or up sharply for a nonrecurring or temporary reason, only so many shares can be bought or sold short at attractive prices before the stock price reverts. Sometimes these trading opportunities are so obvious that hedge funds are tripping over one another to take advantage of the price anomalies.

A second major reason for declining returns is that one of the three primary drivers of Equity Market Neutral performance is the T-bill rate. In recent years that rate has gone down to historic lows. The lower yields have squeezed the amount of interest earned on the credit balances generated by short sales.

ADVANTAGES

There are three key advantages inherent in Equity Market Neutral. First, returns are relatively uncorrelated to the equity and bond markets. Second, volatility is extremely low. Third, adding Equity Market Neutral to a portfolio of traditional assets like stocks and bonds or even to a basket of directional hedge fund strategies, results in increased overall risk-adjusted returns and lowered volatility. This finding is even more crucial today when traditional methods of diversification like adding investment grade international stocks to a domestic portfolio barely reduce risk because of high cross correlations (As of this writing the correlation between the S&P 500 and the MSCI World Index Free was more than 0.90.) A similar problem exists with most hedge fund strategies as their correlations with each other and to the markets have increased as well. Equity Market Neutral continues to add value as a risk diversifier by remaining relatively uncorrelated to the directional strategies. For example, over the past 12 years the strategy's highest correlation with any other hedge type was 0.35 with ELS.[5]

DISADVANTAGES

There are five major risks associated with Equity Market Neutral investing: stock-selection risk; model risk; short squeezes; event risk; and liquidity risk.

1. Because equity market neutral relies heavily on the stock-selecting ability of the manager, it is also its foremost risk. As we noted earlier, managers can hedge their market risk by being beta neutral on many levels, but if the stocks they pick don't behave as expected, they have substituted specific risk for Sharpe's market risk. One example of this risk is the misidentification of a stock either as a value or as a growth play. Managers may identify value stocks as being way overpriced and sell them short. Unbeknownst to them, the market is shifting its perception of the company (possibly because of management changes or a new product line) from

being seen as a value stock to being viewed more as a growth stock. As growth investors become attracted to the stock, the stock rises, quickly going against the short. In this instance, the manager must act quickly as traders have frequently observed that "your first loss is your best loss." Of course the opposite problem can occur if a growth stock long position loses multiple (its P/E ratio contracts) as growth stock investors sell it, fearing a loss of growth momentum.

2. A second major problem for the strategy is model risk. It can be especially frustrating and costly for a fund when its selection analytics, that is, its quantitative models that have worked consistently over the long term simply stop working. What is a manager to do when his models fail and (supposedly) relatively unattractive stocks are outperforming the relatively attractive ones? The answer lies in recognizing and accepting that this peculiarity of markets can go on for an uncomfortable period of time and can produce significant losses. When markets start pricing stocks "perversely" as Dr. Schmitz calls it, an even more serious consequence of model risk occurs called "convergent impact."[6] This phenomenon refers to the situation when a manager's shorts rally and his longs decline, making the strategy a two-way loser. Many relative value managers found themselves in this very position during the formation of the Internet bubble. Historical price valuations went out the window as tech stocks with no earnings and hemorrhaging cash rallied feverishly while value stocks with great earnings and cash-rich coffers declined.

3. We would be remiss not to mention the risks of short squeezes although these are not unique to the Equity Market Neutral strategy. As we discussed and illustrated in Chapter 2, the short squeeze is the bane of all short sellers.

4. A fourth risk that can befall an equity market neutral manager is event risk. The trader and his models find a company that is experiencing serious problems like declining sales or a product recall, and he decides to sell its stock short. Yet what type of company can become an acquisition target? Often it is just such a wounded company that the acquirer hopes to absorb through merger. So the

manager may find himself short the stock only to open the *Wall Street Journal* one morning (or read it online) and discover that his short is the coveted object of a takeover bid. Quantitatively driven managers are especially vulnerable to event risk.

5. A final risk that should be mentioned is the specific liquidity risk that has arisen from the dwindling supply of quality shorts. Equity market neutral managers may need 100 or more names to short and they prefer to sell stocks with a higher degree of liquidity because it is less risky. Schmitz and other managers have turned to less liquid stocks, like Canadian equities for example, for their short book because other hedge fund managers have ignored them and therefore these equities can be borrowed more readily. In doing so, however, managers leave themselves in a position where if the market goes against them, they may not be able to buy back the shares except at inflated prices.

John Schmitz

President and CIO
SciVest Capital Management

Dr. John Schmitz founded SciVest Capital Management based in Toronto, Canada, in 1999 and a year later sold his proprietary quantitative models to Maxxum Fund Management, now a part of Mackenzie Financial Corporation. While a vice president at Maxxum, he refined those models that then helped drive the decisions at Quantum Aggressive Market Neutral Equity Fund, a fund launched by Maxxum in May 2001. In December of that year, SciVest purchased the models for the Quantum Aggressive Fund and renamed it the SciVest Market Neutral Equity Fund in January 2002. SciVest manages about $130 million.

In addition to his responsibilities at the firm, John is an active researcher and has published articles on investing and portfolio management in both academic and professional journals. He earned a Ph.D. in finance from the University of Western Ontario, and a degree in mechanical engineering and an M.A. in economics from the University of Toronto.

SK: *John, how do you characterize the Equity Market Neutral space?*

JS: In reality, it's not a trivial thing to deliver market neutrality. And a lot of the guys that call themselves market neutral are simply cash neutral.

SK: *Can you outline that distinction for us?*

JS: If you're long and short the same dollar value, then you're cash neutral. However, if you think about it a second, it does not necessarily mean that you're market neutral. If you're long $160 worth of tech stocks and short $160 worth of utilities, you probably have a very substantial market exposure. In fact your beta might actually exceed one. So you're not even close to market neutral; not even close to meeting your objective. A true market neutral manager (of which there are not many) will actually beta neutralize the portfolio. In my mind, that's the definition of Market Neutral Equity (Dr. Schmitz prefers this name to Equity Market Neutral). Cash neutrality is a constraint. So if you're long $50 worth of tech stocks and short $150 worth of utilities, then you're probably market neutral. You're not cash neutral, but you're meeting the objective of the space: being beta zero. But maybe that position doesn't sound very good from a marketing perspective.

SK: *So the more important goal is to be beta zero. How do you accomplish that?*

JS: We use an optimization technique. We have a process to build the portfolio in a way to ensure that, in aggregate, the long beta exactly equals the short beta. Now, within the context of optimization you can control a number of different risk factors, including industry and sector exposure. For us, it's not a prerequisite to neutralize industry and sector net exposures. But some guys will neutralize those to get rid of the risks. Others build in an alpha factor within their process. We just control it tightly, we do not neutralize it. For example, right now we're operating at a net sector exposure limit of 5 percent plus or minus. Meaning if we're long 20 percent technology stocks, we're short at least 15 and at most 25. So we're not taking a very large bet that tech's going up or down, but we will have some exposure to that sector. We won't lose too much from that and we probably won't make too much, either. So we use that bet as a small alpha contribution to the overall portfolio. We diversify by our models and by country. For example, right now we're net long transports, industrials, technology, and financials while we're net short consumer services, consumer cyclical, consumer noncyclical, and healthcare. So we're short the consumer in general.

SK: *Okay, so if you're beta zero, how do you generate returns?*

JS: The way you make money in market neutral equity is stock picking. Within an industry sector, picking good versus bad stocks is the ultimate key. The whole objective is to build portfolios where, regardless of market direction, the longs slightly outperform the shorts. So the key question is: How do you define good stocks versus bad? All of us do that in a different way. Right now our stock picking favors earnings-based valuation measures. We also like momentum characteristics of the stocks. So in our portfolio we're strongly net long momentum characteristics and strongly net long earnings valuation characteristics. We're pretty neutral right now on many other characteristics that you could use to pick stocks.

So our returns will depend on two things: whether an earnings-based model is working or not and whether the momentum characteristics are working or not. Our risk is determined by that as well. So the key is to manage those exposures so that you don't blow your brains out on, say, momentum, if it turns. It can turn against you very hard, and very painfully. You could have a drawdown if you have allowed yourself to take too big a momentum exposure. So we don't let the process go unconstrained.

SK: *You've got some checks and balances in place.*

JS: Right. With an optimization process you're always attempting to get to the efficient frontier. So, for the readers who are academics, for a given utility curve,* you're trying to push out toward the efficient frontier at that point where it's tangent to the utility curve. So implicitly or explicitly what you're trying to do is maximize your expected return while minimizing volatility risk of the portfolio. And also minimizing trading costs. And yes, we're subject to a long list

---

*Also called the indifference curve, in economics.

of investment constraints. We have more than 100 investment constraints that have to be met every time we rebalance the portfolio.

SK: *How many positions do you have in the portfolio?*

JS: We're actually up to 800 now because we just recently added Japan to the book. You know, after 11 years of school, one of the key things you walk away with is this: The most powerful risk management technique known to man is diversification. I'm a big believer in both model diversification as well as country diversification. So currently we're up to five live models (or subportfolios) for each of our funds. And the primary reason for that is diversification. So as an example, we've always had a Canadian component to our portfolio. Our U.S. core model and our Canadian core model are basically the same, just applied to the different data sets: different countries.

It turns out, interestingly enough, that the market neutral spread that we develop between the two countries is virtually uncorrelated. So if Canada and the United States are uncorrelated, then almost assuredly Japan and the United States, London and the United States, and Australia and the United States are uncorrelated as well, on our market neutral spreads. We just introduced Japan about a month ago and it has currently drifted up to 25 percent of the portfolio. The Canada core model is another 25 percent. Only 50 percent of the portfolio now is United States. Six months ago it was 85 percent United States, 15 percent other. We're doing that because we think that the spreads available outside the United States today are somewhat bigger than the spreads available in the United States for this type of money management. And even in the United States we've allowed the portfolios to drift more into the Russell 2000, from the 1000. It's the same logic: that among the Russell 1000, the spreads are probably quite a bit tighter than they used to be and quite a bit tighter than, say, the Russell 2000 universe.

SK: *So you're seeking those wider spreads.*

JS: It's a constant search for wider spreads and more volatility as well. We're looking at a market that's at historically low volatility levels and historically low spread levels for these types of strategies.

SK: *The VIX, for example, at all-time lows.*

JS: It's been tough pickin's. Volatility has fallen as correlations between stocks have increased. It's a dramatic convergence.

SK: *What do you see as the causes for that convergence?*

JS: I think it's a combination of two things. First, for a given volatility level (and volatility certainly has been constant over the past three years) I think the spreads have compressed. In the 1990s a normally leveraged market neutral strategy generated 600 to 900 basis points above risk-free. I think that number isn't possible any more. The free lunch is done now. The spreads have compressed to 200 to 500 basis points above risk-free for a given volatility level.

The other issue, of course, is volatility. With the 50 percent decrease in volatility of the markets that we've seen over the past three years you'd expect to earn half as much as you would've three years ago. Unless you've altered or adjusted your risk management process so that you have some hope of achieving your long-term target alpha. If you just allowed the portfolio to fall in volatility with the market, as we inadvertently did through last summer, then your alpha potential would have fallen in half as well. Even if the spreads hadn't compressed.

So over the past 12 months we've widened our investment constraints in an attempt to capture more volatility in the portfolio and, as a result, get a return potential or alpha potential back up to what we feel it should be. So how do you do that? You increase your exposure levels. You let the fund take slightly bigger industry exposures, sector exposures, individual stock exposures, style exposures, and so on. You have to start making compromises between risk and return.

SK: *Either that or do a rain dance, right?*

JS: (Laughing) Yeah, 'cause it's been a drought. It's been a three-year drought, which never happened before in the history of the space. So you've got more brains and more money chasing similar type fundamental spreads. However, it's still a better proposition than equity on a standalone basis, and probably at least as good as bonds. The key though, for the arbitrage industry in general is that we have to stop selling 10, 12 percent returns on an absolute basis. Instead, we have to start selling conservative returns that equity neutral generates above risk-free: from 200 to 500 basis points, and its lack of correlation with the other asset classes an investor holds.*

SK: *Those two selling points make sense. John, we're asking all our managers for war stories. You know, something to illustrate the tough times that everyone goes through. Looking at your numbers I see you had a rough period in 2004, spring and summer. I know a lot of managers did. How did things unfold for you during that period?*

JS: Yeah, those were really bad months. It was characterized by very, very low institutional participation in the equity markets in the United States. And keep in mind, at that time we were 85 percent United States. There was also a massive amount of hedge fund managers trading among themselves. So the long-only and longer-term fundamental money wasn't participating. So you got a lot of quick trades and a lot of industry sector rotation going on. As a result the money was flowing from industry to industry, sector to sector. And we were virtually industry and sector neutral. We had a 2 percent net exposure limit to industries and sectors. We were confined to making all our spreads within industries. We weren't participating in the industry and sector rotation game. I think we lost money partially because I didn't fully appreciate the implications of the drop in volatility over the prior year and a half.

SK: *Well, you weren't alone in that.*

JS: Yeah, we had let our volatility fall to about 5 percent, despite the drawdown. So as a result of that experience we slowly began to increase our exposures, which is really a very difficult thing to do once you're losing money. You know, it's counterintuitive to start widening your risk parameters as you're losing money.

SK: *It's a gutsy reaction, but it does make sense.*

JS: Everyone in our house wanted to tighten things up even more, but I became convinced that there was no way we're going to earn

---

*From January 2001 to December 2005, the HFRI Equity Market Neutral Index outperformed the risk-free rate by 1.80 percent per annum.

anything with the volatility falling to such a low level. So we started widening our parameters trying to get a higher return potential. The other thing is we accelerated our globalization plan as well. Like I said, we were 85 percent United States. If you have too many of your eggs in one basket, you need to take some eggs out and put 'em in other baskets. Hence we aggressively began the globalization program resulting in the launch of Japan last month and the slow increase of our Canadian content.

SK: *That's a terrific story. And let's note that you guys had wonderful performance until then. Look at your returns in 2001 and 2002. You were up 17 percent in 2001 and 9 percent in 2002, which is heroic.*

JS: Well, we won the GAIM Award for the best performing market neutral manager in the world. We'd been managing more than $100 million for quite some time by then.

SK: *John, we're looking for a story, or a specific trade to illustrate how things can go bad.*

JS: I do remember certain trades that went bad in 2004. We actually got nailed with two positions during the year. I bet it was close to 2 percent of portfolio value. They were two very large shorts. And with each one of 'em we got taken for about 60 percent.

SK: *Tell us about that.*

JS: They were both biotech positions; a huge amount of pain from the two positions. They were trades we couldn't get out of because of instant dislocations in the stock prices. A piece of news comes out: Stocks jump 60 percent before the markets open. So you can't get out. You can't stop losses. So it was not a position that ran against us over time. These were 60 percent, one-day hits, twice, on fairly substantial shorts. I think one was in February/March and one was at the end of September. And that prompted us to question "Okay, should we even be trading biotech companies?" Because the biotechs in general are news-driven entities and they have these huge price swings based on test results or FDA announcements.

So the first question was should we be trading them? And the answer to that question was another question, "On average, do we make money from the biotech industry?" The answer to that actually is yes. On average, we have done quite well. So the next question is, "Can we manage the risk better?" And that answer was yes, too. And the solution is that we cut our maximum position allowed in that space by 50 percent. So instead of, say, having five or six biotech longs and five or six shorts, we now have 10 long, 10 short, but with half the weight. So if our biggest weight then was 2 percent, our biggest weight now is 1 percent. Every time we lose money or hit a bump, that's the kind of exercise we go through. That's part of the art of quant investing. It's not a case of waking up every morning and pressing Enter and you're done for the day. The art is the feel for the market, the feel for what's going on in your portfolio with the feedback against what you know the models are supposed to do. And the key is to have that intuition to ask the right questions and then to apply the quantitative skill set to the management of those risks.

SK: *Great. About how long will you generally hold a position?*

JS: We hold stocks an average of two months or so. Since we do that and since our models are designed to slowly adapt to the current investment regime, we're left with some fundamental risks in the portfolio. If the fundamental way the markets price stocks changes very quickly, it takes our models a while to catch up by design. And since we have to hold stocks two or three months, it takes us a while to rotate the portfolio as well. So that's fundamental risk number one.

Fundamental risk number two is that we have what's called a Theory Overlay riding on top of everything. Sometimes the market is pricing stocks perversely across a large number of factors. But we're explicitly not allowed to push the portfolio in that direction. So we got hit with a double whammy in October–November of 2002 that resulted in our biggest, quickest drawdown. In that period, the way the market was pricing stocks flipped 180 degrees literally in one day: October 1. And everything after that regime change was perverse.

SK: *So you ask yourselves some fundamental questions.*

JS: Yes. But most often it comes down to "Okay. We just lost money." And 9 out of 10 times it's just an inherent risk of the strategy and there are no changes necessary. You just go on as usual because you know you'll win it in the long-term. And it's not even really 1 of 10 times: It's probably more like 1 out of 30 times that these outlier events occur.

SK: *How about the flip side: the wins? You're up more than 7 percent this year, well ahead of your Index.*

JS: We've really made a lot of hay in Canada. Canada's been an alpha generating machine for the past 13 months or so. But on a truly market-neutral basis we're up probably about 20 percent gross. And that is again oil up, oil down. It's a pure alpha situation. It's not because we have market exposure and it's not that we have massive oil exposure net long or energy exposure net long. It's actually just been a great wave for the past 12 to 14 months. I think it's somewhat correlated, however, with capital inflows into the country because of the oil, gas, and metals, the natural resource boom in general. So Canada's been kickin' and our models moved into Canada, increased exposure to 25 percent, and lowered United States at the same time. Second, I think our whole program of trying to increase the volatility by widening exposures out has also resulted in picking up much bigger spreads this year than we were capable of producing over the past year and a half.

SK: *You got a double win because you're investing in Canadian stocks that are less liquid and with wider spreads.*

JS: Exactly. There are only 300 stocks to choose from here and we trade 30.

SK: *How about energy?*

JS: The models have been taking some money off the table. We're still net long energy but it's definitely not our biggest net long any more. Within energy though, we like the refining business the best because that's a pure spread, a pure money printing type of business. So I keep trying to avoid the risk of oil up or down and concentrating instead on the lack of capacity in the refining business, which seems to be a place that can just continue to print money regardless of oil going up or down 10 bucks from here. The spreads there, of refined versus unrefined, will remain very high just because of lack of capacity globally.

SK: *A final word to our readers?*

JS: It's been really tough lately for most strategies. It seems like every time the equity markets have a problem, every single hedge fund strategy has a problem. It has been a cyclically tough period. But it will probably reverse out over the next 12 to 14 months. But the old days of 500 to 700 basis points above risk-free? That's not going to happen any more. Those days are gone.

SK: *Thank you, John.*

CHAPTER 8

Convertible Arbitrage

INTRODUCTION

The second of our relative value strategies is Convertible Arbitrage. Convertible Arbitrageurs are currently the bêtes noires of the hedge fund world, having produced distinctly subpar returns in recent years. How bad has it been? In 2004 the HFRI Convertible Arbitrage Index returned 1.18 percent, well below its historical average of more than 9 percent (see Performance section) and was one of the worst performing strategies that year. In early 2005, things got much worse, with the Index down about 7 percent in the first five months of the year. Since then performance has improved and while Convertible Arb ended 2005 as the worst performing strategy, the HFRI Convertible Arbitrage Index was down 2.1 percent. More telling was the performance of the HFRX investable Convertible Arb Index that was down almost 6 percent for 2005.

Since asset flows invariably follow performance, there have been massive redemptions in this space. In the first nine months of 2005, Convertible Arb funds lost 20 percent of their assets worldwide, declining from $49 billion to $38.5 billion.[1] Time will tell whether this bloodletting will help the patient revive.

THE CONVERTIBLE ARBITRAGE TRADING AND INVESTMENT STRATEGIES

Convertible Arbitrage Basics

A convertible security is a hybrid fixed-income instrument that allows the holder to exchange it for the common stock of the issuing company. The specific terms of a convertible bond are governed by the provisions in the convertible's issuance document called the *indenture*. For example, the bond may be callable by the issuer on a given date at a set price or it might have warrants attached to it. The indenture always describes the number of shares into which the security can be converted. In short, a convertible security has some characteristics of a fixed-income instrument and some characteristics of the underlying equity security as well. There are three major types of convertibles issued, senior debt, subordinated debentures, and preferred stock, and they come in the full range of credit ratings from AAA all the way down to junk (CCC) and even Non-Rated.

The most common trade in Convertible Arbitrage is to go long the bond and hedge the specific risk by shorting the underlying stock. To hedge this risk the manager must determine the appropriate ratio of stock to sell. The ratio between the number of shares sold short and the number of shares into which the bonds are convertible is called the *hedge ratio*. Let's use the following example to illustrate. A manager buys 10 convertible bonds at a discount to par value, say $800/bond, for a total of $8,000. The bond's conversion ratio as set by the indenture is 20; thus the total number of shares into which the 10 bonds can be converted is 200. If 100 shares are sold short, the hedge ratio in this example is 0.5.

Several factors, including whether the bond is trading at a premium or a discount, the volatility of the stock, and the interest rate environment, will determine whether a manager has hedged effectively. For this example, let's assume that shorting 100 shares makes this position quite market neutral at inception. As the stock moves further away from the start point, either additional shares will need to be sold short or some shares will need to be covered in order to maintain the neutral posture. Alternatively, if a short or long bias is the portfolio manager's wish, a greater or lesser number of shares can be sold short and the desired bias preserved by adjusting the short position as the stock price moves up or down. Thus positions must be very closely monitored and managed.

Warrants or options may be used instead of or in addition to stock for hedging purposes. This complicates the analysis considerably since they require more position management as share prices change. This is especially true in the case of options, as puts or calls may be used, or a combination of both, and options selected may be at-, in-, or out-of-the-money as well as having near or far expiration dates.

Delta is a measure of the relationship of the price movement of a convertible security to the price movement of the underlying stock, option, or warrant that has been used as a hedge. The value of delta changes as share prices move up and down. For example, convertibles that are very in-the-money, that is, the share price is well above the conversion price, have deltas that approach 1. For every 1 percent change in the price of the stock, the convertible price also moves nearly 1 percent. For very out-of-the-money convertibles the delta will be close to zero, that is, the convertible price is quite insensitive to stock price changes. *Gamma* is a measure of the sensitivity of delta to changes in the stock price, defined as the change in delta related to the change in the price of the underlying stock. Gamma is calculated by dividing the delta by the change in the stock price. In calculus, gamma would be considered the first derivative of delta.

Convert arb managers are long gamma and long volatility in the sense that large increases in the stock's upward volatility and share price lead to outsized profits on the convert. Because delta and gamma are constantly changing as stock prices move, convertible arb managers must monitor positions carefully and adjust long and/or short positions accordingly in order to maintain the desired market exposure.

There are many variations on the strategy, depending on market conditions, market outlook, the outlook for the companies whose securities are being arbitraged, the characteristics of the convertible security in question, and the manager's personal management style. Some managers prefer convertibles that are beaten down and selling near their bond value. An out-of-the-money convert's delta is not very sensitive to changes in the equity's price, and the stock will have to appreciate a great deal before the debenture begins to increase much in value. As such, a beaten down convert may make the long position low risk (assuming no credit downgrades), but the position's value if converted is way below market. Hedging in such situations must also protect against credit risk such as a downgrade or default. An arbitrage using a depressed convert can produce a profit if the share price declines while the convert holds its ground due to proximity to its bond value. Managers will often hold off on establishing a position in a depressed convert until they see an increase in the stock's upside volatility and the delta begins to increase. Once that happens the manager can establish his arbitrage, and if the share price continues to increase, he will then cover portions of the hedge from time to time, in order to maintain the optimal hedge ratio.

The Trade of an Out-of-the-Money Convertible

One of your authors still vividly remembers one of his previous firm's largest convertible debenture purchases, made while it served as investment advisor to the Lincoln National Convertible Securities Fund.[2]

"As a closed end fund we were unable to hedge this purchase; nevertheless, the situation beautifully illustrates the profit potential and attractive risk/reward characteristics of an out-of-the-money convertible debenture. The convertible had been issued years before when MCI was a high-flying stock. The stock had then fallen into extreme disfavor, selling near its book value at about $5 per share. It had no friends and little analyst coverage, a classic fallen angel. The convertible was in the basement as well, selling at a deep discount to par value and yielding more than 10 percent. Its conversion value was even lower, a small fraction of the convertible's price.

"Our objective in managing the fund was to accomplish combined returns from income and appreciation, and at a superficial glance this security offered only the former of these two. It seemed inconceivable that the company would be able to return to profitability or that the stock would ever rise from the ashes. Cash flow was positive so the bond seemed money good, but it, too, was dead in the water.

"One of our analysts developed a bullish thesis on MCI stock as a turnaround play. It seemed to have the potential to increase, he thought, by at least 50 percent. After considerable further study millions of shares of stock were purchased for the firm's stock portfolios. Meanwhile, the manager of our convertible fund, Ed Petner, was well aware that MCI had this all but forgotten convert outstanding. The problem was that even a double on the stock would not bring the stock value of the bond near the price at which it was selling. Now came what in retrospect was a brilliant call. We had considerable experience in turnaround investing, having made a major killing on Chrysler shares several years before as it emerged from bankruptcy. The lesson from that and other turnarounds we had studied was that they seemed to have a way of vastly outstripping everyone's expectations. On that basis Petner took a large position in the MCI convertibles. As it happened, MCI not only turned around but once again became a high-flyer (before years later falling back again into financial distress, ultimately declaring bankruptcy). The stock doubled and doubled again and then again over the next several years. The MCI convertibles were the most profitable position in the fund by far until they were finally called."

At the time, Convertible Arbitrage was barely in its infancy. But in retrospect, this convert would have been a convertible arbitrageur's dream. The long side would have provided high yield and such low risk that little or no hedging would have been needed initially except to hedge against possible further credit downgrading. Once the turnaround became evident, the stock price began to move up and sponsorship developed for the stock, attractive hedging opportunities would have presented themselves including the purchase of puts to preserve upside potential while hedging against the downside risk. Given the still low delta, a large short position would have offered good downside profit potential. As the stock continued to appreciate and upward volatility increased as well, the delta increase would have necessitated covering portions of the short from time to time to maintain the desired hedge ratio. Needless to say the price of the convert skyrocketed and the gains from the long would have far outstripped losses from the hedge. This example illustrates the power of being long gamma and long volatility, two of the keys to making money in Convertible Arb.

Other Convertible Arb Trades

The converse of the deeply depressed situation is that of a high-flying stock that has carried with it the price of the convertible security. The convertible might have been issued when the stock was in the low 40s, for example, with a conversion price of $50 (convertible into 20 shares). In this example, with the stock at $100 the convertible is worth $2,000 if converted. If the convertible is callable, the premium over conversion parity will likely be very small, reflecting primarily only the income advantage that the convertible has over the common stock. In the case of a convertible that is not callable, the premium will be somewhat greater, reflecting the fact that the convertible may be considered more attractive on a risk/reward basis than the common. In the event of a major decline in the share price, the convertible price decline will gradually decelerate and ultimately stabilize at its bond value while the stock can theoretically decline to zero. Thus the short side of the position has greater profit potential than the long side has risk.

Convertible securities valuations are also influenced by conditions in the bond market. From a yield perspective, a convertible may be of little interest if it carries a 5 percent yield while corporate bonds yield 6 percent or more. In a rising bond market, as corporate yields decline to, say, 5 percent the convertible may be an attractive value if it is now yielding 4.5 percent. The modest yield discrepancy may be viewed as a small price to pay for the possibility that the price of the underlying shares may rise and the convertible will also appreciate, even in a flat or declining bond market. The benefit of a high-yielding convertible, therefore, is that unlike a straight corporate bond, there are two ways to make a profit.

Many convertible arbitrageurs are relatively agnostic regarding the attractiveness or unattractiveness of the prices of underlying shares, preferring to set up hedges that are likely to create profits regardless of whether the stock price moves up or down. Others, especially those with stock analysis backgrounds, are more inclined to express their attitude toward the common stock via the hedge ratio established. Either a bullish or bearish bias is easily created, and may be based on their market view or view on the underlying stock, or both.

Nirvana for the convertible arbitrageur is a convertible that is selling not too far above its bond and stock values. Such pricing is sometimes found in the new issue market for convertible securities, which explains why convertible arbitrageurs are active participants in such financings. Depending on market conditions, new issues may be priced attractively, with premiums in the aftermarket more likely than not. This phenomenon often happens in the late stages of bullish market cycles. At such times many stocks are sufficiently fully priced to offer attractive short sale and hedging opportunities.

SOURCES OF RETURN

Convertible arbitrage managers have four steady sources of return: positive carry, credit arbitrage, volatility trading, and leverage.

Positive Carry

At the heart of successful and low-risk convertible arb trading is the positive carry the fund receives from two sources. First and foremost is the coupon payment or, in the case of a convertible preferred, the dividend. The second part of the carry is the short rebate, discussed in Chapter 7. Together, these two pieces form the core of what the manager is trying to protect and augment through his hedging. To get a maximum positive carry, some managers prefer high-yielding out-of-the-money convertibles as their longs. Because high-yielding convertibles are often issued by companies with low credit ratings, the manager may see fit to hedge against default risk by putting on a larger equity hedge. This in turn means a higher short rebate earned that when added to the high yield results in a larger positive carry.

Credit Arbitrage

The credit or capital structure arbitrage (with converts) strategy is designed to earn profits from mispricings in the credit risk inherent in the convertible security. For example, the convert might become mispriced relative to the company's stock after the announcement of disappointing earnings alters the historical price relationship between the underlying stock and the convertible.[3] It may also become mispriced versus other debt instruments on the balance sheet. There are usually three reasons for the convertible's mispricing: illiquidity of the issue, small issue size and therefore little interest in it, and, most importantly, the complexities of the terms of the security that make valuation difficult. Whether they use quantitative or qualitative analysis to find these pricing inefficiencies, managers constantly search for these wrinkles that are imbedded in the DNA of the bond.

Not every convertible bond is created equally. Some bonds have unusual characteristics such as convertibility into part cash and part stock or payment of interest in equity as opposed to cash. Other interesting bonds will, if the company forces early conversion, pay the bondholders some consideration in return for forcing that early conversion. In all of these instances, the standard black box pricing model doesn't do well, and in other cases, the model doesn't handle them at all. Some managers prefer to trade in this not-so-small universe of unique convertible securities. Others are reluctant to invest in bonds that do not model-up cleanly. Recognizing these undervaluations before the market does creates trading opportunities and the possibility of generating low-risk profits.

Credit arbitrage can be accomplished by going long the bond while selling short the stock and also using interest rate derivatives or swaps to hedge against interest rate hikes that would lower the bond price. Normally this is a low-risk strategy but in 2005 it took down a multibillion dollar convertible arb fund.

Marin Capital was managing about $1.7 billion when it made a huge credit arb bet on General Motors. In April 2005 GM bonds were downgraded to junk status while the stock actually rose due to a tender offer. The losses on this position dealt a crushing blow to this fund.

While many other hedge funds were hurt by the downgrade, Marin was out of business within two months.[4]

Volatility Trading

In the vernacular of the street, convertible arb is a "long vol" strategy. What this refers to is the fact that a convertible security may be viewed as having imbedded in its price an option representing a call on the future price appreciation of a certain number of shares of common stock. Thus the price of the security tends to fluctuate with the price of call options on the stock into which they are convertible. The price of call options, in turn, is in part dependent on the expected volatility of the underlying stock. Therefore, convertibles tend to rise in price as volatility expectations increase and decline as volatility expectations decrease. By recognizing volatility mispricings skilled arbitrageurs can earn risk premiums that add to their returns.[5]

Leverage

Leverage is commonly used by convertible arbitrageurs, as it is for most fixed-income arb traders. It allows them to increase the number of positions in the portfolio or increase position sizes. If the profitability of these portfolio changes is greater than the incremental interest paid on the increased borrowings, net profits benefit. As we discuss later, the amount of leverage used by convert arb managers has declined in the past five years to somewhere in the range of 2.5 to 3 times assets. Nevertheless, it remains an important source of potential returns. In the past two years as Convertible Arbitrage has struggled, the degree of leverage used by various hedge funds has become a significant distinguishing factor. Experience is the major element in knowing when to use leverage and when discretion is the better part of valor. Savvy arb managers have all heard and never forget the old Wall Street saying, "Bulls can make money and bears can make money but pigs get led to slaughter." When greed leads to excessive use of leverage, in Convertible Arbitrage as in any other strategy, the outcome can be most unpleasant.

PERFORMANCE

The CISDM hedge fund study for the 15 years ending in 2004 showed that Convertible Arb returned 10.23 percent per annum, with a stellar Sharpe ratio of 1.50.[6] Our study, which tracked performance from 1994–2005, showed a slightly less rosy picture.[7] Convertible Arb, while outperforming equities and bonds, returned only 9.1 percent with a Sharpe ratio of 1.39. Convertible Arb had the best performance of the relative value strategies but greatly underperformed four other strategies and the average fund as represented by the HFRI Fund-Weighted Composite Index. See Figure 8.1.

Over the most recent five-year period with equity markets lagging, the HFRI Convertible Arb Index has easily outperformed the S&P 500 and was on a par with bonds. Figure 8.2 shows that for this period the Index returned more than 30 percent cumulatively to investors, averag-

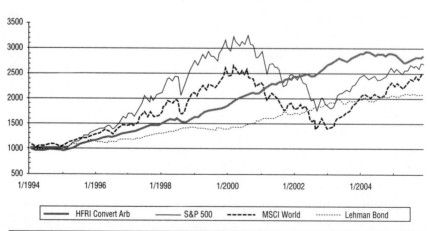

FIGURE 8.1

Cumulative Performance of HFRI Convertible Arbitrage Index versus Benchmarks

Growth of $1,000 USD, 1/1/1994–12/31/2005

Sources: Mayer & Hoffman Capital Advisors, HFRI, and PerTrac.

FIGURE 8.2

HFRI Convertible Arbitrage versus Benchmarks, Trailing Five Years

Growth of $1,000 USD, 1/1/2001–12/31/2005

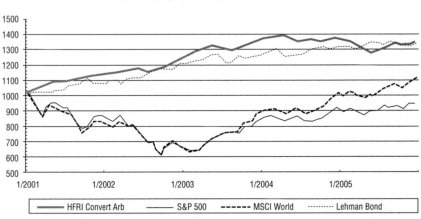

Sources: Mayer & Hoffman Capital Advisors, HFRI, and PerTrac.

ing more than 6 percent per annum. Yet, the strategy was the second-worst performer next to Equity Market Neutral.[8]

What Has Happened to Performance?

Controversy has been raging over whether the time has come for Convertible Arbitrage to rise Phoenix-like from the ashes and return to its prior pattern of attractive returns. Few, however, have been willing to stand up and say it is time again for the good times to roll. Some managers have told us that poor performance will continue as long as redemptions continue, and they're not sure how long that pattern will go on. Peter deLisser, who founded the convertible arb fund Sage Capital back in 1988, and is our featured interviewee, said, "What it feels like to me is that we're at the end of a very long correction cycle. It's been a fairly miserable time to be in this business for the past two years, but we're definitely starting to see the light at the end of the tunnel . . . But I would just add this one cautionary note: I don't think you're going to see returns come back to where they were pre-2003, probably ever."

What has changed, then, that has deLisser and others less than sanguine about Convertible Arb's future performance potential? There are five very good reasons that explain the dramatic decline in the strategy's performance: too much money chasing too few securities; the quantitative edge has largely disappeared; volatility has declined and remained at all-time lows; generation-low interest rates have tremendously impacted the positive carry; and the significant reduction in the amount of leverage used has also hurt performance.

Too Much Money.   This is the mantra heard most often. In a convertible market that totals only about $260 billion in the United States, the dominant players are now hedge funds ($40 billion of assets × 2.5 leverage = $100 billion of buying power). This is especially so in consideration of the active trading of most convertible arbs versus typically buy and hold strategies for most other convertible investors. Since the vast majority of transactions in the market are done by hedge funds, and since they tend to buy or sell the same merchandise at more or less the same time, it is not difficult to comprehend the difficulty in generating alpha. Mickey Harley, whom we featured in the Event Driven chapter, says that once upon a time, there were 50 *natural convert buyers** for every 1 arbitrageur. Now it's the other way around.[9] A flood of money drove convert prices to unreasonable levels and when there were no more buyers, prices began to tumble and with them arbitrage performance. As performance deteriorated, the massive redemptions that took place in 2005 forced more sales, compressing values further.

The Quantitative Edge Has Disappeared.   In Chapter 5 we made the point that the attractiveness of Merger Arbitrage had been permanently diminished by changes in technology that in turn caused the

---

*Long-only investors who purchase convertible securities.

disappearance of an information advantage that once existed in the space. Similarly, technology changes in computing power and instantaneous information about any security have permanently altered the Convertible Arb landscape. Quantitative models that once found inefficiencies and mispricings because of their proprietary nature are no longer difference makers. As one manager told us, "I think it's reasonable to say that in the past, whoever had the best quantitative map had a competitive advantage. But what's happened over time is the math has gotten very good and very cheap. Now any convertible player who enters the arena has access to the same map. It's not only the buy side that has it but the sell side as well. That part of the playing field has been leveled."

Lower Volatility. The poor performance of convertible strategies in recent times has also been in part a function of the decline in volatility expectations to decade-low levels. The CBOE VIX, the most widely used measure of volatility, has declined from a high of about 45 in 2002 to near 11 as 2005 comes to a close and has been trading in a narrow range at or near its all-time low for more than a year.[10] Since volatility trading is one of the three steady sources of return, the low vol environment of the past two years has knocked out this strategy as a performance booster.

Low Interest Rates. The positive carry is at the heart of most convert arb performance. With generation-low interest rates having settled in, both sides of the carry have been negatively affected. First, yields on the convertibles are dramatically lower than they were 5 or 10 years ago. The second source of income in the positive carry, the short interest rebate, has been reduced because lower interest rates mean that the broker's payments to the short seller are also lower. Together, these reductions in income add up to a significant hit to the core of convertible arb's historic profit attribution.

Lower Leverage. In the past five years, convertible arb managers have greatly reduced the amount of leverage they use. In a recent Goldman

Sachs research paper the authors found that leverage had dropped from an average of 10 times to around 2.5.[11] In the interview that follows this chapter, Pete deLisser, whose fund, Sage Capital, uses no leverage, asserts that the industry trend is moving in the direction of low leverage. Even though we know that leverage cuts both ways, if the norm for convertible arb leverage has indeed dropped to 2.5 times, then returns have undoubtedly been adversely affected.

Goldman Sachs announced on December 19, 2005, that it was dropping its Convertible Arb Index at month end.[12] One might infer from their actions that they think the strategy is near death. We believe, however, that it's premature to play a funeral dirge for the strategy, but for the foreseeable future we agree with deLisser that convertible arb funds will be unable to generate the returns of yesteryear.

ADVANTAGES

Historically, Convertible Arb has enjoyed two major advantages as a strategy: market neutrality with low correlations to bonds, equities, and other hedge funds, and fairly stable return patterns.

As previously noted, Convertible Arb shielded investors during the most recent bear market. Like the other relative value strategies, when added to a portfolio of traditional assets, Convertible Arb will lower volatility and improve risk-adjusted performance. In our study, Convertible Arb was the best performer in the relative value group. Of course, that's over the past 12 years. More recently, Fixed Income Arb has surpassed Convertible Arb as the leader and Equity Market Neutral has gained ground. Figure 8.3 shows the performance of the three relative value indices over the past five years. Note the turning point that occurred in early 2004.

A second advantage of the strategy has been, until recently at least, the stability of its return patterns. Because of the positive carry, funds had low volatility and predictable sources of return that were aug-

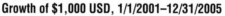

FIGURE 8.3

HFRI Relative Value Arb Indices versus MSCI World, Trailing Five Years

Growth of $1,000 USD, 1/1/2001–12/31/2005

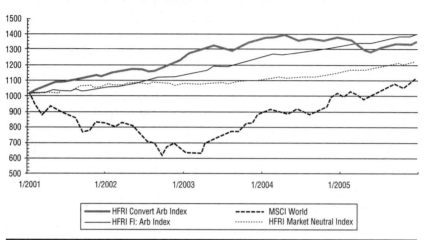

Legend:
- HFRI Convert Arb Index
- HFRI FI: Arb Index
- MSCI World
- HFRI Market Neutral Index

Sources: Mayer & Hoffman Capital Advisors, HFRI, and PerTrac.

mented by leverage and position trading profits. It is no longer clear that this pillar of the strategy is still standing after the changes in the market place that we have previously catalogued.

DISADVANTAGES

In the section "What Happened to Performance?" we chronicled the convergence of several risks that have shaken the Convertible Arb world to its core. Two of these risks, declining volatility and low interest rates, we've already discussed. There are, however, two other risks that still impact the convertible arb manager: the change in converts supply and demand characteristics and the so-called Greek risks associated with declining delta, gamma, and *vega*.*

For much of the past 15 years, the supply of convertibles exceeded demand and allowed many converts to trade at attractive valuations. When money poured into the strategy in 2001–2004, those discounts vanished and an easy source of profits disappeared.[13] The relative attractiveness of the convertible market versus other investments declined and the natural buyers disappeared leaving only the hedge funds to trade with each other. As 2005 came to a close, yields continued to be low and premiums to conversion parity high, thus converts were still generally lacking good risk/reward characteristics.

Another consequence of the changed marketplace is the convertible new issue calendar, which is highly cyclical. As we discussed earlier, new issues can be a good source of profits for the arbitrageur. In the past two years, however, since pricing has become richer and offerings have been fewer in number, a source of profits for Convertible Arb has been removed.

Finally, we have the Greek risks. When some convert arb managers deliberately set up a hedge with a bullish or bearish bias because they have a view on the stock, the market, or both, they leave themselves open to both market and specific risk because they are not fully neutral. In a market that is crashing, not only will delta be impacted but gamma will be as well. Negative gamma, the opposite of what convert arb managers want, occurs when there are violent and often sudden drops in the value of a stock that also take down the bond. A variation on this scenario is discussed in Chapter 9 when we look at the triggers and consequences of the flight to quality phenomenon. Suffice it to say that a flight to quality can destroy the value of most converts and, as liquidity dries up, exposes convert arb managers to liquidity risk as well. In 1998, when this last happened on a global scale, the HFRI Convertible Arb Index dropped about 5 percent

---

*Vega is a measure of the change in an option's implied volatility.

in August–October. Their cousins in Fixed Income Arb weren't as lucky, as you'll see in the next chapter.

Since Convertible Arb is a long volatility strategy, our final Greek risk is vega. As volatility decreases, vega values decline, in turn reducing convert premiums.[14] In fact, this has happened to the entire market for almost two years.

Peter deLisser

Founder and Portfolio Manager
Sage Capital

THE FLAVOR OF OUR CONVERSATION WITH PETER DELISSER, WHO FOUNDED Sage Capital as a Convertible Arbitrage shop in 1988, is perhaps reminiscent of the kind of talk one might hear from an infantryman after you've jumped into his foxhole, seeking shelter from heavy shelling. His candor seems almost brutal and he does not downplay the dire circumstances, yet he's tough and knows he is going to survive. For 2005, Sage Capital was down a mere 0.57 percent while the investable HFRX Convertible Arbitrage Index was down 5.69 percent for the same period. Since inception, Sage has turned in a respectable annual average return of 9.05 percent.

For Sage, based in Sarasota, Florida, the vicious Convertible Arbitrage market of 2005 felt like one more named storm in a savage hurricane season—roofs torn off, walls collapsing, debris in the streets. While Convertible Arbitrage was becoming the worst-performing hedge fund strategy over 2004 and 2005, redemptions tore at the foundations like storm surge, funds closed, and there was no one new moving into the neighborhood. A strategy that was once a centerpiece of the hedge fund world had been reduced to near ruin. Consequently, rather than featuring a newer manager, we chose the veteran Pete deLisser for this interview. Pete's insights and perspective have been honed through his experience of running a Convertible Arb hedge fund for more than 17 years.

SK: *Things were different back when you started Sage, right?*

PdL: It was a totally different market environment in the late eighties than you have today. I started with the notion that we could create a portfolio that would act as a bond substitute which would give the investor better returns than the bond market, with significantly less risk and volatility.

It was something I knew we could do. There were billions of dollars going into bond funds and I thought of that as our marketplace. At that time, there were probably only half a dozen guys in the country who were actually doing Convertible Arbitrage.

The idea was to take the Convertible Arbitrage strategy and eliminate from it the key areas of risk. This was six months after the equity market crash in 1987 and everybody was naturally concerned about downside protection. I was on the Morgan Stanley desk at the time [from 1982 to 1988] and we were amazed at how poorly our convertible arbitrage portfolio had performed in the crash.

We recognized that the major culprit behind the poor performance was the use of leverage. So it seemed to me that there was a business opportunity of entering the convertible arbitrage business and offering a product that employed no leverage. Clearly, your returns wouldn't be as high as they might be in a positive year for the strategy if you were leveraged. But operating without leverage would bring the volatility of the portfolio way down and reduce the risk to the investor.

In 1988 we built a business that since then has basically attracted the most conservative types of investors who invest in hedge funds. We're way over on the conservative end of the spectrum in terms of convertible arbitrage managers because risk avoidance has always been a primary feature of our portfolio management style.

At the time that wasn't a big deal. But over the next 10 years, the way the hedge fund industry business was growing, it seemed that the world was happily taking on more risk and adding more leverage in the effort to get bigger returns. The average convertible arbitrage manager was leveraging up to the max. Some of them were five, six, eight, ten times leveraged! So, as time passed, our risk profile looked less and less like the other convertible arb funds.

SK: *Is that true even over the last few years?*

PdL: No. Now, many of the managers have come back to us. The market's been so bad for the last couple of years, a lot of convertible arbitrageurs have had to cut way back on leverage. Guys have been wracked by redemptions, and others have gone out of business. Suddenly the survivors look a lot more like us.

SK: *So you guys don't have any leverage in your fund?*

PdL: Our core strategy has always been zero leverage with a highly diversified portfolio: diversified among industry groups, types of convertibles, and sizes of issuers. Our goal is to size the positions so that we avoid a situation where one position can overly and dramatically impact the whole portfolio.

SK: *So, your sweet spot is plain-vanilla convertible arbitrage.*

PdL: Very vanilla. Unfortunately, that sweet spot has been kind of sour in the last couple of years. But we'll see. We're actually starting to see yields versus premium relationships almost back to where they were years ago, when the business made a lot more sense.

SK: *Is it a case of too much money chasing too few deals?*

PdL: That's a fair assessment. But as bad as it's been, if you consider how profitable this business was, and then you look at the last two years, the damage to us really has not been very extreme. Two thousand four was a crummy year, but we still made a little bit of money, up 1.9 percent. In 2005, we were down a teeny amount (0.57 percent). It could have been worse.

Another way that we're a little bit different from other managers is that their businesses are very model-driven now. Whether they're proprietary or whether they purchase these packages, these models have tended to make the convert markets more efficient. That's because the convertible model is still a relatively simple one and everybody's is pretty much the same.

But there are factors that just can't go into a model. A model is nothing more than a pretty good way to separate the universe into issues that may be marginally attractive versus those that are absolutely not attractive at all. In the buy-sell decisions that we make, we're not model-driven at all.

We buy convertibles based on what we see as an opportunity to make money. We're not trying to capture volatility or capture gamma.* We're not trying to outbet the credit analysts. We're trying to make money by putting together a portfolio that captures streams of income from the short side and the long side.

SK: *What market changes are you looking for to help you make money?*

PdL: There are a few key things. I think one factor that has put a lid on our profitability is the Fed. As long as they are raising rates, and as long as there's the fear that the Fed will keep raising rates, it's very difficult to quantify what the inherent fixed-income value of any convertible really is. And that makes buyers reticent.

Another overhang on the market is that we have to get out of the redemption cycle in the convertible universe. I'm inclined to think we're pretty close to that, although I wouldn't be surprised if there's some more damage at the end of the year.[†] I would imagine a lot of money's going to move around at the end of the year. But I would be willing to bet that starting in January 2006 investors who kept money in Convertible Arbitrage are going to stick with the strategy for a while.

SK: *Has the redemption cycle hit you hard?*

PdL: We're not immune. We have $225 million under management right now. Two years ago, we had $425 million. So, we've gotten redeemed just like everybody else. In fact, in some ways, it's harder on us because we supply monthly liquidity, which most hedge funds do not. Therefore, at the beginning of a redemption cycle, we tend to get hit hard.

On the flip side, though, when we get past that cycle and things start to get better, we tend to be able to raise new assets a little faster

---

*See Convertible Arbitrage Basics section in this chapter for a complete definition.
[†]As deLisser had guessed, Convertible Arbitrage did sustain further net redemptions at year-end 2005.

than other funds. After all, we've been through a few cycles and we've been here a lot longer than most other managers.

SK: *Is it harder or easier for you to manage the portfolio now that you're a smaller fund?*

PdL: The simple, sad reality is that it's easier to manage small amounts of money than it is to manage big amounts of money. You know the bigger your fund gets, the more you get sucked into the same kind of problems that everybody has and that you've probably made your reputation on avoiding. You lose the ability to be quite as selective. When you're smaller like we are now and don't have to buy every issue that comes along, we can analyze and go over every convertible pretty hard before we say, "Okay. That one will work."*

But for us, large or small, our strength has been to maintain a high level of discipline. I think being successful in the investment business is really more about discipline than it is about being a genius. When investments meet our criteria, we buy them. When they get to a point that they're outside our criteria, we sell them. The biggest mistakes we've made over the years are when we've ignored either our buy or sell discipline because we liked the story, or because we had a feeling, or because of some information we got from somebody. Interestingly, though, the biggest losses that we've had or the individual positions that have hurt us the most have been cash takeovers.

SK: *Any particular securities come to mind?*

PdL: In 2005 we have had more losses due to cash takeovers than we did in our previous 16 years in business put together. Takeovers are among the most serious risks facing the convertible arbitrage market and in the past there was no real takeover protection that meant anything.

Right now you have a corporate environment that is very favorable to takeovers. Lots of stocks are trading at much lower prices than they were a few years ago. At the same time, you have corporate America loaded with cash since interest rates are low. We knew that takeovers

---

*We cover the advantages enjoyed by smaller funds in Chapter 11.

were possible. We just hoped that we'd be pretty good at avoiding them. In fact, we did avoid a lot of the really bad ones, but we also got caught in a number of them.

Today, one major positive change that's occurred is that a company can't get a new-issue convertible done without real takeover protection. It's finally being done the way it has always needed to be done.

Up until very recently, people thought takeover protection was to put a par put on a convertible bond, so that if there's a hostile takeover, you're guaranteed to get par and you're out. The par put doesn't really address the problem that the convertible owner has, because when you buy a convertible security, no matter why you bought it, you bought a warrant with a time duration that is determined by the call protection. Of course, that warrant is extinguished in the event of a cash takeover, because there is no stock to convert that warrant into. Basically, it's a violation of the covenants that you purchased in the first place. Finally, the market has begun to address that whole issue.

SK: *And that built-in takeover protection has actually led to a very interesting phenomenon.*

PdL: Yeah, because now you have a bifurcated market where all the new issues are takeover-protected. All the Arb guys are buying the takeover-protected stuff, because they just can't take the hits anymore.

As a result, the non-takeover-protected names are cheap! I'll tell you, we've been buying a lot of them. And we think that with a diversified bunch of those names, even if we get a hit here and there, we're being more than adequately paid for taking the risk.

SK: *That is a very interesting strategy.*

PdL: Yeah, we'll buy that type of security and instead of shorting the underlying stock maybe we'll just buy puts. That way the upside is still open if the stock rises. But if the stock goes down, we're still hedged to some degree. The put strategy is not quite as systematic as hedging with a stock-short. But it's a way to take advantage of an opportunity.

If an investor asks, "Well, how can you make money on this position?" I can give him an answer.

SK: *How about a recent example of your trading strategy?*

PdL: Let's use Axcan Pharmaceutical (Nasdaq: AXCA). Axcan develops and manufactures gastroenterology products. In April 2003 the company issued a convertible that matures April 15, 2008, with a coupon paying four and a quarter percent. It was convertible into 71.4 shares of the common.

SK: *At a conversion premium of . . .*

PdL: About 38 percent. This was a small issue with about $125 million outstanding. The bond has a call price of $101.70 but runs out of call protection April 20, 2006. Oh, and it doesn't have takeover protection.

SK: *So it's a small issuance with no takeover protection. Sounds like your cup of tea?*

PdL: Exactly. We started buying in the fall of 2005 with the stock trading at $12.60 per share and paid $105 per bond. Since the conversion value was $900 [$12.60 × 71.4] we were paying only a 16 percent premium. Now the premium had narrowed because there was a high likelihood that the bond would be called in April.

SK: *So you shorted the stock?*

PdL: No, that's the thing. Because we had a positive carry from the coupon and the bond was maturing in April 2008, we considered it relatively low risk. Figuring the upside, with no takeover protection, was huge, we liked the risk/reward of simply being long the bond.

SK: *These days, pharma is certainly popular in the M&A world.*

PdL: Well, sure enough, the stock moved up to $18 per share on takeover rumors. The bonds went to $130, shaving the premium to 1.5 percent.

SK: *But no real deal for the company.*

PdL: So in late January 2006 to protect our position we sold the stock short with about 90 percent coverage.

SK: *So what was your carry then, including the short interest rebate?*

PdL: A beautiful 7 percent. Unfortunately, we knew the clock was ticking on the bond so we enjoyed it while we could, which turned out to be one month.

SK: *What happened?*

PdL: It was great, actually. One of Axcan's products was rejected by the FDA during clinical trials and the stock got clobbered down to $12 again. At that point we sold the bonds at 105, collected 6 points on the shorts, and closed it out.

SK: *That's a beautiful thing, especially because so few shops would even look at that issue. On the other hand, this past April [2005] the GM bond downgrade coupled with the stock rise just hammered a lot of people in the hedge-fund world.*

PdL: You would've had a hard time finding any convertible arb guys in April who didn't own GM. We were one of those who did not own it.

SK: *Yet, you got hurt in April anyway.*

PdL: Partly for different reasons. Initially, we didn't own it. Then GM started to get hammered and funds were losing money all over the place. At some point after that, we decided to buy some GM, basically because everybody was bleeding to death on it. We tried to pick the bottom, but we were a little too early, and we lost a couple of points, too.

We made some of that money back in May. After that, we kicked it. So we didn't entirely miss the debacle in GM, but we missed a good part of it.

SK: *Given the tough times for the strategy, why should investors consider putting money back into Convertible Arb?*

PdL: The convertible arbitrage strategy is extremely unique because there is a systematic relationship between your longs and your shorts. Every convertible bond, or every convertible preferred stock, is convertible into a fixed number of shares of the common. So the relationship between how the common moves and how the convertible moves is relatively easy to figure out. Because of that, it offers a unique opportunity. When you hedge convertibles, it's a systematic hedge; it's not guesswork. So there is a discipline there that doesn't exist in most hedge businesses. It's also unique in the sense that you get income from both sides of your positions. Your longs obviously have coupons. Your shorts get rebates, and you actually add to the income of the portfolio by reducing risk. That being said, some times are better for the strategy than others, for sure.

SK: *What's ahead, Pete?*

PdL: What it feels like to me is that we're at the end of a very long correction cycle. It's been a fairly miserable time to be in this business for the past two years, but we're definitely starting to see the light at the end of the tunnel. Most importantly, we see an environment where we can start to make money again. But I would just add this one cautionary note: I don't think you're going to see returns come back to where they were pre-2003, probably ever.

CHAPTER 9

Fixed Income Arbitrage

INTRODUCTION

The final strategy in our Relative Value trilogy is the one that's received the most notoriety over the years, Fixed Income Arbitrage. Stated simply, this strategy seeks to exploit small price discrepancies in fixed-income securities of all kinds. Because of the very small scale of these discrepancies, Myron Scholes, a Nobel Prize winner in economics and a principal at Long Term Capital Management (LTCM), once explained that the fund would make money by "being a vacuum sucking up nickels that no one else could see"[1] thus coining a phrase that would become forever attached to Fixed Income Arbitrage.

The fixed income instruments most often used in this strategy include:

- Treasuries of all stripes.
- Corporate bonds.
- Municipal bonds (munis).
- Mortgage-backed securities (MBSs) and other asset-backed securities.
- Interest rate swaps.
- Interest rate futures.
- Emerging market bonds.
- Collateralized debt obligations (CDOs).
- Credit default swaps (CDSs).

An entire book could be written today on all the variations of Fixed Income Arbitrage (FI Arb), but it would become largely outdated soon after its release. In response to the demands of the marketplace, the complexity of these instruments and their derivatives is becoming greater each year. Generally speaking, the greater the complexity and the newer the security, the greater are the potential trading opportunities for the sophisticated arbitrageur. It is common to find traders with math doctorates working alongside premier database programmers who in turn have constructed large databases crunched by top-of-the-line computer hardware in the pursuit of identifying and capitalizing on opportunities before a competitor does.

It's no surprise then that specialization has become increasingly common. Each area of specialization entails its own unique barriers to entry (beyond the advanced mathematical requirements) that naturally suppress the numbers of traders entering the space. For example, an arbitrageur who specializes in MBSs, the largest single trading strategy under the Fixed Income Arb banner, has elaborate models specifically for these instruments, including forecasted prepayment rates, balanced portfolio risk exposure, liquidity, and *convexity* (a measure of the curvature in the relationship between bond prices and yields). In addition, the MBS manager must have substantial experience and exceptional trading skills. Because of the unique characteristics of the instruments, MBS arbitrage does not correlate with other fixed income arbitrage strategies or indices. The barriers to entry are great, ensuring the specialist fewer competitors than most other hedge funds have. In the Hedgefund.net database that contains about 7,000 hedge funds, you'll find only 22 MBS funds.[2]

Fixed Income Arbitrage has not been found atop the leaderboard of hedge fund strategy performance. From 1996 to 2005, FI Arb did not once rank in the top four strategies, but in 1998 the HFRI FI Arb Index lost more than 10 percent making it the worst-performing strategy. In that span of years it was typically ranked around third from last.[3]

Surprisingly, losses such as those suffered in 1998 by most FI Arb funds have not killed the sector. On the contrary, the strategy has rebounded with strength. In 2002, HFRI indicated that $10.4 billion flowed into MBS funds alone.[4] Since 2001, the total amount of hedge fund capital devoted to FI Arbitrage has grown from $11 billion to $58 billion.[5]

THE FIXED INCOME ARBITRAGE TRADING AND INVESTMENT STRATEGIES

As we've noted, the variety and complexity of trading in this strategy is increasing. Each shop has its own proprietary valuation models that factor in multiple data points in determining the fair value for any fixed income security or its derivatives. Even a slight discrepancy, just a few basis points, can be sufficient impetus to initiate a trade if a suitable hedge can be identified. It is reasonably safe to state that nearly all trades made within this strategy share three commonalities: They involve a long offset by a corresponding short; they use leverage; and they rely on mean reversion as a core assumption.

FI Arb managers look for pricing discrepancies between two related instruments in order to set up a long–short trade that will result in positive cash flow while hedging interest rate risk. In this way, FI Arb attempts to make money while remaining market neutral. The most common trades exploit anomalies in yield spreads; yield curves; credit spreads; cash versus futures spreads; and swap spreads. Let's first look at examples of each of these trades and then examine the strategy's sources of return.

Yield Spreads

Yield-spread trades might involve going long a high-yielding corporate bond and short a lower-yielding Treasury of the same duration to capture the positive cash flows equal to the spread between them. Note, however, that it can be difficult to find an offsetting trade that completely hedges away market risk.

In practice, then, arbitrageurs in yield spreads, credit spreads, and swap spreads try to match the *duration* of the long and short positions as closely as possible. The duration of a bond measures its change in value resulting from a 1 percent change in interest rates, stated in years. For example, a duration value of 2 means the bond will decrease in value by 2 percent if interest rates increase by 1 percent or, conversely, the value will increase by 2 percent if interest rates decrease by 1 percent. Duration also expresses the weighted average of the maturity of all the income streams from a security.

When a trader seeks a hedge, it will ideally be an offsetting trade of the same duration as the initial position. If there is a discrepancy in duration within a hedged pair of trades, that discrepancy can be offset by an equal and opposite discrepancy in another hedged pair in order to achieve market neutrality within the portfolio.

Yield Curves

Yield curve arbitrage involves two similar bonds but with different maturities. Here, the manager goes long, say, an underpriced 10-year duration municipal bond and shorts a relatively overpriced 11-year municipal bond. A variant on this trade is more directional and less market-neutral yield curve arbitrage. In this trade (assuming a normal yield curve), the manager is long the longer end of the yield curve, that is more than 10 years, and short the shorter end (under 5-year maturity) because he believes that the yield curve will flatten.

Credit Spreads

A third type of trade involves credit spreads. There are many variations on the theme but at their heart they involve going long a riskier credit instrument and shorting the less risky one. A manager can arbitrage within the capital structure of a company (as do convertible arb managers) with different tranches of debt, between Treasury futures and Euro futures (the TED spread), and between the debt instruments of two companies in the same industry that have different credit ratings. MBS traders in particular use credit spread trades as a primary source of profits. Their most common trade is going long higher-yielding but riskier Fannie Mae-backed MBSs and going short the safer but lower-yielding Treasury bond of the same maturity.

Cash versus Futures Spreads

Going long Treasury Futures versus shorting a cash instrument is another trade designed to generate a positive carry by exploiting a credit spread coupled with a yield curve arbitrage. Managers including our featured interviewee, Michael Pasternak of Pinewood Credit Markets, execute basis trades that are an arbitrage between a physical instrument and an underlying derivative. For example, the manager goes long a municipal bond and short an over-the-counter (OTC) or exchange-traded derivative.

In addition to the long–short hedged aspect that all of these trades have in common, they also share another trait: the use of substantial leverage. FI Arb involves capitalizing on small price discrepancies and frequent trading, and the more liquid the market is, the fewer and smaller the price discrepancies become. Profits therefore can only become meaningful when amplified by leverage. That is the reason that FI Arb managers use leverage, on average 20 to 30 times assets,[6] significantly greater than any other hedge fund strategy.

Finally, all of these trades share the same theoretical basis: the principle of mean reversion, that is, a return to fair value in the historical pricing relationship between the instruments arbitraged. Remember the same principle at work in equity market neutral trades? The arbitrageur's fundamental investment thesis is that spreads between instruments that are out of line with their histories will eventually converge. In that sense, it is fair to characterize most FI Arb trades as *convergence* trades.

SOURCES OF RETURN

There are four identifiable sources of return in FI Arb: the positive carry, the risk premium paid, the complexity premium earned, and leverage.

Positive Carry

Like the other relative value strategies FI Arb has a positive carry that is an important source of returns. Let's examine a commonly used trade in swap spreads to illustrate how the carry is generated. The swap-spread strategy was made famous at LTCM.* The strategy has two components. First, it exploits differences between the long-term swap spread and its short-term counterpart. Then it shorts a Treasury with similar maturity to the swap and invests the short interest rebate in a margin account that earns the *repo rate*. The repo rate is the rate embedded in a repurchase agreement, usually in overnight transactions with the sale taking place one day and being reversed the next. Positive cash flow is generated by the difference between the interest received from the fixed coupon of the long-term swap plus the repo rate for the short interest minus the sum of the payments for the Treasury rate and floating LIBOR (the London Interbank Offered Rate, a proxy for the short-term swap rate). Breaking this trade down further, we have a long-term component that is the difference between the fixed coupon of the swap and the Treasury note and a short-term component that is the difference between floating LIBOR and the short rebate. In a sense, then, the strategy is a bet that the profit on the long-term component more than offsets the cost of the short-term one. What makes this bet a probable winner is that under normal circumstances the short-term component, the spread between LIBOR and the repo rate, is highly stable with a very low standard deviation and it always reverts to the mean. Thus, when FI Arb managers see a spread of more than 20 bps between the long-term arbitrage and the historic mean of the short-term spread, they are comfortable in putting on the trade.[7]

Risk Premium

One way of looking at the performance of any hedge fund strategy, especially a more esoteric one like FI Arb, is that any alpha generated is

---

*We return to LTCM and the swap-spread strategy later in the Disadvantages section of this chapter.

a result of the risks taken by the fund. These risks, including credit, interest rate, and liquidity risks are not covered by the Capital Asset Pricing Model (CAPM) or Fama's Efficient Market Hypothesis (EMH),[8] and therefore *holding less liquid and riskier instruments* should be rewarded by some type of risk premium. In FI Arb, traders who are long illiquid securities and short more creditworthy and liquid instruments must be compensated for taking on additional risks that at times can be substantial. Later in this chapter we discuss what happens when an exogenous crisis occurs and spreads blow out followed by illiquidity. By assuming the risks associated with these types of events, FI Arb managers, in turn, earn a risk premium, that is, the higher return obtained by holding relatively illiquid securities.

Complexity Premium

FI Arb's third source of return, the complexity premium, is, like the risk premium, also not covered by CAPM or EMH. A complexity premium is earned by a trader who has the ability to identify the price anomalies that can occur between instruments when poorly understood and complex variables interact. These variables include the interaction between options, credit quality, swap spreads, and yield curves to name just a few. The EMH in its most conservative form holds that there is no price-relevant information available to all investors that is not already reflected in the market's prices. Since many FI Arb traders work in less than efficient markets, there is no doubt that some information edge still exists. Their reward, therefore, for gaining that information is the complexity premium.[9]

Leverage

We have already noted that leverage in FI Arb is higher than in other strategies because the price anomalies found are nickels in comparison with ones found, say, in ELS. On the one hand, without that substantial leverage it would be virtually impossible for an FI Arb manager to make sufficient profits to survive. On the other hand, we discuss the pitfalls of leverage, using the case of LTCM as an example, in the Disadvantages section.

PERFORMANCE

Over the period 1994–2005, Fixed Income Arbitrage was the worst-performing hedge fund strategy (other than Short Sellers). FI Arb returned 5.9 percent per annum and had a Sharpe ratio of only 0.53, a risk-adjusted return that was higher than equities but lower than bonds and all other hedge fund strategies.[10] Figure 9.1 shows how the strategy performed against equities and bonds over that 12-year period.

Over the past five years, however, the strategy has outperformed bonds in total return, has substantially outperformed equities, and even had a slightly better annualized return than the HFRI Equity Hedge Index with a much lower standard deviation (see Table 9.1). Figure 9.2 shows the cumulative return of the HFRI FI Arb Index versus the MSCI World, the S&P 500, and the Lehman. Note that FI Arb funds returned about 40 percent over the period while long-only managers lagged far behind. In 2005, the FI Arb Index returned 5.6

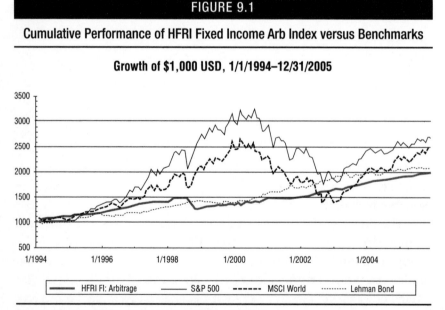

FIGURE 9.1

Cumulative Performance of HFRI Fixed Income Arb Index versus Benchmarks

Growth of $1,000 USD, 1/1/1994–12/31/2005

Legend: HFRI FI: Arbitrage — S&P 500 — MSCI World — Lehman Bond

Sources: Mayer & Hoffman Capital Advisors, HFRI, and PerTrac.

FIGURE 9.2

HFRI FI: Arbitrage versus Benchmarks, Trailing Five Years

Growth of $1,000 USD, 1/1/2001–12/31/2005

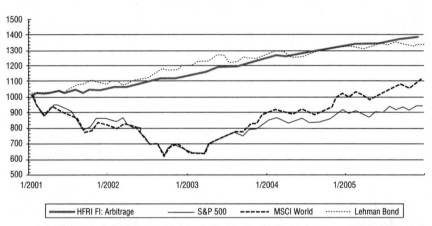

Sources: Mayer & Hoffman Capital Advisors, HFRI, and PerTrac.

percent and while that was below the average hedge fund perform-ance for the year, it still was ahead of both the S&P and the Lehman indices.

ADVANTAGES

FI Arb has two primary advantages: It shows low correlation and low volatility of returns compared with all asset classes and performs rea-sonably well in nearly all market conditions.

The primary benefit of investing in this strategy is its low correlation to the stock and bond markets and to other hedge fund strategies. In our study covering 12 years, FI Arb had small negative correlations to both traditional asset classes and a 0.13 correlation to the HFRI Fund-Weighted Composite Index.[11] As such it is a good diversifier when added to a portfolio of either traditional assets and/or other hedge funds.

Secondly, a well managed fixed income arbitrage fund has very little risk and low volatility under nearly all market conditions. Referring to Figure 9.1, it is apparent that the strategy has given a good account of itself consistently over the past 10 years except for 1998. If one chooses to view that year as an outlier that is highly unlikely to recur, and is willing to underwrite that event risk, then the strategy looks quite enticing on a risk-adjusted basis.

DISADVANTAGES

There are four major risks to the strategy: high use of leverage, liquidity risk, interest rate risk, and, for MBS traders, prepayment risk.

Leverage

The strategy's primary risk is its reliance on significant amounts of leverage, without which returns would be low. Leverage, as we all know, is a two-way street. It is all well and good when its use amplifies profits, but not pleasant when losses are amplified. The sad tale of LTCM is not only an object lesson in the risks of leverage but also in the disastrous consequences of the strategy's second major risk, liquidity risk.

Liquidity Risk

In times of crisis, markets, especially illiquid ones, can dry up quickly and almost completely. If significant leverage has been used, positions may need to be unwound in order to stem the bleeding and meet the inevitable margin calls that come with excessive borrowing. In an illiquid market characterized by a flight to quality, anyone needing to place a sell order can run into the dire situation when there are no buyers. Experienced traders never want to run into the proverbial "to whom?" question when trying to sell a position. The resulting losses can be staggering as positions are forcibly unwound at deeply distressed prices.

Unfortunately, this worst-case scenario played out for LTCM and its investors and revealed quite clearly that the fund was vacuuming up nickels in front of a steamroller.[12] To parse this colorful phrase, the nickels represent the small spreads the fund sought to exploit. The steamroller represents the confluence of negative events that flattened LTCM.

Long-Term Capital Management

The lineup that launched LTCM in 1993 could not have been more golden if Midas himself had been on the team. Founder John Meriwether was the central genius who made the arbitrage group at Salomon Brothers famous for spectacular record earnings. Robert Merton and Myron Scholes who jointly had won the Nobel Prize in economics were there along with many other luminaries from the faculty of Harvard and M.I.T. Investors practically expected this team to hit a home run with every pitch, such that no one complained about the steep terms. At a time when most funds charged a 1 percent management fee and a 20 percent incentive fee, LTCM charged 2 percent and 25 percent, with a three-year lockup and a minimum investment of $10 million. Yet Meriwether raised $1.3 billion when he opened up shop, at that time the largest-ever hedge fund launch.[13]

For the first five years of operation, everything seemed to be going according to plan. LTCM engaged largely in swap spread arbitrage, making significant profits on various convergence trades including:

- Convergence between European sovereign bonds.
- Convergence between U.S., Japanese, and European bonds.
- Convergence between on-the-run (new issue) and off-the-run (more seasoned) U.S. government bonds.
- Long positions in emerging markets sovereigns hedged back to dollars.

The nickels yielded by these trades were magnified into dollars through an astronomical leverage ratio in the neighborhood of 30 to 1. This meant if the fund had a rate of return on capital only 1 percent higher than its interest paid on borrowings, it could achieve the performance that everyone seemed to think was its birthright. Couple this with the fact that LTCM was able to accomplish its leverage borrowing at very favorable rates. In hindsight it is clear that a cornerstone of LTCM's early triumphs was the fund's ability to exploit miniscule arbitrage opportunities by leveraging low interest rate loans at 30 to 1.

In both 1995 and 1996 the fund returned almost 40 percent. That performance dipped below 30 percent the following year as many of the spreads had tightened considerably, prompting Meriwether to return $2.7 billion in capital to investors saying "investment opportunities were not large and attractive enough." Still, the fund entered 1998 with around $4 billion of assets under management. It also entered the year with a number of leveraged positions in the Russian market (most would say a form of Russian roulette).

In August of that year Russia devalued the ruble and defaulted on its sovereign debt (par value 281 billion rubles, approximately $13.5 billion). Although LTCM took a large loss on its Russian equity option positions,* the more devastating result was a flight to quality throughout the worldwide markets. The resulting liquidity crisis lit the fuse that led to the LTCM explosion. The high leverage that had once magnified gains now equally magnified shattering losses. LTCM's convergence plays were crushed under the steamroller of widening spreads. As a result, the firm began receiving margin calls and was forced to liquidate positions at huge losses until it could no longer do even that. Before the end of September, the fund was down to $600 million in equity, an unprecedented catastrophe necessitating the Federal Reserve Bank of New York to step in with a $3.5 billion bailout.[14] Throughout the world, fixed income arbitrage funds suffered major losses[15] and ended the year down more than 10 percent on average according to HFRI.[16] Because this index weights performance for all hedge funds equally regardless of size, this figure clearly understates the magnitude of dollar losses investors suffered.

---

*The game of roulette was lost. The chamber containing the bullet rotated into position and the gun went off, resulting in a mortal wound.

Interest Rate Risk

FI Arb managers always attempt to hedge against interest rate risk. Unfortunately, when riskier and less liquid instruments are used for the longs, sudden interest rate hikes, suddenly widening spreads, or a flight to quality can result in cascading margin calls. That's what happened to David Askin and his three hedge funds. In the 1990s, investment banker Kidder Peabody had built up a controlling share in the market for collateralized mortgage obligations (CMOs). It turns out that Askin invested heavily in the most risky of the CMO instruments, which were known as "toxic waste."[17] He also traded principal-only strips (POs) that protect investors from prepayment risk (see later). Like the MBS traders of today he went long the CMOs and short Treasuries and leveraged the positions.[18]

Askin and Kidder did well while interest rates on residential mortgages stayed under 7 percent. During the second quarter of 1994, the interest rate on new 30-year mortgages jumped to an average of 7.45 percent, an increase from the first to the second quarter of 50 basis points. The CMO market, which was heavily leveraged, collapsed under the weight of widening spreads. The POs that Askin held were also buried because they are priced in part by certain prepayment expectations that vanished when interest rates rose.* As a result, Askin's funds were forced into liquidation. Askin also held $2.5 billion in CMOs, mostly purchased with borrowed money. The liquidations set off a tsunami that destroyed the venerable more than 100-year-old Kidder and threw the CMO market into disarray. It was necessary for the Federal Reserve to enter the market in order to restore order.

Prepayment Risk

Prepayment risk distinguishes the MBS market from all other FI Arb markets. MBS traders have developed pricing models that value MBSs by their option-adjusted spreads and reflect the MBS's yield premium to Treasury bonds of similar maturity. The spread is a function of the

---

*In other words, people prepay significantly less under rising rates, and therefore the holders of POs don't get their money back as quickly.

probability of prepayment, hence the risk.[19] It can become a significant problem when interest rates decline unexpectedly and refinance activity escalates. This causes early repayment of mortgage principal. Since prepayments are made at par, MBSs trading over par will suffer price declines while MBSs trading at a discount will be marked up. Prepayments are notoriously difficult to predict, so even expert traders can be surprised when they occur. Assuming the MBS is a long position and is trading at a premium, the arbitrageur faces sudden risk as the value of his long position declines while his short position is at best stable and more likely increasing in price. Therefore, to act as a hedge against prepayment risk, MBS traders go long POs (described earlier) and may also short the other stripped-out instrument, the interest-only (IO) tranche. Then, when rates decline, the POs rise as prepayments occur and can offset losses to the MBSs. The short of the IOs also makes money because IOs decline in value as interest rates decline.

MBS valuations can also decline when interest rates rise and prepayments slow down beyond expectations. We saw the consequences of this scenario in the David Askin story earlier. When MBS managers expect interest rate hikes by the Fed as they have for quite some time, they will hedge their MBS positions by going long the IOs and short the POs. This arbitrage has been very successful recently as the Fed has raised rates 14 consecutive times since June 2004.[20] These various trades illustrate the importance of experience in the mortgage industry, the sophistication of pricing models, and, last but not least, the keen trading instincts of the successful MBS trader.

HEDGE FUND PERFORMANCE RECAP, 2001–2005

Having now completed our single strategy chapters, we think it is interesting to show how the various asset classes have performed over the past five years across a full market cycle. Table 9.1 shows the returns, standard deviations, and Sharpe ratios for a variety of hedge fund strategies and equity and bond benchmarks along with certain correlation data. The risk-free rate for the period was 2.26 percent.

Several important observations are readily apparent. First, all of

TABLE 9.1

Hedge Fund Strategies, Performance, and Correlations to Stocks and Bonds, Trailing Five Years

Performance: Hedge Fund Strategies and Traditional Assets (1/1/2001–12/31/2005)

	Annual Return	Standard Deviation	Sharpe Ratio	Correlation with S&P 500	Correlation with Lehman Gov-Credit
HFRI Convertible Arbitrage Index	6.15%	3.48%	1.12	0.04	0.17
HFRI Distressed Securities Index	14.76%	4.48%	2.79	0.43	0.07
HFRI Equity Hedge Index	6.57%	6.48%	0.67	0.81	−0.21
HFRI Equity Market Neutral Index	4.09%	2.28%	0.80	−0.28	0.13
HFRI Event-Driven Index	10.68%	6.01%	1.40	0.71	−0.09
HFRI Fixed Income: Arbitrage Index	6.89%	1.97%	2.35	0.08	0.34
HFRI Fund-Weighted Composite Index	8.00%	5.20%	1.10	0.81	−0.13
HFRI Fund of Funds Composite Index	5.89%	3.30%	1.10	0.58	0.02
HFRI Macro Index	9.26%	5.03%	1.39	0.17	0.29
HFRI Short Selling Index	2.58%	15.24%	0.02	−0.91	0.34
CISDM CTA Asset-Weighted Index	7.72%	8.25%	0.66	−0.19	0.39
Lehman Government-Credit Bond Index	6.10%	4.86%	0.79	−0.33	1.00
MSCI The World Index—Net	2.18%	14.67%	−0.01	0.97	−0.29
S&P 500 Price Index	−1.11%	14.90%	−0.23	1.00	−0.33

Sources: Mayer & Hoffman, HFRI, PerTrac, and CISDM.

the individual strategies that we've discussed plus the HFRI Fund of Funds Composite Index outperformed equities on an absolute-return and risk-adjusted basis. As you can see, both the S&P 500 and the MSCI World have negative Sharpe ratios over the past five years. Second, all of the strategies (except the CTA Index) and the HFRI Fund of Funds Composite Index have also outperformed the Lehman Government Index on a risk-adjusted basis even though bonds were relatively strong performers over the period. Third, Distressed, Event-Driven, and Global Macro had the highest annualized returns while Distressed and Fixed Income Arb had the highest risk-adjusted returns. FI Arb had the lowest standard deviation while the S&P had the highest, a volatility number more than seven times higher than that of FI Arb. Finally, correlations between ELS and equities have moved higher and perhaps as a result annualized performance over this period of 6.57 percent, which was substantially lower for ELS managers than their performance of 14.48 percent from 1994–2005.

INTERVIEW

Michael "Boris" Pasternak

Chief Investment Officer
Pinewood Credit Markets, LP

IN 2003 MICHAEL PASTERNAK AND DANIEL FITZGERALD CO-FOUNDED Pinewood Capital Partners, LLC. By April 1, 2004, they launched Pinewood Credit Markets, L.P., as a Fixed Income Arb fund. Michael Pasternak (his friends call him Boris) serves as CIO and Dan Fitzgerald is COO. The fund utilizes a range of strategies that exploit fundamental and technically driven valuation anomalies in the credit markets. The strategies are designed to benefit from a range of idiosyncratic (company or industry-specific) and systematic (market-level) risk and return factors that the managers anticipate will be weakly correlated.

Our interviewee, Michael Pasternak, was a managing director and senior portfolio manager at Goldman Sachs from 1997 to 2003 with responsibility for developing the dedicated high-yield franchise for Goldman Sachs Asset Management. From 1986 to 1997, he held various positions with Saudi International Bank, where he developed and managed global high-yield corporate bond and loan portfolios. He earned his B.A. with honors in natural sciences from Cambridge University in 1985. He sat with co-author Sam Kirschner and spoke openly about Pinewood Credit Markets and its investment strategy.

SK: *Michael, give us an overview of Pinewood.*

MP: Glad to. Pinewood Capital was formed in 2003. The Fixed Income Arb fund Pinewood Credit Markets began trading on the first of
April 2004. Right now, the fund is managing $170 million. Our goal is
to take it up to $750 million. In our portfolio we have about 200 line
items. That represents about 140 trade tags spread over numerous
strategies.

SK: *Tell us about your style and overall investment strategy.*

MP: In the context of credit and fixed income, our style is pretty unusual. We manage very idiosyncratic credit risk, so we're taking views
on the valuation of debt instruments such as bonds, loans, or credit default swaps (CDSs). We're looking for movement on both the long side
and the short side in such a way that we then end up developing a
portfolio that is market neutral. By market neutral I mean we're not
heavily exposed on a forward- or rearview-looking basis to any primary market risk.

So we're really looking for movements of spreads and prices that
we can capture on a three- to nine-month basis, ahead of the market.
And we're looking at the single security level.

SK: *To help illustrate your own approach, what is your view of the approach more typically taken by a vanilla fixed income arb shop?*

MP: I would characterize most fixed income or fixed income arb
strategies to be some derivative of mean reversion or carry. Lots of
people generate return basically by leveraging up small movements
or leveraging up carry. That carry might be a curve trade or it might
just be a leveraged position and a leveraged loan that can be fi-
nanced attractively.

We try to avoid doing those things. We tend to look for events or
major changes to drive spreads in and out. We like to find operating
changes, things that are happening in the business makeup or the
management makeup of a company, or the world environment of a
company. Things that we think the market hasn't anticipated yet.

We think that fixed income, by its nature, is essentially an instrument for carry or mean reversion trades. It's an extra abundance instrument, meant to be contractible. It's meant to be very predictable, and

so it's almost genetically hard-wired to be predictable. Therefore it's the nature of most participants in the fixed-income industry to think in these terms. But our approach is fundamentally different. We're looking for gapping events and to break out of the usual ranges.

If we find a paradigm shift in terms of the prospects of this company, then there's got to be a whole new valuation matrix. The market in general is still very focused on symmetrical or mean reverting kinds of outcomes. But we're looking for asymmetrical outcomes. The market is going for the 90 percent of things that work out right. We're trying to find the 10 percent of things that work out wrong, and be exposed to that the right way.

We believe that most of our money over the long term is made from shorts. We are willing to incur negative carry (since we pay coupons) so that we can capitalize on the potential price action on our shorts. And that we think is extremely unusual within the fixed income arbitrage space.

SK: *Fascinating. With a strategy like that, how do you benchmark your performance?*

MP: Good question. The typical industry indices and benchmarks really don't apply to us. We wouldn't use the Lehman High-Yield Index. We don't think that would be appropriate for us at all because we don't rent that market exposure. There isn't really a good economic benchmark other than Treasury bills.

Volatility in the rear view is on the order of $2\frac{1}{2}$–3 percent. We would like to target something like 5–6 percent. Some might say that's a risky number, but it's risk on our skill, it's not risk on an external market number. So we could set an absolute benchmark, like you might just say we should have a 6 or 8 percent absolute return hurdle.

One factor in our returns is the general level of short-term interest rates, particularly in U.S. dollars. Primarily what we put as initial margin or collateral is driving an element of our returns in a way that's outside of our control. And that's fine. We accept that.

SK: *It looks like your performance has tracked pretty closely with the HFRI Fixed Income Arb Index.*

MP: I don't know all the components of that, but I would consider it a pretty inappropriate benchmark. I mean that's kind of getting into the peer group argument, and, again, we do things very differently. Keep in mind, Sam, that if we had been running at our target of volatility, 5–6 percent, I'd suspect our tracking error to that Index would be substantial. It would be more obvious how different we are.

SK: *Got it. Michael, give us an example of a good trade, a real winner that illustrates your unique approach.*

MP: Okay. I've said we tend to make more money on the short side, but this is an example of making money on the long. But it's helpful at least in that it shows credit intensity.

In 2004 AT&T had fallen on hard times and the bonds had been downgraded to junk. We felt both AT&T and one of its major competitors, MCI, which was emerging from bankruptcy between 2004 and 2005, were fundamentally very poorly understood by the investment community. And we considered them actually to be pretty valuable companies in the context of their relationships and the services they provided. We felt the market was sort of throwing out the baby with the bathwater in terms of looking at the fundamental enterprise evaluation of those two entities. On top of that, technical evaluations of AT&T were extremely ugly. We reviewed the capital structure and the information available on the company and basically hit on an instant trade. There was a bond issue that had step-up features covering both upgrades and downgrades to the credit.

We thought that was very interesting in that it protected you on the downside even if you gave up some of the room on the upside. So we constructed a trade where we bought a very long-dated bond, and we shorted the default risk through some *credit default swaps* (instruments designed to *transfer credit risk* of fixed income products between parties), but we were long AT&T in the forward market. That meant we could make a lot of money if there was a positive merger or acquisition. And also we could not lose much money if things continued to deteriorate, so that was an unusual profile, right?

SK: *Definitely contrarian.*

MP: Well, here's a payoff that looks pretty asymmetrical. So the idea was just to capture some movement at some point. We were willing to think that that might be 12 to 18 months, or somewhat longer than our normal investment horizon. But we felt that it was a good bet.

As events unfolded, SBC [SBC Communications] bought the company. This was one of the most profitable trades we've ever had in the fund. The position was at the top end of our range, in terms of exposure, because we had a lot of conviction and we liked the upside/downside profile.

SK: *How did the SBC acquisition affect the bondholders?*

MP: Well the nice feature about the bonds was that once the acquisition was finally approved, the coupons actually went down. So ironically there was still quite a lot of value in the bond because the coupon was still very high. So we made lots of money on the acquisition, and then we changed the trade into a new trade where we were just long the bond, because the market's left, let's say, one or two points on the table.

We captured all the economics in what's called the trade tag, and that trade tag populates a certain strategy. In this case it's an intra-capital strategy, because we've taken advantage of anomalies in pricing between markets as well as having a directional view in the name.

SK: *Tell us a little bit about the other side of this trade, which are the CDSs that you used as your hedge.*

MP: Right. The CDSs were basically a way of us getting exposed in the short end of the forward curve, as it were. These CDSs were linked to the timing of a default, had one occurred for AT&T Corporation. We were paying a premium, and that premium collapsed once SBC stepped in. So yeah, we lost a lot of money on that. But it was more than offset by what we made on the bond side. We gave up 6 points on the short side, but we made 16 on the long. And that was all part of the scenario that we worked out.

SK: *That's a great trade. But then, let's look at the dark side, too. In April and May, a lot of fixed-income guys were in GM and just got hammered. You, too?*

MP: Well, no . . . and yes.

SK: *No and yes?*

MP: Here's what happened. We held a view from late 2004 that the prospects of the auto sector, and the auto supplies in particular, were extremely ugly in a way that was completely undiscounted by the marketplace. So we basically entered into a short bias industry trade. We entered into a lot of long/short trades where we were net short. So we actually benefited enormously from the sell-off that then happened. We really had it nailed, completely nailed.

SK: *Nice. Although I sense a "but . . ." coming.*

MP: Right. We nailed the GM sell-off, but we really got burned on Visteon Corporation, the global automotive supplier. We were still short and the payoff on a Visteon default would have been enormous in our portfolio; a default would have added three to five points to our NAV [net asset value]. We felt that the operating prospects of Visteon were so horrific that it was a worthwhile speculation that they would file Chapter 11 and restructure. And we were wrong. Visteon didn't default and the draw-down was on the order of one to one and a half percent of our NAV. It swung against us. So we called it right on GM, but soon after that we got burned.

SK: *That was a bad trade.*

MP: Our worst in terms of economic impact but still a good decision. You know, at the end of the day, you just have to say, "It's okay." You always have regret. You'd like to win on everything. But you have to recognize that you can't and you won't. In terms of tradecraft, we could have done better. But every day's a new day.

SK: *True. In what market conditions would you say you do best?*

MP: What we've observed is that we actually do better in dire markets. By design, we would anticipate doing our best when default rates accelerate, dispersion rises, and credit spreads widen.

We get kickers from being correctly positioned on default expectations to specific names. Those shorts really run away from us in a great way. We get much bigger payoffs on our shorts than we even thought possible three or six months earlier, as the market sort of melts down and people get depressed.

SK: *Great stuff, Michael. To wind it up, what advice would you have for potential investors in your space?*

MP: Short term, there are going to be a number of reasonably profound model and valuation issues around credit. There's been such an explosion in new technologies around credit risks and portfolio credit risks. I think it's similar to what happened in the mortgage market in 1994.

In a more structural way, I think probably the biggest risk in credit and fixed income will not go away. That is, basically the whole industry is biased to reverting to the mean. I don't see that ever changing.

SK: *So what are the effects of that?*

MP: The effects are, if you go and build a diversified portfolio of fixed-income managers, probably all you're doing is kidding yourself about the diversification benefit. So, you should bear that in mind, because a lot of managers do the same trade. Most fixed-income managers, like 95 percent of the managers, are generic positive carry people. And I think it's very difficult to find the 5 percent who aren't. Communicating that difference, our value proposition as it were, is challenging. In that respect then, the strength is the weakness, right? We are so different that it actually makes life more difficult for us in the short term, but I expect that.

SK: *But long term?*

MP: Well, as far as our business, in the long term, it should be really good. We just have to get there.

CHAPTER 10

The Newer Strategies

INTRODUCTION

If one delves into managers' motivations for starting a hedge fund and injects them with a dose of truth serum, inevitably the discussion will reveal that this type of investment vehicle allows for the payment of significant incentive fees based on performance. It's been said that achieving this goal is harder than it used to be. In fact, it's never been easy. While the many great successes in the hedge fund world are well-known, there have also been many instances of mediocre or even poor returns. These do not get the headlines. The authors prefer to say that the methods for successfully achieving the goal are constantly changing and are definitely different from what they used to be.

Now that the viability of the private investment partnership has been established beyond doubt, both new and existing managers are looking for new and novel ways to invest using the hedge fund structure. While hedge funds have always attracted many of the brightest investment minds from all corners of the investment world, these individuals are less likely to open a new convertible arbitrage or equity market neutral fund today, for example, than they were just a few years ago. There's just too much money already at play in those arenas, and fresh opportunities have begun to resemble endangered species. It is also, practically speaking, near impossible to raise assets in a strategy that has been producing generally subpar returns. Capital is usually leaving, not entering, such strategies.

Many of the newer strategies are practiced by just a few hedge funds, generally because of the small size or immaturity of the markets for the instruments traded or because of a lack of liquidity. Other strategies have attracted substantial assets and accordingly many hedge funds. At the outset of this chapter, we briefly describe four of these new trading areas. Then we feature Direct Financing, a strategy that has seen many hedge funds and billions of dollars enter the space in recent years.

REAL ESTATE

Investors might consider real estate hedge funds to be a novelty, although the space has seen a dramatic increase in asset flows over the past five years. Real estate hedge funds invest in real estate investment trusts (REITs), public home builders, land companies, real estate service providers, mortgage providers and specialty finance companies, hotel and leisure companies, retailers and healthcare providers, and other public companies with substantial real estate assets. There are now about 50 real estate hedge funds globally, with most of them focused on the U.S. market. In addition, a number of recently launched funds invest globally.

In 2004 real estate hedge funds in the United States managed, according to estimates, less than $1.5 billion in combined assets. Since then, Blackacre Capital Management, LLC, an affiliate of the hedge fund giant Cerberus, has raised close to $1 billion for its fund; Mercury Real Estate Advisors, LLC, which runs two funds, has increased its total AUM to $470 million; and Marathon Real Estate Opportunity Fund has raised $260 million in a little over a year. Even the legendary real estate investor Tom Barrack has gotten his $15 billion private equity firm, Colony Capital, into the real estate hedge fund game.

Real estate funds have also been popping up in Europe, Asia, and Australia. We mention three recent successful launches. The Swiss Finance and Property Corporation started up a new long/short real estate fund in August 2005 focusing on European-listed real estate companies. LIM Asia Alternative Real Estate Fund, Hong Kong, launched in July 2004, invests in Asian real estate and real estate–related securities. The Australian fund, Pengana Absolute Return Real Estate Fund, launched in August 2004, invests globally in real estate–related securities.

There are two common ways for managers to hedge the longs in a portfolio of real estate stocks. The first method is to short relatively overvalued REITS or other real estate equities. According to James Lang of real estate hedge fund Cashel Capital Advisors, "You can short these securities, but it just can be more expensive because they are dividend payers."[1] Another way is by shorting one or more of several real estate ETFs, which do not pay dividends and are actively traded.

At a time when the average REIT has an historically low yield, roughly equivalent to the current risk-free rate, some hedge funds are of the view that many REITs are overvalued. The basis for this view is that the underlying assets of REITs, commercial real estate properties, are selling at the lowest capitalization rates in history. This has led CalPERS, the largest U.S. pension fund, to divest most of its core portfolio of commercial real estate over the past year or so.[2] These sales have amounted to some $8 billion, and boosted CalPERS' return on its real estate portfolio in the fiscal year ending June 2005 to more than 40 percent.

INSURANCE AND REINSURANCE

Like real estate, the insurance industry is gradually gaining more attention from hedge fund managers. Nephila Capital opened in 1998 to profit from insurance risk by trading the early catastrophe bonds (CAT bonds) that had first appeared a few years earlier. CAT bonds can offer a better risk profile than similarly rated corporate bonds. Since then Nephila has shifted gears, now emphasizing the purchase of traditional OTC reinsurance contracts. Other players in this field include Citadel and Coriolis Capital.[3]

Some hedge funds are structured much like reinsurance companies, assuming catastrophe risks across many markets above preestablished limits. The year 2005 was indeed a "perfect storm" for such funds, but with reinsurance rates soaring, 2006 could be very profitable for this hedge fund niche if hurricane damage reverts to the mean, or even close to it. Therein lies one key risk in such funds. Are the more frequent, more intense hurricanes of recent years part of a secular global warming trend or just random events in the sporadic pattern that hurricane activity has long shown? The answer to that question will have much to do with future performance in this sector, but at least the funds are getting compensated handsomely in the near term for taking these risks.

ENERGY

Traders in this sector invest in energy-related equities, derivatives, and commodities. This space is occupied predominantly by multistrategy firms like Citadel, D. E. Shaw, Vega, and Ritchie Capital but also by specialty funds like Lucas Energy Total Return Partners. It is further marked by a number of former Enron traders like John Arnold of Centaurus and his counterparts from other power companies, as well as several well-known former buy and sell side Wall Street energy analysts and a number of former energy industry executives. One of the highest-performing hedge funds in this space is BP Capital, LLC, headed by 77-year-old T. Boone Pickens, former head of Mesa Petroleum. Pickens's success has been largely based on his firm belief that oil and gas prices would soar over the past two years. He put his money (and that of his investors) on the line in that belief, and the payoff has been extraordinary.

Investing in oil equities becomes intensely volatile from time to time. Indeed, many forecasts of oil and gas prices by leading experts have proven way off the mark again and again over the years, and the stocks have a very high correlation with prices in the oil patch. Herein lies a classic hedge fund quandary. In the past few years buy and hold strategies in oil and gas equities have been enormous winners. A number of junior Canadian gas plays, for example, have risen 1,000 percent or more. Times like this are salad days for long-only investors who are knowledgeable in the sector, and potentially for hedge funds as well, except that most hedge funds are very conscious about downside volatility, and it is practically impossible to capitalize on such massive upside plays without also incurring large corrections along the way. It is difficult to hedge away such significant drawdown potential without also reducing returns far below those of long-only players.

Investors in energy-oriented hedge funds know that the road will likely be bumpy, but there is an important benefit from having this exposure. Large run-ups in oil and gas prices can raise havoc with corporate profit margins, consumer pocketbooks, the economy, and the stock market. In such an environment hedge funds in this sector figure to be big winners, offsetting likely losses in long-only portfolios and some hedge fund strategies as well.

EMISSIONS TRADING

Under the Kyoto Protocol, the industrialized countries have been granted emissions allowances in line with their commitments to reduce greenhouse gas pollutants by 2012. The European Union (EU) member nations, all of which signed the Protocol, then specified mandatory emissions allowance targets for known polluting industries like oil refineries, steel and glass makers, and power plants. For example, with carbon dioxide, an emissions allowance is the right to emit 1,000 kilograms (a metric tonne) of the gas.

The EU then set up a trading plan in October 2003 that gave emissions credits to these industrial companies. Companies that reduce greenhouse gases and achieve their targets can sell unused credits on the open market to those that exceed their specified goals. Otherwise, the violators must pay substantial fines that are far more costly than buying the credits.[4]

Even though the United States didn't sign the Kyoto Protocol, U.S. companies have been subject to emissions allowances since the Environmental Protection Agency (EPA) began issuing them in 1995. Every March, the Chicago Board of Trade holds auctions of new EPA allowances for sulfur, carbon monoxide, nitrous oxide, and renewable energy credits. As in the EU, companies can buy credits from others who have reduced their pollutants and therefore have surplus credits to sell. Sensing arbitrage opportunities, at least 12 hedge funds like the giant event-driven Centaurus Fund are trading emissions rights, and more are expected to enter this evolving space. Sulfur trading volume is currently at the $10 billion level while carbon trading is only at $2 billion but expected to grow exponentially over the coming decade.[5]

Early returns for the funds are very promising as prices for credits are on the rise and vary widely between countries. These markets are highly illiquid and volatile, further creating great opportunities for the most knowledgeable traders, but large risks for those on the other side of their transactions.

DIRECT FINANCING FOR PUBLIC COMPANIES

While the four markets just discussed have attracted considerable interest, direct financing has already become a $20 billion market with the potential to grow considerably larger. Dynamic changes in both the investment banking and commercial banking markets have in recent years provided hedge funds with the opportunity to provide financing to smaller public companies. Let's examine this transformation more closely.

As trading and commission margins have been increasingly squeezed, brokerage and investment banking firms have cut back on research budgets. Particularly hard hit has been coverage of small companies whose shares generally do not trade actively. Lack of coverage has created a void in the securities markets for information on small and micro caps, which in turn has made it difficult to bring to market secondary financings for such companies. Investment bankers have nearly all come to the conclusion that large "deals" are the way to go.

Similarly, commercial banks have been increasingly losing interest in lending to small companies. Consolidation in the industry has meant that many small regional banks are now part of giant bank holding companies. The buzzwords in banking have become "fee-based services," which have the benefit of not tying up capital. Banks are selling mutual funds, separate account management, and trust services, and many have built large trading operations rather than focusing on loans. When lending is done, it is usually at scale, and whenever possible large loans are packaged and resold to investors. Small loans are by and large a thing of the past. When banks are asked to make a loan to a small company, which most are not terribly interested in doing anyway, the process is usually so laborious and time consuming that the borrower immediately becomes a good prospect for a fast-moving direct financing hedge fund.

Against this backdrop there are thousands of low-profile small public companies in every major industry and service area. These companies are always looking for ways to finance their growth. Once they realize that their friendly banker is not the answer, they often look to the new funding community started by hedge funds.

The types of financing offered vary by manager, but the most prevalent are in the form of collateralized loans, debt with warrants, convertible securities, and common stock (often at a discount). The financing option in each case is invariably a compromise between the desire of the hedge fund to make a high return with minimum risk and the need of the company to secure financing that suits its business needs, which makes sense balance sheet-wise and is fair to shareholders. It is quite common for companies to return again and again to the direct financing hedge fund that they have dealt with before. The smart hedge fund does not lose sight of the obvious fact that terms must be fair to ensure repeat business.

THE DIRECT FINANCING TRADING AND INVESTMENT STRATEGIES

Most of the transactions in the space are covered by Regulation D of the 1933 Securities Act, the regulation that governs private placement exemptions. Reg D allows smaller companies to raise capital through the sale of equity or debt without having to register their securities with the SEC. When there is an equity component in the deal, and nearly all transactions include one, the hedge fund will usually require that the company commence the registration process with the SEC within 30 days. Registration usually becomes effective within 90 days after filing, at which time shares can be sold into the market. If the financing has included warrants or convertible securities, no selling is done until the share price rises above the warrant or convertible exercise price. When/ if that occurs, shares may be fed into the market, generally very carefully so as not to impede the rising share price. In this way, liquidity for the shares is improved, the company's shareholder base is broadened, and the company's balance sheet benefits.

At the other extreme, should the company fall on hard times, most direct financing hedge funds enter the picture to protect their investment. Interventions might take the form of additional capital infusions or even assistance with a merger or takeover.

Privately placed equity and debt are compelling for smaller public companies for one or more of the following reasons:

- Avoids upfront SEC registration process for timing-related reasons.
- Maintains confidentiality throughout the capital-raising process.
- Hedge funds can provide loans of all sizes from $1 million to $50 million.
- Deals can be executed on an accelerated basis, often in 30–45 days.
- Expands shareholder base.
- Inexpensive financing costs.
- Flexibility in the financing structure.

In addition to these benefits, hedge funds may also provide ongoing mentoring and guidance to the borrower in terms of improving the company's ongoing operations and raising the company's profile in the investor community.

Direct financing hedge funds are suppliers of capital to those sectors of the economy where capital is in the greatest demand. In recent years, biotech, healthcare, and especially oil and gas have been hot investment areas. According to Gary Vasey, vice president of energy consultancy Utilipoint in Houston, "The traditional lenders are either not interested in providing the terms that they (the small exploration and development companies) need, or they are simply not interested."[6] Banks are generally unwilling to lend against proven reserves if they are not yet hooked up to a pipeline, whereas the more opportunistic hedge funds are delighted to enter into discussions where such collateral is available. And in a related development, Randy Castleberry of Intrepid Financial Partners, a Houston-based adviser to the energy sector, reports that hedge fund money will help rebuild the energy infrastructure in the Gulf of Mexico in the wake of Katrina.[7] Needless to say, when a business sector is very strong and there is a shortage of capital, there is the potential for high returns for those willing to invest.

As of late 2005, there were at least 35 funds in the space with more opening regularly. In 2005 about 1,300 deals worth $20 billion were completed,[8] 40 percent of them by hedge funds. Contrast that total with the $1.3 billion invested in 114 deals that were done in 1995.[9]

There are many permutations and combinations of financing techniques, including common stock and warrants, convertible preferreds, convertible debentures, and senior loans with warrants. All loans require interest and/or dividend payments either at or above conventional market rates. Monthly interest payments are the backbone of the steady returns generated by many of these funds, with equity kickers serving as the potential rocket fuel. In 2005, more than 90 percent of the deals involved common stock or a convertible instrument.[10] Table 10.1 highlights the benefits and terms of the four most common types of Direct Financing.

Besides deal terms, another variable that differentiates these funds is the source of deal origination. Some rely substantially on the service providers who represent companies seeking financing, including deal brokers, accountants, lawyers, and investor relations firms. Others participate in informal syndicates of Direct Financing funds who join together in financings too large for any one of them. Many prefer to act alone, structuring their own deals in direct negotiations with borrowers. Some funds rely to a large degree on repeat business, in some cases refinancing a smaller deal done earlier.

In our opinion a key differentiating factor between these funds is how they handle the inevitable problem investments. A related factor is the type of covenants these funds write into their financings,

TABLE 10.1

Four Types of Financing

Type of Security	Benefits to the Company	Additional Considerations
Common Stock	• "Plain vanilla" structure • Broad target investor base • May be executed with limited marketing	• Buyer may require warrant coverage • Dilution given discounts
Convertible Preferred Stock	• Can result in less expensive cost of capital than common stock—depending on terms • Usually convertible at market price or at a premium to market price into a fixed or variable number of shares • May be executed with limited marketing	• Buyer may require warrant coverage • Dividend payment • Redemption features
Convertible Debt	• Can result in less expensive cost of capital than common stock—depending on terms • Usually convertible at market price or at a premium to market price into a fixed or variable number of shares • May be executed with limited marketing	• Buyer may require warrant coverage • Interest payment • Maturity features
Structured Equity Line	• Ability to draw funds on as-needed basis • Discounts typically smaller than common stock deals • May be executed without marketing	• Securities must be registered via shelf filing prior to any drawdowns • Uncertainty of total funding—depends on stock volume/price variables • Stock overhang perception • Narrow investor universe

Source: Mayer & Hoffman Capital Advisors.

which can come into play in the event of default. The actions open to a direct financer range all the way from write-off to active involvement in a corporate restructuring. Such workouts can be very time-consuming but the value gained for investors can be significant. Sometimes bankruptcy and/or sale of the company may be forced in order to repay the hedge fund.

In the early days of this strategy, financing often took the form of stock at a discount to the market with returns hedged by short selling. This type of activity was subject to abuse and has fallen under the regulatory spotlight (see Disadvantages), and it is not commonly used today.

PERFORMANCE

Since 1996 when it was first launched through 2005, the HFRI Regulation D Index* has been an outstanding performer returning almost a "five bagger" in that time, averaging almost 17 percent per annum.[11] During this period, the Reg D Index outperformed all of the principal hedge fund strategies and as Figure 10.1 shows, it significantly outperformed the Wilshire Small Value Index. The Reg D Index also more than doubled the Lehman Government/Credit Bond Index. Note also that the strategy has widely outperformed the HFRI Fund-Weighted Composite Index. Direct Financing funds' performance, however, was negatively impacted by the market downturn in 2001 and 2002, with the HFRI Reg D Index down 1.72 percent in 2001 and 5.49 percent in 2002.

---

*This index is not a perfect proxy for the types of hedge funds described here because it reflects only Reg D financings that are primarily for straight common stock. We believe that the returns of today's Direct Financing hedge funds are less volatile than those of this Index.

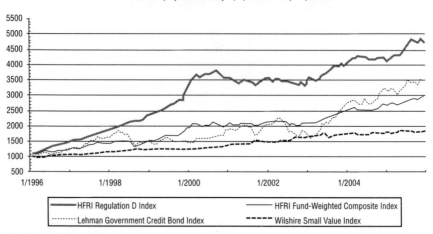

FIGURE 10.1

HFRI Reg D Index versus Benchmarks 1/1/1996–12/31/2005

Growth of $1,000 USD, 1/1/1996–12/31/2005

HFRI Regulation D Index
Lehman Government Credit Bond Index
HFRI Fund-Weighted Composite Index
Wilshire Small Value Index

Source: Mayer & Hoffman, HFRI.

ADVANTAGES

Steady performance bolstered by occasional upside volatility coupled with the downside protection of interest and dividend payments have been the hallmark of Direct Financing hedge funds. The
strategy has significantly outperformed all the major hedge fund
strategies since 1996 and, as always, there are certain funds that have
turned in even more spectacular results. For example, Laurus, one of
the largest Direct Financing funds, has averaged slightly more than
20 percent in its first five years, with no down years or quarters, and
a very high Sharpe ratio of 3.5.

A second major advantage of the strategy is that it is a direct, conservative way to capitalize on the long-term superior performance of
small-cap stocks, especially small-cap value stocks. According to Ibbotson Associates, from 1928 through 2004 the mean return of small-cap

value stocks averaged a stunning 19.5 percent as compared to 15.3 percent for large-cap value stocks and 11.1 percent for large-cap growth stocks.[12] Over the past 10 years, the Wilshire Small Value Index has averaged 13.3 percent annually while the HFRI Reg D Index has averaged 17 percent, suggesting that the direct financers have produced significant alpha.

DISADVANTAGES

Notwithstanding their valuable role in providing much needed capital to the important small business sector and their excellent returns of the past decade, Direct Financing hedge funds are still controversial. In fact, some institutional investors will not invest in them as a matter of policy. There are four major reasons that investors give:

1. *An 18-month ongoing SEC investigation into private financings to public companies.* At the crux of these investigations are three different types of violations: whether hedge funds that were approached by public companies for possible loans turned around and, using this inside information, shorted their stocks; whether hedge funds shorted the companies' shares after deals were closed with the resultant decline in prices triggering deal provisions giving the funds in question even more shares; and whether investors other than the direct financers were given confidential information about pending transactions allowing them to profit from short sales of the companies involved.

    To date, one hedge fund manager has been disbarred by the National Association of Securities Dealers (NASD) while several brokers involved in private transactions have been prosecuted and fined. No formal charges, however, have yet been brought against any major hedge funds that transact in the space.[13] Nevertheless, the ongoing SEC investigation has placed a cloud over the industry and its players.

2. *Exposure to economic recessions and bear markets.* In a typical bear market, without profits from warrants and convertible securities that

become in-the-money due to stock appreciation, net returns from this strategy can be less than the interest or dividend income. In a severe bear market, as occurred in 2001–2002 (see Figure 10.1), modest negative returns can occur. In the event a massive recession leads to large numbers of defaults and poor recoveries, direct financers could suffer greater performance pain.

3. *The liquidity risk inherent in these private transactions.* The stocks of the borrowers often have small floats and are highly illiquid. In the event of adverse corporate performance or other event risk, shares can suddenly plummet in value by a large percentage without much trading occurring.

4. *The lack of standard accounting practices for valuing warrants and other securities held by these funds.* Different approaches are used by different funds, and there is a fair degree of flexibility as to how assets are valued. As a result, monthly NAVs issued by the hedge funds may be revised on year-end audits.

CONCLUSIONS

As of this writing, institutional aversion to this strategy has been slowly dissipating. Mutual funds, including the legendary Bill Miller's Legg Mason Value Trust, have accounted for more than 22 percent of private deal volume in 2005 compared with 9.7 percent in 2004.[14] In addition, large multistrategy hedge funds like Ramius Capital and Highbridge have allocated substantial capital to these transactions, thus adding additional credibility to the space. The reason for the increased interest, in a nutshell, is that the strategy has stood the test of at least one major down market cycle and has proven to be relatively uncorrelated to equities.

Furthermore, hedge fund investors have begun to acknowledge that default rates are generally low and that audited results have confirmed the outsized returns generated by many funds. For example, Laurus claims that since inception in 2001, it has had to foreclose on less than 2 percent of the more than 160 deals completed.[15]

Investor skepticism, legion in the early days, has gradually shifted to the point that in 2005 $20 billion of such financings occurred. Time will tell whether this strategy will continue to do as well in the future as it has in the past. It could, in fact, do quite a bit less well and still be producing returns that are above average versus equities and/or other hedge fund strategies.

CHAPTER 11

The Search for Alpha

FACED WITH A BEWILDERING ARRAY OF COMPLEX STRATEGIES AND NEW investment opportunities, professional investors and researchers alike have attempted to discover the major drivers of hedge fund risk-adjusted and absolute performance and where the best future sources of alpha might be uncovered. This chapter explores these and related questions. It is divided into four sections. The first part discusses alpha and then analyzes the research on alpha in hedge fund performance. The second section presents an analysis of studies that have compared younger versus older funds and draws a set of conclusions from the research. The third part offers two original studies on the Class of 2003 managers and the lessons the senior authors have learned as managers of a fund of hedge funds that primarily invests in newer funds. The fourth and final section offers a set of best practices for conducting due diligence on new funds.

THE SEARCH FOR ALPHA

What is Alpha?

If we follow CAPM,[1] *alpha* is the excess investment return that a fund generates that is above and beyond the risk-free rate plus its performance derived from its beta to the market. The preferred equation for calculating α (alpha) of a fund's performance used by Schneeweiss[2] is:

$$\alpha = (\text{fund return} - \text{risk-free rate}) - \beta (\text{market return} - \text{risk-free rate})$$

where:

$\beta = \rho$ (fund return, market return) $\times \sigma$ (fund) $\times \sigma$ (market)/ σ^2 (market)

ρ = the correlation between the fund's return and the market's return

σ = the standard deviation over the period measured

Because most hedge fund strategies have relatively low betas to the stock and bond markets, it has been presumed that their significant outperformance has been due to skill, luck, or unknown factors.

Furthermore, the very idea that alpha can persist in a group of managers goes against Fama's EMH discussed in Chapter 9.[3] As a result, many researchers have rejected the EMH in its strictest forms and have concluded that hedge funds, because of their asymmetric return patterns* and the particular risks that they take that are beyond CAPM's market risk, do not fit under the rubric of the EMH.[4]

We agree with Jaeger[5] that almost all hedge fund strategies are therefore best understood in the context of Arbitrage Pricing Theory (APT), a multifactor extension of the one-factor CAPM hypothesis. First described by Ross in 1976[6] and subsequently refined by others including Ross,[7] APT details additional variables that may contribute to a hedge fund's performance beyond its beta to market risk. These include unanticipated inflation, changes in industrial production outputs, unanticipated shifts in risk premiums, and unanticipated moves in interest rates.[8] The latter two risks in particular have significant applicability since, as you recall, they form the basis for the returns of certain hedge fund strategies like Convertible Arb and Fixed Income Arb to name but two.

Multifactor models like APT allow us, therefore, to view alpha generation in hedge funds as a combination of the manager's skill and mostly his willingness to take on and successfully profit from the additional risks of liquidity, interest rates, credit, complexity, and events, which we have detailed throughout this book. For taking on these

---

*See Chapter 13 for a full discussion of asymmetric returns in hedge funds.

and other risks, hedge funds earn risk premiums that add to their performance.[9]

How Much Alpha Do Hedge Funds Produce?

How much alpha hedge funds produce has been a topic of great debate in the literature. As we've just observed there are four primary sources of return in hedge funds: the risk-free rate, the manager's (traditional) beta, the manager's beta to additional and more exotic market risks, and the risk premiums earned for skillfully handling those risks. A fifth source of return could also be luck, which we consider as well.

A good way of evaluating manager skill and alpha is to see whether outperformance persists. Schneeweiss and his colleagues at CISDM[10] have found evidence of performance persistence but that it varies by strategy and that it is largely due to the exotic risks that hedge funds take and the premiums that they earn. The most recent studies on alpha in hedge fund performance further conclude that performance persistence is quantifiable and that it is mostly a by-product of these exotic betas and the passive risk premiums associated with them.

Based on a three-year study on hedge funds, Asness has found that the average hedge fund produces a positive alpha but that it isn't very strong.[11] Furthermore, he distinguishes the beta to exotic risks from true alpha while suggesting that these hedge fund–specific betas are indeed value-added propositions driven by manager skills. Asness goes on to say that these particular betas might be considered as part of a new "working definition of alpha."[12] Finally, by adding these particular hedge fund betas to traditional portfolios Asness argues that this strategy will increase portfolio Sharpe ratios, as we've shown throughout this book.

Three other recent studies have been able to quantify the contribution of hedge fund betas and manager alpha to overall hedge fund performance. Fung and Hsieh found that 80 percent of hedge fund returns were attributable to the unique beta risks that hedge funds face.[13] Kosowski, Naik, and Teo found that managers with superior alphas were not just lucky.[14] They found that the alpha differences they observed persisted over a three-year period. We return to their study in the next section because one of their other findings was that smaller funds created the largest amount of alpha. Finally, in a review of the literature by Ibbotson and Chen the authors found that in a 10-year study of the CSFB/Tremont database on a 9.1 percent net annual compound return (after accounting for various database biases), alpha was equal to +3.7 percent and beta, +5.4 percent.[15] Alpha, then, contributed about 41 percent to the total return.

THE SUPERIOR PERFORMANCE
OF NEWER MANAGERS

Having found that hedge fund manager skill and their exotic betas do contribute significantly to performance, what other factors contribute to higher risk-adjusted returns? *A slew of studies have concluded that newer and smaller funds have produced more alpha in comparison with their more seasoned peers.* Figure 11.1 summarizes three of the first studies conducted on the relative performance of newer funds.[16] The left side of Figure 11.1 shows a 700 basis point advantage between

FIGURE 11.1

The Superior Performance of Emerging Hedge Funds (1990–2000)

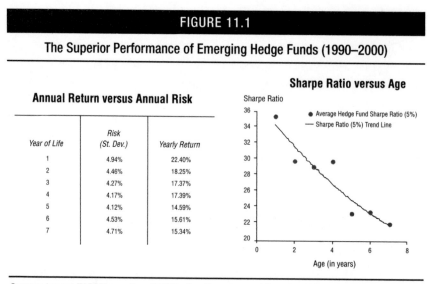

Annual Return versus Annual Risk

Year of Life	Risk (St. Dev.)	Yearly Return
1	4.94%	22.40%
2	4.46%	18.25%
3	4.27%	17.37%
4	4.17%	17.39%
5	4.12%	14.59%
6	4.53%	15.61%
7	4.71%	15.34%

Sources: Lazard, TASS/Tremont, and HFR in Jen, Heasman, and Boyatt, 2001.

funds in their first year versus year seven. Note that volatility as meas-ured by annualized standard deviation is relatively unchanged regard-less of the fund's year in business.

On the right side of Figure 11.1, the Sharpe ratio is presented for the period 1990–2000. From years one through seven, Sharpe ratios declined about 33 percent from 3.5 to 2.2, using a risk-free rate of 5 percent. Clearly, according to these studies, investing in newer hedge funds was not only more rewarding but also less risky than investing in older funds.

As we discussed in the opening chapter of this book, studies have concluded that survivor bias has a 2–3 percent impact on performance for most databases.[17] In fact, five different studies have concluded that survivor bias has a greater effect on newer funds than on more sea-soned ones in reducing performance.[18] This impact on performance has been estimated to be 2.9 percent in year one of existence declining to about 0.9 percent in year six. *Accordingly, Jen, Heasman, and Boyatt adjusted Figure 11.1 to reflect this negative impact on performance.*

Cross Border Capital's[19] landmark study found that even after ac-counting for survivor bias, funds in their first few years outperformed older funds by about 1,000 basis points per annum. Their analysis for the period 1994–2000 showed that after adjusting for survivor bias, funds in their first two years show the highest returns, a finding that has been replicated in many other studies.

Two additional studies cited earlier, Schneeweiss et al.[20] and Kosowski et al.,[21] also found that smaller funds outperformed either be-cause they took on more risk or because of manager skill. Nevertheless, superior performance diminishes over time either because of mean re-version and/or because of other factors that we will now explore. First, let's understand what factors contribute to the outperformance that we've seen. A number of explanations have been forwarded, some be-havioral and some trading and markets related.

Psychological and Behavioral Explanations

The behavioral and psychological hypotheses focus on fear and greed as key drivers of hedge fund manager performance. In the early going, most managers with smaller asset pools need to outperform in order to garner incentive fees and additional assets. Their very existence may depend on their ability to put up bigger numbers than their peers. Fear of failure, then, makes them work harder and perhaps smarter.

Later, as they've become successful, these same managers may focus more of their attention on asset accumulation and retention especially on the institutional side. With a 2 and 20 fee structure, a fund with $1 billion AUM generates $20 million a year in management fees. With 8 percent performance, the fund will add another $16 million in incentive fees. All in all, the manager has made revenues of $36 million for what would have been slightly below average performance in 2005!* Managers are disincentivized from taking risks with that type of cash flow. Imagine the temptations in a $5 billion or $10 billion fund.

Another nuance in the asset retention game is the impact of institutional investors on manager performance. Because institutions dislike surprises and often have modest performance expectations, managers adjust their trading techniques to dampen volatility. A fixed income arbitrage manager whom we were considering for investment told us that, given his new institutional clientele, he was toning down his performance targets from 20+ percent to around 12 percent. The higher number was off-putting to prospective institutional investors. To accommodate them he decided to tighten his risk controls and lower his leverage.

The final psychological explanation has been called "the Ferrari syndrome." This is an apt description of certain managers who become very wealthy and delegate the management of the business to others while they drive off in their new Ferraris. Clearly, when a manager starts being paid $50 million a year or more, the possibility of a midlife crisis looms large. Stories of managers learning to drive race cars, leaving their wives, or just simply turning to other pursuits abound in the hedge fund community. How prevalent is this syndrome? It's probably more urban legend than anything else, yet it's also probably true that most managers are hungrier and more driven early on and more protective of their wealth later in their fund's life cycle.

---

*The HFRI Fund-Weighted Composite Index was up more than 9 percent in 2005.

Market and Trading Explanations

Newer managers are generally smaller and therefore can exploit niche trading opportunities. Whether trading in illiquid bonds or small-cap stocks, the smaller managers can go where the behemoths cannot. If there is insufficient trading volume or not enough volatility to place money, larger funds typically go elsewhere leaving these markets to their more nimble and smaller peers. In fact, some enlightened managers simply close their funds to new investors at $150–200 million because to not do so would mean compromising future returns. Sitting in cash is generally not what hedge funds are about.

It is possible, then, that superior returns by younger managers may depend on their ability to find new markets or niches to exploit. This explanation would account for the explosive growth of the types of new investment ideas that we featured in Chapter 10. These new areas have generally been targeted by smaller start-up funds, some of whom have grown tremendously as demand for their product heightened. Today, for example, the direct financing space has a dedicated $1 billion hedge fund to go along with the many $50 million to $100 million players. We anticipate that as asset flows continue to pour into hedge funds, emerging managers will continue to pave the way in generating new investment ideas.

LESSONS LEARNED IN SELECTING
NEWER MANAGERS

Size Matters

While 900* to 1,000 new funds emerge in a given year,[22] some begin life with less than $30 million and others with $1 billion or more. Though having more money is great for the manager, investors should proceed with caution, given that performance may be inversely correlated with size. As research on the Class of 2003 indicates, there appears to be a

---

*900 in 2003, according to HFRI's 2005 Year-End Industry Report.

sweet spot investing in managers with $30 to $250 million AUM. We certainly think so. Our average manager has about $100 million when we make our initial investment.

In a series of studies conducted by Kirschner et al., managers from the Class of 2003, that is, funds that commenced operations during calendar 2003, were compared with relevant benchmarks on their performance in 2004 and 2005.[23] Our stratified sample of 167 managers was selected on the basis of AUM and primary strategy. Therefore, we eliminated multistrategy funds. Managers under $30 million were eliminated due to the likelihood of insufficient infrastructure and operational inadequacies. They represented about 50 percent of all managers in the Class of 2003. A smaller group of managers, those more than $250 million in AUM who represented about 15 percent of the Class of 2003, were eliminated as being already too large to be considered emerging. Another 15 percent were eliminated for being long-only, short-only, or unclassifiable. Our sample then represented about 20

TABLE 11.1		
Stratified Sample of the Class of 2003		
Strategy	**Average AUM**	**# of Funds**
Convertible Arbitrage	$103,868,379.89	9
CTA	$ 74,520,555.89	18
Distressed	$ 93,070,000.00	20
Equity Market Neutral	$ 97,696,000.00	10
Fixed Income	$ 87,971,042.16	19
Global Macro	$101,574,250.08	12
Equity Long/Short	$ 91,381,203.42	59
Merger Arbitrage	$105,000,000.00	1
Reg D	$171,000,000.00	1
Special Situations	$127,193,253.17	18
Average AUM	$105,327,468.46	
Total Number of Funds		167

Source: Mayer & Hoffman Capital Advisors. Data as of 12/31/04.

percent of the Class of 2003. Table 11.1 shows the breakdown of our sample by strategy and assets under management.

Figure 11.2 shows the performance of the group in 2004 and 2005 compared with the Credit Suisse/Tremont Investable Hedge Fund Index (CSFB) and the MSCI Equal-Weighted and Asset-Weighted noninvestable indices. We selected the CSFB and MSCI indices as proxies for the established hedge fund group because they primarily contain large managers with long track records. None of our emerging managers was found in either the CSFB or MSCI. CSFB was selected as a benchmark because it was the best-performing investable index over the two-year period 2004–2005.

Over the two-year period 1/1/2004–12/31/2005, the Class of 2003 widely outperformed the MSCI indices on a total return basis by 45 percent equal weighted and by over 60 percent asset weighted, and more than doubled the CSFB Investable Index. The performance advantage was significant in both years. For purposes of analyzing performance, closed managers' returns and AUMs (for the asset weightings) were calculated through the last month of their operations. Returns and AUMs were reported by either the managers or the management company.

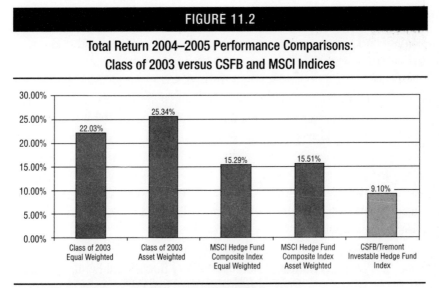

FIGURE 11.2

Total Return 2004–2005 Performance Comparisons:
Class of 2003 versus CSFB and MSCI Indices

Source: Mayer & Hoffman Capital Advisors, MSCI, and CSFB.

All New Funds Are Not Created Equal

We have found that the best new funds are started by existing fund families, by managers who have formed strategic relationships with existing funds so that they can use their infrastructures, and by managers experienced in a particular strategy who have graduated either from other successful shops or from brand-name proprietary desks. Following are three recent examples of new funds that typify these origin points. The first two are not identified, as Mayer & Hoffman Capital Advisors has invested in them.

Fund A: An Existing Fund Family Launches a New Fund.   Fund A focuses on distressed debt and equity opportunities within the emerging markets of Latin America, Eastern Europe, and Asia. The fund targets valuation driven instruments, particularly distressed debt and equity, with longer-term horizons. This fund launched in January 2004, while the management team has been in place since the early 1990s. The fund family manages two large funds already, specifically in emerging markets debt and equity strategies. Fund A returned in excess of 25 percent net of fees in 2004 and nearly that in 2005.

Fund B: New Fund with Strategic Relationship to Existing Established Fund.   Fund B is a multistrategy global commodities fund consisting of a relative value trading program (75 percent of positions) and a diverse portfolio of systematic commodities trading strategies (25 percent of positions). The relative value strategy generates returns primarily from inconsistencies that occur across the global commodity markets, particularly within the energy sector. The fund arbitrages the costs of transportation and storage, the marginal economics of production of related commodities, the calendar between delivery periods, and volatility. The infrastructure and trading platform is provided through a large fixed income arbitrage firm with which the fund has a strategic relationship.

Fund C: A Spin-Off from an Existing and Very Successful Fund.   Michael Zimmerman left his job as portfolio manager in the consumer sector at

Steve Cohen's megasuccessful SAC Capital Management to start Prentice Capital, an equity long/short hedge fund focused on the retail and consumer sectors. The fund is seeded with money from Cohen and Zimmerman. Prentice Capital, which launched in early 2005, primarily engages in ELS, but will also have up to one-third of the portfolio in Special Situations. These event-driven opportunities will include convertible debt and equity securities issued directly to the fund by distressed companies facing financial and operational challenges.

Beware of Managers with Long-Only Experience

Ever since Jeffrey Vinik and Michael Gordon left Fidelity Investments to start Vinik Asset Management, a host of long-only managers have followed in their footsteps, lured in part by the incentive fees that are part and parcel of the hedge fund business model. With these and related hopes and dreams, successful managers like John Muresianu (Fidelity) and John Schroer (Invesco) started their own hedge funds. What happened? While Vinik and Gordon were highly successful, Schroer and Muresianu closed their respective shops, Itros Capital and Lyceum Partners, after a few years.[24] We have seen many such situations. Without experience on the short side, long-only managers are pressed to learn on the job. And the market can be a harsh teacher.

DUE DILIGENCE BEST PRACTICES

While Chapter 13 delves deeply into general hedge fund due diligence best practices, here we address specific concerns related to vetting newer funds. Due diligence of new funds is somewhat more specialized than with older and more established funds. First, quantitative analysis is generally not useful on new funds since there aren't enough data points from which to draw conclusions. In general, if given only monthly returns, then two years of data are the minimum that quantitative analysts consider meaningful in making peer or benchmark comparisons. Of course, if the managers bring a track record from another fund and they can lay legitimate claim to it, that record can be subjected to analysis. But in the end, the qualitative and operational aspects of due diligence are by far the most important.

Qualitative Due Diligence

There are several areas of investigation that, in our view, deserve more attention than others. For the purposes of this chapter we focus on only three: career track record, quality of the team, and portfolio management and trading skills.

Career Track Record.   Interview the managers' former employers and colleagues. Find out if they had profit/loss responsibility with real money. Even more critical is to interview fellow managers. Finding out how they are viewed by competitors in the marketplace can give you insight into the managers' integrity and trading acumen. Often, when new managers spin off from existing funds, their former bosses will invest significant sums to get the fund started. This vote of confidence says a lot. When Goldman Sachs gave $300 million to Eric Mindich, the firm's youngest partner ever, it ensured that the fund Eton Park would launch on November 1, 2004, in style. Indeed, in his first year Mindich raised more than $3 billion and turned in a modest 5.3 percent return to investors. To his credit, Mindich followed up his slow start with an almost 10 percent gain in the early months of the second year.[25]

Quality of the Team.   The people risk, as venture capitalists call it, is substantial in hedge funds. Has there been a fracture in the founding partner group? Has there been litigation? Has the team worked together before, or is this the first time? Is each member of the team playing to his or her strengths and skill sets? Who is the CFO? Who is running operations and how much hedge fund experience do they have? How much of their net worth have they invested in the fund? As an investor, you should walk away from these interviews with a distinct feeling that the manager and team are decent people with high integrity who are on an aligned mission to succeed and make money. If you have any doubts or your gut tells you otherwise, *don't invest.*

Portfolio Management and Trading Skills.   While much can be written about this one topic, we will limit ourselves to one aspect: failure. We all know that different hedge fund strategies require differing trading and portfolio management skills. What is less well-known is that these skills are often learned as a result of making serious mistakes that caused the manager real pain, both psychic and financial. We like to ask about these mistakes. What happened? What did they learn? How did they change their risk controls? Did they make changes in their team? How were they transformed as traders or portfolio managers? Be sure to ask these questions. You want to know that your managers have truly learned from their errors. The best ones always do.

Attrition and Operational Due Diligence

In Chapter 1 we reviewed the studies on hedge fund attrition rates across all fund ages and concluded that 8.8 percent per year was a reasonable estimate.[26] What about new managers? Estimates of failure rates have been all over the map, ranging from 7.4 percent in year one[27] to more than 20 percent in year two.[28] Some studies have shown no significant difference in mortality rates between older and newer funds. For example, Brooks and Kat[29] found that 30 percent of new funds do not make it past three years due to poor performance, a mortality rate comparable to older funds over a comparable period. While it is true that some have found that poor-performing young funds drop out of databases at a higher rate than older managers,[30] it is also true that many younger funds drop out as soon as they hit their asset-gathering targets.[31] For example, some of the ultrasuccessful managers mentioned in this chapter have never registered with any database. A more recent report[32] shows that younger funds are more likely to fail in their first few years of operation. The review of 564 managers demonstrates that mortality rates reach their peak in year three (14.50 percent) and then diminish by more than 50 percent to 6.39 percent in year seven. Newer funds fail at a 10 percent rate at the end of year one, but then are more vulnerable in years two (14.14 percent), three (14.50 percent), and four (12.91 percent).

In our studies of the Class of 2003, none closed during 2004, only two closed and liquidated at year-end 2004, and another 12 had closed down by year-end 2005. The total failure rate for the group was 8.4 percent. Lipper-Tass and Hedgefund.net have published their estimated attrition rates for the hedge fund universe in 2005 at 10.5 percent and 6.6 percent, respectively. Table 11.2 breaks down the closures in the Class of 2003 by strategy. Note that Global Macro had the highest failure rate by far, even higher than that of Convertible Arbitrage.

What do we know about the variables that may be responsible for the demise of these young funds? A recent study[33] found that operational failures were the number one contributor followed by investment-related issues. More than 56 percent of the failed funds did so because of operational and business issues, while 38 percent reported the primary reason for failure as performance related. Four key operational issues were cited: false reporting of valuations; misappropriation of funds through theft; style drift; and inadequate technology, service providers, and human resources.

TABLE 11.2

Closures by Strategy as of Year-End 2005

Strategy	Class of 2003	Closed	Incomplete Data	In Business[a]
Convertible Arbitrage	9	2	0	7
Managed Futures[b]	19	2	0	17
Distressed	20	1	0	19
Equity Market Neutral	10	0	0	10
Event-Driven	20	1	0	19
Fixed Income Arbitrage	19	2	0	17
Global Macro	11	4	0	7
Equity Long/Short	59	2	0	57
Total	167	14	0	153

[a]As of 12/31/2005.
[b]In the original published study one manager was classified as Global Macro and is now Managed Futures.
Source: Mayer & Hoffman Capital Advisors.

At Mayer & Hoffman Capital Advisors, only one person can veto a potential investment at the Investment Committee: the Chief Risk Officer. It is his job to conduct operational due diligence on every potential fund, and he has developed a thorough evaluation process and accompanying scorecard that uncovers the types of operational issues mentioned earlier. In Chapter 13 we detail that process thoroughly.

CONCLUSION

Over the past five years numerous studies have concluded that newer hedge funds outperform their more seasoned peers in their first three years of existence. Our studies on the Class of 2003 validate this hypothesis. Despite investors' concerns that newer funds have significantly high attrition rates, our studies show that by eliminating the smallest funds from consideration, the remaining cohort's mortality rates are generally in line with those of the general hedge fund universe. We conclude that newer funds remain an important source of alpha for investors.

CHAPTER 12

Funds of Hedge Funds

INTRODUCTION

Funds of hedge funds (FOFs) are exactly what their name implies, pooled investment vehicles that invest in individual hedge funds. FOFs were first introduced into the United States in 1971 by Richard Elden and his team at the Chicago firm Grosvenor Capital Management, LP. They are, however, an invention of the Rothschild family in Europe who started the first FOF, Leveraged Capital Holdings (LCH), in 1969, as a primarily U.S.-focused Equity Long/Short fund. The fund still exists today and manages more than $1.3 billion.[1]

Over time, FOFs began to employ a strategy with greater diversification than LCH had. FOFs offered investors a chance to reduce their risk by investing across all hedge fund strategies and in funds that were relatively uncorrelated to one another. The resulting portfolios were expected to be less volatile than investments in either individual funds or in a single strategy (see Advantages section). Furthermore, if any one of the funds in a given FOF portfolio had a performance problem, the effect presumably could be offset or at least dampened by the performance of the other managers.[2]

Many of today's FOFs, especially those that cater to the institutional market, have become considerably more sophisticated in their risk controls so that they diversify away most of the risk of investing in single managers.[3] They also often have volatility levels equal to or below those of bonds. As returns tend to correlate with volatility, investors in low vol FOFs expect relatively stable returns, not high ones. They also expect very few down months or quarters, regardless of what equity markets are doing. In this way, conventional and very large FOFs, with standard deviations ranging from 2 percent to 4 percent, are competing for investment allocations that historically have gone to bonds. Remember that in Chapter 1 we showed that a 2005 survey of 300 large family offices revealed that allocations to hedge funds and FOFs exceeded those to bonds.

Other FOFs have emerged that offer greater upside potential with somewhat more risk by concentrating in a particular strategy like Event-Driven or in newer managers with shorter track records. Climbing up the risk ladder, we find FOFs that have somewhat more systematic risk in that they focus on a particular country or geographical region, or even on a particular strategy in a region. Potentially, the highest risk for investors is an FOF that uses significant leverage. FOFs are nearly as different from one another as are hedge funds, so investors are advised to read this chapter carefully. It could help them invest in the right FOF and, more importantly, to avoid a potentially disappointing one.

Multi-Strategy FOFs, the most popular type of vehicle, attempt to reduce the risk of investing in a single strategy. As Table 12.1 shows, the effectiveness of any one hedge fund strategy varies widely from year to year. Yesterday's winners like Convertible Arbitrage in 2000 can be tomorrow's worst performers (Convertible Arbitrage in 2005). Conversely, ELS funds were 2002's worst performers yet since then have once again been among the leaders. Lest we forget, investors in ELS from 1997–1999 must have thought they were in nirvana until the strategy became the poorest-performing group in 2001 and 2002. By investing in a Multi-Strategy FOF, institutional investors hope that the manager has the ability to avoid overly concentrating in hot strategies just when they may be poised to get cold. In fact, over the past five years, many investors who had been allocating directly to single managers have switched over to Multi-Strategy FOFs due to concerns over poor performance, blow-ups, or general risk management. For many institutional investors, then, these multimanager vehicles have become the preferred way to invest in hedge funds.

TABLE 12.1

Strategies Ranked in Order of Performance from Best to Worst

1996	1997	1998	1999	2000	2001	2002	2003	2004	2005*
Event Driven	Equity Hedge	Equity Hedge	Equity Hedge	Short Selling	Convertible Arbitrage	Short Selling	Distressed Securities	Distressed Securities	Equity Hedge
Equity Hedge	Event Driven	Managed Futures**	Event Driven	Equity Market Neutral	Distressed Securities	Managed Futures**	Event Driven	Event Driven	Distressed Securities
Distressed Securities	Global Macro	Equity Market Neutral	Global Macro	Convertible Arbitrage	Event Driven	Convertible Arbitrage	Managed Futures**	Equity Hedge	Short Selling
Managed Futures**	Distressed Securities	Convertible Arbitrage	Distressed Securities	Equity Hedge	Short Selling	Fixed Income Arbitrage	Convertible Arbitrage	Fixed Income Arbitrage	Event Driven
Convertible Arbitrage	Equity Market Neutral	Global Macro	Convertible Arbitrage	Event Driven	Global Macro	Global Macro	Global Macro	Global Macro	Managed Futures**
Equity Market Neutral	Convertible Arbitrage	Event Driven	Fixed Income Arbitrage	Managed Futures**	Equity Market Neutral	Distressed Securities	Equity Hedge	Managed Futures**	Equity Market Neutral
Fixed Income Arbitrage	Managed Futures**	Short Selling	Equity Market Neutral	Fixed Income Arbitrage	Fixed Income Arbitrage	Equity Market Neutral	Fixed Income Arbitrage	Equity Market Neutral	Global Macro
Global Macro	Fixed Income Arbitrage	Distressed Securities	Managed Futures**	Distressed Securities	Managed Futures**	Event Driven	Equity Market Neutral	Convertible Arbitrage	Fixed Income Arbitrage
Short Selling	Short Selling	Fixed Income Arbitrage	Short Selling	Global Macro	Equity Hedge	Equity Hedge	Short Selling	Short Selling	Convertible Arbitrage

*HFRI Indices as of December 31, 2005. *Sources:* HFRI and PerTrac. **CISDM CTA Index. *Source:* CISDM.org. *Additional source:* Mayer & Hoffman.

245

The FOF Industry

The FOF business has grown dramatically. From the fourth quarter of 2004 to the third quarter of 2005, assets under management jumped by $120 billion. Assets under management now total more than $650 billion as more than half of the assets in the hedge fund industry are managed through FOFs.[4] There are more than 2,000 FOFs worldwide, adjusting for clones, onshore/offshore duplications, multiple share classes, and multiple currencies in the same fund.[5] Yet, as is the case with single hedge funds, the majority of FOFs have less than $25 million under management.[6]

Who then have been the primary beneficiaries of these large capital inflows? The lion's share has gone to the largest single FOFs and the largest FOF families. The top 10 FOF groups led by megafirms Man and Permal[7] Investments controlled about 30 percent of FOF assets according to Watson Wyatt's last global survey.[8] And just as there are now more than 250 single manager funds with AUM more than $1 billion, there are about 80 FOFs with at least that level of assets. Table 12.2 lists the top 10 global individual FOFs by AUM as of 9/30/2005.[9]

Despite these massive inflows, the largest investor groups, the public and corporate pension plans, are still largely on the sidelines. Recent industry surveys report that only 1.6 percent of these assets[10]

TABLE 12.2	
The Top 10 Funds of Funds by AUM	
Permal Investment Holdings N.V.	$3,800,000,000
Selectinvest Arbitrage/Relative Value Ltd.	$3,300,000,000
Arden Strategic Advisers, L.P.	$3,010,500,000
Aurora Offshore Fund Ltd.	$2,853,700,000
GAM Diversity USD Class	$2,788,920,000
Green Way Arbitrage (Class C—USD)	$2,583,000,000
Coast Diversified Fund, Ltd.	$2,217,400,000
J.P. Morgan Multi-Strategy Fund, Ltd.	$2,104,980,000
Silver Creek Low Vol Strategies, L.P.	$2,100,000,000
Pentium Fund	$2,000,000,000

(roughly $90 billion) have found their way into hedge funds or FOFs, although commitments are increasing annually. Will the largest institutions continue the trend of investing primarily into the largest hedge funds and FOFs? We examine this question shortly.

PERFORMANCE

The HFRI FOF Composite Index has performed very well relative to other benchmarks, especially in the past five years. During this difficult period, it has returned about 6 percent per annum with a Sharpe ratio of 1.1. Equities, in contrast, struggled and had a negative Sharpe ratio.[11] Figure 12.1 shows that over the past five years the FOF Index is up more than 35 percent and has greatly outperformed the S&P 500 and the MSCI indices. In 2005, the HFRI FOF Composite outperformed both equities and bonds with a 7.4 percent return compared with a 3.0 percent return for the S&P 500 and a 2.4 percent return for the Lehman Index.

FIGURE 12.1

HFRI FOF Composite versus Benchmarks, Trailing Five Years

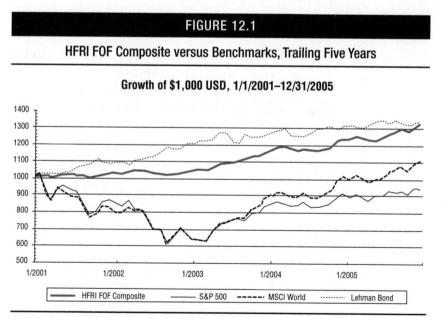

Growth of $1,000 USD, 1/1/2001–12/31/2005

Sources: Mayer & Hoffman Capital Advisors, HFRI, and PerTrac.

Clearly, FOFs have shown that they can help to preserve capital in bear markets. Witness 2001 and 2002: The S&P 500 was down 13 percent and then down more than 23 percent, respectively, while the average FOF was up 3 percent in 2001 and 1 percent in 2002.[12] Investing in and diversifying through FOFs was fortuitous for astute long-only investors.

Figure 12.1 also shows that the HFRI Fund-Weighted Composite Index, an equally weighted index of all funds in the HFRI database, returned more than 45 percent to investors over the past five years, averaging 8 percent per annum, about 2 percent per year better than FOFs.[13] FOF underperformance relative to hedge funds continues a long-term trend.

Figure 12.2, covering the period 1994–2005, shows that FOFs outperformed bonds and on an absolute basis nearly equaled global equities. However, as Table 1.1 showed, FOFs outperformed the S&P, the MSCI World, and Lehman indices on a risk-adjusted basis over the 12-year period.[14]

FIGURE 12.2

Cumulative Performance of HFRI FOF Composite Index versus Benchmarks

Growth of $1,000 USD, 1/1/1994–12/31/2005

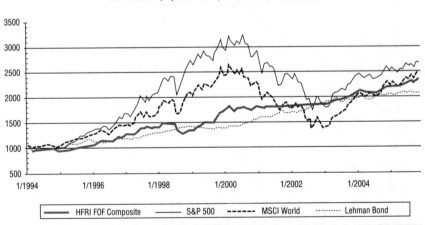

Sources: Mayer & Hoffman Capital Advisors, HFRI, and PerTrac.

Is FOF Performance Real or a Mirage?

In Chapter 1 we explored the methodological issues that plagued early hedge fund data collection. We concluded that survivor bias, backfill bias, and even attrition rates were now quantifiable and that some major database operators had rectified their procedures to eliminate these flaws. What about FOF performance? Does it have to overcome the same biases as single managers? According to several recent studies, the returns of FOFs are less susceptible for two reasons:

1. FOFs file audited performance reports that contain their managers' performance regardless of whether these managers report to databases.
2. As Fung and Hsieh in their review article put it, "Past investments in funds that ceased operation will also remain in the track record of the FOF. Consequently, the actual track record of a FOF has no survivorship bias."[15]

We agree with Fund and Asieh's assertion that FOFs' performance data found in databases is more accurate than that of single managers' performance reports.[16]

ADVANTAGES OF FOFS
VERSUS INDIVIDUAL FUNDS

As we saw earlier, FOFs have underperformed single manager hedge funds over time. This has been shown to be largely due to the extra layer of fees amounting to about 2 percent per year, which is then compounded.[17] FOFs charge an average of 1 percent to 1.25 percent annual management fees and an incentive fee that ranges from 5 percent to 15 percent sometimes subject to a hurdle rate. So why not invest directly in hedge funds and avoid paying the FOFs? As the two senior authors are FOF managers, we, of course, have an obvious bias. But this bias has been born out of a conviction that comes from years of investment experience.

Eldon Mayer is a pioneer in the hedge fund industry having designed and implemented, in 1968, the very first mutual fund hedge fund. That fund, The Hartwell and Campbell Leverage Fund, became one of the top 20 performing mutual funds of the decade 1970–1980.[18] Years later, he ran several outstanding hedge funds at his former company, Lynch & Mayer. After that, he helped start and consulted with a number of funds. And during this entire period he's been a hedge fund investor. What did he learn? Sourcing, selecting, and monitoring the performance of single funds are demanding and time-consuming tasks. They require travel, research, and ongoing risk management. He concluded, as did Sam Kirschner, that in today's market environment unless you have a professional research team coupled with good risk management professionals, it would be difficult to do a first-rate job investing directly.

Likewise, most institutional and family office investors do not have a dedicated hedge fund team whose sole mission is to source, select, and conduct due diligence on managers. Therefore, there are six primary advantages offered by FOFs that may offset the extra layer of fees charged. They are portfolio diversification, access to new or closed funds, reducing blow-up risk, professional due diligence, postselection monitoring, and risk management. As Chapter 13 is devoted entirely to best practices in conducting due diligence, postselection monitoring, and risk management, here we discuss only diversification, access to new managers, and reducing the risk of blow-ups.

Portfolio Diversification

Diversification is at the heart of Modern Portfolio Theory (MPT) and drives contemporary portfolio construction and optimization. For the institutional investor, there are two aspects to this crucial variable. The first is diversifying the investor's overall portfolio of stocks, bonds, and other alternatives like real estate and private equity by adding a portfolio of hedge funds or FOFs. Second, having decided to add FOFs, the investor looks for diversification within the FOF.

On a macro level, institutional investors can use FOFs to diversify their overall portfolios of stocks, bonds, and other alternative investments. Let's review data that we analyzed in Chapter 1. As you recall, a portfolio that was invested 50/50 in the MSCI World and Lehman Government/Credit Bond indices significantly underperformed and had higher volatility over the 12 year period, 1994–2005, than a second portfolio that was invested 40/40/20 with the 20 percent invested in a composite of hedge funds. The portfolio that included hedge funds outperformed the portfolio that did not by 105 bps per annum while enjoying lower volatility of about 50 bps per year. Our findings are consistent with those of CISDM.[19]

How then were these superior risk-adjusted returns achieved? Let's recall that in Chapter 1 we reviewed Sharpe's seminal work on systematic risk and asset-specific or idiosyncratic risk. To lower equity market risk for a given portfolio of assets by adding an FOF, for example, you must ensure that the FOF's beta to the market is sufficiently low. If we use the HFRI FOF Composite Index over the period 1/1/1994–12/31/2005, the correlation to the S&P 500 is 0.53.* The beta of the FOF Index is *0.21*. This low beta demonstrates the proposition that by adding an FOF with the preceding characteristics we are contributing to the lowering of the portfolio's market risk.

Multi-Strategy FOFs that want to keep their betas as low as possible to the market while not sacrificing the upside potential deliberately construct their portfolios by investing in most of the hedge fund strategies we've detailed in this book. As the reader has seen, a market environment that might benefit one strategy can make for rough sailing for another.

Many FOFs further diversify away domestic market risk by investing globally. Witness 2005. European and Asian bourses thrived, so hedge funds trading in those regions outperformed their counterparts that invested only in the United States. The FOFs that recognized the importance of international investing presumably benefited as well.

---

*See Table 2.1 for all the data.

Finally, FOFs provide portfolio diversification by investing in different asset classes, including commodities of all kinds, currencies, global bonds, and, of course, equities. As we showed in Chapter 3 on Managed Futures, adding this particular asset class reduces the risk of both hedge fund and traditional portfolios. For the professional investor these three levels of diversification provide several layers of protection that are not provided by investing in single managers.

How exactly does a Multi-Strategy FOF build its portfolio so that its beta to the market is relatively low and its volatility of returns is lower than equities, while still capturing significant upside? After identifying top-performing potential candidate funds from the desired strategies, asset classes, and geographic regions, the team will run pro forma calculations on the correlations of all hedge fund pairs on the list. The goal is to create a portfolio with as many low or even negative pair correlations as possible with an overall correlation between managers that is not statistically significant. In practice this means that certain funds might be eliminated because their correlations to the equity markets, for example, and to other managers in the portfolio from totally different strategies are too high. The FOF manager hopes that through this process his portfolio will not only withstand market corrections or shocks but also perform well in healthy market environments.

Figures 12.3 and 12.4, developed by Barry Wintner of Asset Alliance, show there are two efficient ways to lower volatility. Figure 12.3 demonstrates that a portfolio of only six funds each with relatively high standard deviations of 15 percent can still produce a portfolio with surprisingly low volatility. If pair correlations are reduced to about 20 percent, overall portfolio volatility drops to just above 8 percent.[20] Bear in mind that over the period just analyzed, the S&P 500 had an annualized standard deviation of 15.61 percent.

Wintner also demonstrated the effect of lowering the standard deviation of each fund on overall portfolio volatility versus the standard practice of adding many funds to the portfolio. Figure 12.4 illustrates this principle. As the reader can see, adding four additional funds is less powerful at reducing portfolio volatility than by simply selecting

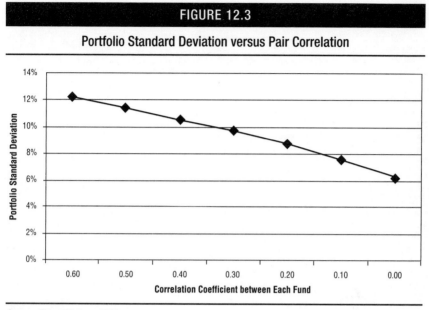

FIGURE 12.3

Portfolio Standard Deviation versus Pair Correlation

Source: Barry Wintner, 2001.

funds that are less volatile to begin with. A combination of lower individual standard deviations coupled with low pair correlations is the most effective way to produce lower portfolio volatility.[21]

Other studies have shown that a portfolio of only 15 to 20 hedge funds can diversify away 95 percent of the specific or idiosyncratic risk associated with single managers.[22] Despite these findings, many FOFs continue to build portfolios of 40 to 100 funds only to find that they have overdiversified and brought their performance results in line with the mean or an FOF Index. To combat this outcome, some FOFs will lever up their portfolios 200 percent or more in order to boost returns. As we described in Chapter 9, adding significant leverage is a risk that can bring a manager and his fund down. It is our view that a concentrated but diversified portfolio of well-selected funds with low pair correlations and reasonable individual standard

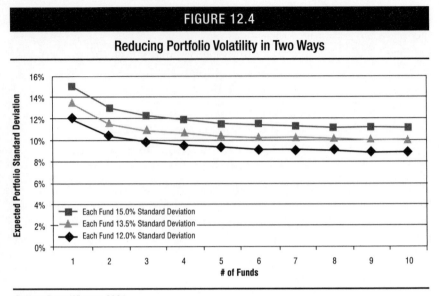

FIGURE 12.4

Reducing Portfolio Volatility in Two Ways

Source: Barry Wintner, 2001.

deviations (15 percent or so and under) is the best way to achieve above-average risk-adjusted returns.

Access to New and Closed Funds

At some early stage in their life cycle many good hedge funds close to new investors. FOFs often make side agreements or arrive at understandings with hedge funds that allow them to continue investing, usually up to agreed upon limits, even after closure to new investors. As a result, FOFs have a clear advantage over most direct hedge fund investors, certainly versus all but the largest and most sophisticated hedge fund investors such as the Yale Endowment.

As Chapter 11 showed, if an investor is looking for a performance boost, newer managers are a fertile place to look. The problem is how one identifies them in the first place. Many do not provide performance figures to databases. And, of course, they cannot advertise. Since 900 to 1,000 new hedge funds have been starting annually since 2003,[23] finding the best ones early on is difficult. In fact it's a full-time job. Once identified, they are often very difficult to analyze. Their track records are too short, many lack the operational resources necessary to meet the criteria of large institutions, many have an inexperienced CFO or COO or none at all, and/or they may lack an inexperienced auditor and/or administrator. As a result, it takes much more time and effort to perform due diligence on newer managers than it does on more mature hedge fund organizations that are definitely institutional in nature. By sourcing, conducting due diligence, and ultimately selecting the best newer managers for their portfolios, FOFs that specialize in this area can add significant value to their investors. In fact, despite the extra layer of fees top-performing FOFs have outperformed the average single manager hedge fund.

Reducing Blow-Up Risk

The final and perhaps most important advantage offered by FOFs is the minimizing of the possibility of major capital losses and "headline risk"* as a result of a fund blow-up. It has been our experience that because of the rigorous due diligence that today's FOFs conduct, they are less likely than most other investors to invest in such a fund. Secondly, because of the diversification they offer, even in the event of such a catastrophe, they still have a chance of remaining relatively unscathed. Finally, the chance of an FOF blowing up as compared with that of an individual fund is *de minimis*.

DISADVANTAGES OF FOFS

The first and primary objection to FOFs is invariably the extra layer of fees. It is in some senses a fair objection. Indeed, many endowments and large family offices avoid FOFs and invest directly. David

---

*See Chapter 13 for details.

Swensen, Yale's CIO, has built an enviable record by building a strong investment team in-house that has the capability to source managers, perform the necessary due diligence, identify the top performers, and carefully monitor them after selection. As of the most recent fiscal year, Swensen had allocated about 25 percent of Yale's $15 billion portfolio to hedge funds, his largest single allocation to any asset class.[24] However, building and managing such a team is very difficult, costly, and time-consuming and is therefore beyond the reach of most institutions.

But there are also other reasons besides fees that account for the relative underperformance of some FOFs: lack of understanding certain strategies; lack of best practices in due diligence; and a deliberate dampening of volatility (thus lowering returns) in order to gather assets.

We suspect that a number of FOF managers have underestimated the difficulty of selecting excellent hedge funds across strategies. To us, logic suggests that in order to do a good job in this quest, FOF managers and their teams must be expert in understanding and analyzing all of the major hedge fund strategies. That is a very tall order, indeed.

If an FOF manager does not conduct thorough due diligence, does not provide adequate risk management, and fails to monitor properly, then his performance results will suffer. In selecting an FOF, then, the more diligent one's research, the more likely it is that the investor will find an FOF that produces satisfactory performance equal to or better than the average hedge fund with lower risk. Chapter 13 helps you do just that.

Another reason for FOF underperformance is that with assets pouring in from institutional investors, there has been a reduction of the risks some FOFs are willing to take. In order to gather assets from these new and generally more conservative investors, many of the largest FOFs have been keeping vol down by avoiding new markets, new managers, and funds that might produce alpha but are inherently also riskier. We must ask, therefore, if institutions will at the end of the day demand better performance from their FOFs. We sincerely believe so. In 2005, institutions redeemed billions of dollars from giant FOFs that had underperformed, seeking better returns from substantially smaller FOFs that had shown better performance.

We close with a final word on FOF fees. If an investor has substantial resources, the time, the ability to engage in thorough hedge fund research, and the deep skill sets found in good investment teams, there are few if any reasons to invest in FOFs. But very few investors, including most family offices, corporate and public pension funds, smaller and medium-size university endowments, and private foundations have these skills, and most are unwilling to expend the financial resources to build a professional hedge fund selection and due diligence team, not to mention manage it. Thus, the question of FOF fees is for most investors a moot point.

MULTI-STRATEGY HEDGE FUNDS AND INVESTABLE INDICES

This chapter would not be complete without a discussion of two topical investment vehicles: multistrategy funds and investable hedge fund indices. There is considerable buzz these days about multistrategy funds as an alternative to funds of funds. We have yet to see a study that analyzes the performance of the one approach versus the other, but the multistrategy funds do not carry the extra fee burden, so they are certainly worth consideration. Their supposed advantage is the ability to reallocate resources quickly, whereas FOFs can typically do so only at month or quarter end, usually with at least 30 days notice. The FOF advantage is that they have the pick of the litter in any given strategy whereas the multistrategy manager is limited to in-house resources. The discussion will undoubtedly go on and on. For now the fee conscious will certainly prefer multistrategy funds, whereas performance-oriented investors will go wherever they find the greatest rewards net of fees.

The reader has, of course, noticed that we use the noninvestable HFRI indices as benchmarks for each strategy discussed. There are several other notable noninvestable indices including the indices at www.hedgefund.net, the CTA and other indices at CISDM.org, the Managed Futures and other indices at www.barclaysgrp.com, and the global indices including Asia and Latin America at www.eureka hedge.com, among others. They all employ widely different sampling techniques and contain substantially different hedge funds in their respective databases. Not surprisingly, then, their resultant performance numbers are sometimes quite different from one another. Appendix D contains the names and contact information for all major global hedge fund databases.

With this as context, Standard & Poor's in 2002 put its blue chip name on the first investable hedge fund index. Others, like Credit Suisse, MSCI, the Financial Times Stock Exchange (FTSE), and HFRI (called the HFRX indices) quickly followed suit and within a couple of years had garnered about $12 billion of institutional assets. Much has been written about them, both pro and con. The investable indices do offer good liquidity provisions, good capacity, and better transparency than standard FOFs. Their fees include sales and management fees but no incentive fees.

On the other hand, they are not true indices. A true index like the S&P 500 replicates the performance of all the securities in the class by first knowing what they are and then weighting them all according to market cap. None of the investable hedge fund indices can include all the funds, and they are therefore at best large stratified samples of a particular type of hedge fund: usually very large with a multiyear track record. In the S&P Index, for example, the average fund has $800 million AUM with at least a three-year track record.

But that objection would seem to beg the question, which is whether these investable products will outperform FOFs. Thus far, they have not. For example, the best-performing investable index, CSFB, returned 9.10 percent over the two-year period 2004–2005. Over that same period, the HFRI FOF Composite Index returned 14.68 percent.[25] As we noted, the hedge funds selected by the indices are typically very large with long established track records. Selecting these types of funds hasn't generally proven to be the best way to achieve good performance.[26]

Furthermore, there is a built-in selection bias in these indices that further limits the selection process. This phenomenon arises because the indices are limited to hedge funds that will sign separately managed account agreements with liquidity, valuation, and capacity agreements. These constraints may be unacceptable to top-performing funds that can attract investors who aren't as demanding and difficult to service. This adverse selection bias may ultimately lead to mediocre performance by these investable indices.

Matthew Hoffman

Partner and CIO
Mayer & Hoffman Capital Advisors, LLC

MATTHEW HOFFMAN HAS WATCHED THE EVOLUTION OF THE HEDGE FUND industry since his days as a derivatives trader in the 1980s. Hoffman is the chief investment officer and a managing member of the firm, two of whose other principals are the primary authors of this book.

After earning his M.B.A. at the University of Chicago in 1982, Hoffman went to work for the Chase Manhattan Bank in the interest rate and currency derivatives areas. He developed derivatives sales and trading businesses for the bank in both Tokyo and Hong Kong, later serving in a similar capacity for Merrill Lynch in London. In 1991 he moved to O'Connor Partners as a senior manager of the European equity derivatives business. Then prior to founding Mayer & Hoffman, he headed hedge fund manager research, selection, and portfolio creation at Credit Suisse Asset Management, which invested in hundreds of hedge funds. During his tenure, hedge fund assets grew from $700 million to more than $5 billion.

SK: *Matt, give us an overview, if you will, of the way the fund of funds vehicle has evolved.*

MH: Sure, funds of funds were really developed as a cautious exercise for institutional clients to get into the hedge fund markets. It was a very prudent way of getting hedge fund exposure early on, because it was a much lower-risk play than investing with a single manager. The diversification afforded by a portfolio of managers offered protection from potential bad performance by any one manager.

As more and more individuals, family offices, and, finally, institutions started placing money in this space, the firms that had created the early funds of funds grew phenomenally. That was yesterday. Today, the hedge fund market is more mature. The mystery is evaporating quickly and the danger has been downgraded to a simple risk that is understood to be no more dramatic and probably less so than what exists with any asset class.

The first-generation type of fund of funds still exists today: aggregations of managers chosen solely for low volatility. This model functions in much the same way as an investable index of hedge funds. But some FOFs represent an evolution of the model. These second-generation funds seek to aggregate managers that invest in either newer or less efficient markets in the hope that they will produce greater alpha. These FOF managers believe that these potentially higher returns are still protected on the downside by the inherent risk management tool of diversification that is the bulwark of the first-generation funds. Mayer & Hoffman Capital Advisors is one of these second-generation FOF firms.

SK: *What led you toward this second-generation approach?*

MH: One thing that I've always done throughout my career is to look for the next type of inefficient market. When I first started out in the early 1980s trading foreign exchange, it was a relatively novel concept. Most corporations weren't hedging their foreign exchange even though they were becoming global firms. But by the mid 1980s, the market had become more sophisticated and hedging more prevalent. Then the interest rate and currency swaps markets emerged and I began trading those.

By 1990, equity options emerged and I joined a team at O'Connor Partners that was instrumental in developing options trading globally. Yet there was a global inefficiency in pricing options; it was great. And it took almost 10 years to mature to the stage where there were multiple competitors pricing options on single stocks.

So you've got to find the next inefficiency and the next profit opportunity. Or you can sit back and wait for the next big thing to find you. And when it does, rest assured it will be too late for you to take real advantage of it. The market will already be efficient.

SK: *So part of that inefficiency is inevitably market volatility, right?*

MH: Right. And that's just what is lacking these days, across all the major asset classes. In 2004 and right through 2005, we've had unprecedented low levels of volatility globally. Everything that we've looked at, fixed income, foreign exchange, equities on a global basis, the volatilities have hit all-time lows.

The markets are oddly complacent. Look what happened when London was bombed, the terrorist attack in July 2005. Normally, markets would have gone haywire. But what happened? The market dropped for about an hour and then popped right back up again. The equity markets actually ended the day up. Fixed income had a negligible change. I mean, there was just no volatility. It was unbelievable. The managers we have in our portfolios are perfectly capable of dealing with volatility. Most traders have been trained through volatile markets. A lot of people would be doing significantly better if the market volatility wasn't so flat.

SK: *The lack of volatility is like the time in a prizefight between rounds. Nothing is going to happen until the bell rings, right? Until the next round of volatility emerges.*

MH: Right. And who is going to benefit the most from that? Of course, many people will benefit from a more active market, but who is going to benefit the most? We think we have a very good idea about that. We say it's going to be emerging managers. At Mayer & Hoffman we've built three FOFs specifically for that. Our funds select newer managers who have two essential attributes: one, a deep understanding of an inefficient market and the unique opportunities it presents and, two, the trading discipline to play their positions well.

SK: *Aren't the funds' capacity constrained because of the managers' niche markets?*

MH: We're always going to keep the sizes of our portfolios relatively small in comparison to other fund of funds so that we keep the performance advantage that a smaller fund gives us. Instead, as our funds close, we will create new portfolios with emerging managers. There are, after all, 900 to 1,000 new ones launching every year.

SK: *Please tell us about the firm's due diligence process.*

MH: We split the up-front effort into a sequence made up of three phases: qualitative, quantitative, and operational. The qualitative phase is where you learn all about the manager and his strategy. It's certainly not the best use of our time to call the names that the manager gave as references, people who are going to say only good things. We try to find sources that have no vested interest in the manager's business. One reference should be a previous employer. One should be a trader, someone who knows the manager and his market. And a third might be a service provider who has worked with the manager. We ask open-ended questions. We like to ask, "If you were to be critical of this person, what would you say?" And believe me, that's when they'll start telling you stories. If the guy doesn't play well with others in the sandbox, that's when we'll find out. We spend significant time in this phase because when we're investing in a business, we know we're investing in people.

Next comes the quantitative phase where we're looking at peer group comparisons, risk control policies, analytics relating to the performance, and the types of exposures they're willing to take. We look at the way they hedge to protect their downside.

Finally comes operational due diligence. If they made it past the first two steps, we check out the firm's auditor, the administrator, and the prime broker. We look at their audits, Uniform Application for Investment Adviser Registration (ADV), everything. We make sure that everything is properly signed off. A lot of other firms may not do quite as much on this phase. But with newer managers we think it's crucial. For example, if there's a personal connection between the audit firm and the CFO or any significant person on the hedge fund side, we'd probably eliminate them for that reason alone. There are too many potential conflicts of interest. Likewise, if the CFO is related to any of the decision makers on the trading side, we don't like that, either. We eliminated an otherwise interesting manager where the trader had hired his brother-in-law to be the CFO. I'm not saying that they were dishonest. It's just that the potential conflict is there.

After a manager passes all three steps, Mayer & Hoffman may invest in him. However, the firm's due diligence does not stop there. Our postselection monitoring process is very stringent as well.

SK: *Any other exciting market opportunities that our readers should look at?*

MH: Emerging managers are hungry, work hard, and are exploring new avenues. For example, there are newly developing markets in carbon dioxide trading, pollution control credits, and the direct lending space. These are not yet efficient markets and therefore the hedge fund managers who set up in them now could make significant profits in the years ahead. We are looking very closely at these types of managers.

CHAPTER 13

Due Diligence Best Practices

IN THE HEDGE FUND INDUSTRY, RIGOROUS DUE DILIGENCE HAS TRADI-tionally been a subject that has been taken for granted as an essential precondition for investing, yet many investors don't really know the nuts and bolts of the process. Instead, investors have focused on the dramatic stories that surround the industry: from the soaring of Soros to the crashing of LTCM, and from the spectacular gains of Eddie Lampert to the devastating losses suffered by Bayou's investors. The principal authors, like other industry insiders, are hard-pressed to explain this lack of thoroughness, knowing that without rigorous due diligence one may as well be shooting dice.

Before we dig into our overview of what good due diligence really is, a word about what it is not. A great many investors are persuaded to pick a manager through capital introduction events (organized by prime brokers to introduce potential investors to managers who custody or trade with the bank), an industry conference presentation, or the word of a trusted friend. This is not due diligence.

Up until now, this book has detailed the various hedge fund strategies, their trading styles, their advantages and disadvantages, and how they fit into portfolios of both traditional and alternative investments. All of that knowledge is worthless unless the investor knows how to select the right managers. Without that skill, the investor may end up with underperformers or even blow-ups. Selecting from among the 8,000 or so single managers and more than 2,000 FOFs is at the very heart of successful investing. Therefore, this is the most important chapter of the book.

Locating a manager via enlightened selection can result only from a systematic, detailed, and thorough investigation. There is no mystery to it. Done properly, it can take 50 person-hours or more to judge an individual fund. And, after all that effort, the result will often be a failing grade. Does this mean that before allocating dollar one, every potential hedge fund investor must first allocate untold hours of research? Not necessarily. But every potential hedge fund investor should make sure that his or her consultant or fund of funds has done this painstaking work. If not, walk away and find the adviser who believes in doing the requisite homework. That's the person or firm who stands the best chance of helping you preserve and grow your capital. This chapter enables you to ask all the right questions to ensure that your money or that of your institution is prudently managed.

We've asked two savvy professionals, Terry Bilkey and Ron Panzier, to help guide us through the process. Terry Bilkey, CFA, is the founder of BilkeyKatz Investment Consultants in Pittsburgh, Pennsylvania, and has more than 25 years experience advising institutional clients on manager selection and portfolio construction. Terry is featured in the interview at the end of the chapter. Ron Panzier, CFA, FRM, is chief risk officer and CFO at Mayer & Hoffman Capital Advisors, LLC, and a member of the firm's investment committee.* Ron has also been on the receiving end of intense due diligence by institutional investors while serving as CFO at several single manager hedge funds during his 17-year career in the industry.

This chapter walks you through a complete due diligence process for selecting either single managers or FOFs that includes the following sequence of steps:

1. Sourcing and identifying candidate managers.
2. Qualitative analysis.
3. Quantitative analysis.
4. Operational analysis.
5. Postselection monitoring.

---

*Ron Panzier co-authored this chapter.

Each stage is detailed in three important ways: First, we describe the process; next, we list some of the most important questions to be asked or information to be covered during this step, and, finally, we refer you either to a table in that section or to the appropriate appendix that lists all the questions and requests for information that are pertinent to that stage. By the time you've studied this chapter you will understand the underpinnings of a complete due diligence process. In this manner, we have endeavored to make this as readable as possible. In the end, however, if at times wading through the writing mirrors the laborious nature of the due diligence process, so be it. Like training for a long race or finishing a Ph.D., it's not necessarily fun, but it's what you have to do to succeed.

STEP ONE: SOURCING AND IDENTIFYING CANDIDATE MANAGERS

This step alone could fill at least a chapter if not the better part of a book. For great FOFs, sourcing, identifying, and gaining access to managers that can generate alpha is at the heart of their value proposition. Most investors, however, do not have a worldwide network of industry contacts to refer potential fund candidates. For most investors, therefore, other sources like marketing firms, conference presentations, prime brokers, or trusted friends or consultants, while not substituting for due diligence are valid ways of identifying potential managers or funds. The operative word here is *potential*. In step one you begin by deciding if a particular hedge fund strategy or fund of funds might be a good fit for your portfolio.

For example, perhaps you've done a database search looking for an ELS Emerging Markets manager. Or you've heard from a fund in which you're invested that it is spinning out a new fund in a similar strategy led by the head trader. You've scanned the marketing materials from the top-performing funds in the strategy and have completed a small peer group and benchmarking study to identify the best risk/adjusted and absolute performers. You've identified one fund in particular that started in January 2003 and has had a terrific run. He's up 209 percent through October 2005.

Your next move is to learn more about the manager. This is often done by conducting a short interview with the manager on the phone in order to make an initial qualitative assessment as well as to request documentation that will be used later when performing more in-depth due diligence. If a manager is not dismissed from consideration at this point, comprehensive due diligence can begin.

STEP TWO: QUALITATIVE ANALYSIS

This is the most important step in due diligence and it contains three major components: an evaluation of the manager and his team as people and as professionals; a clear understanding of the strategy, investment process, and portfolio; and thorough reference and background checks on the principals. A good place to begin is with a Due Diligence Questionnaire (DDQ). There is nothing proprietary about a DDQ. The DDQ for hedge funds has been refined for more than 20 years and good examples have also been published by the AIMA[1] and in John Mauldin's excellent book *Bull's Eye Investing.*[2] Every fund manager expects to receive these questionnaires from potential investors and they should be equipped to respond promptly. In many cases, a fund will simply send you an existing document that they have drafted in response to the questions that are frequently asked of them. If some of your questions do not fall into this category, persevere until they, too, are answered. The answers to the questions posed in the DDQ will run about 30 pages or more not including additional required documentation.

The Due Diligence Questionnaire covers the following areas:

- The history, the principals, and ownership structure of the firm.
- Compliance issues.
- Fund details, provisions, performance, and service providers.
- Investment strategy.
- Risk management.
- Investor service/reporting.
- Business continuity.

Look carefully at this list. Note that the DDQ covers every major aspect of the firm's life. In fact, reviewing the firm's answers to the DDQ will become increasingly important if you move ahead with steps two, three, and four. That's because you will be asking the firm's principals many of these same questions over and over again as you dig deeper into each of the areas. And you will be looking for discrepancies, inconsistencies, half-truths, and outright deceptions in the process.

As mentioned earlier, your candidate manager will also be asked to provide all pertinent fund documentation detailing the terms and conditions of investing. For domestic U.S. funds, for example, these documents will include a subscription document, a partnership agreement, and a private placement or offering memorandum that explains the lockup and redemption conditions, fees, high-water mark provision if any, NAV pricing and monthly reporting, degree of leverage used, names of the principals, potential conflicts of interest, any litigation or arbitration proceedings involving the firm or its principals, and all other terms and conditions of investing in the fund.

Review the fund documentation and compare the answers you will get from the DDQ to the terms and provisions in the fund documents. For example, if there is a discrepancy between them on redemption provisions or potential conflicts of interest, there may be a big problem lurking with this firm. You could pass on the manager for one of these discrepancies alone. If you discover that the discrepancy is minor, you might prepare a second round of questions and, if answered to your satisfaction, you can choose to move forward. If you choose to throw the fish back into the lake, be content that you've done a good day's work in eliminating a manager. This is the proper attitude to have in conducting due diligence; that is, your first instinct should be to say, "No, we'll pass." Only the best firms and the best managers, be they new or more established, should succeed in completing the marathon that is due diligence.

Often, the first face-to-face contact with a manager takes place with a presentation at our offices. After all, we're the prospective investors.

But if we're interested after that, there is no substitute for meeting the manager and his team in their office.*

After the meetings are over, Mayer & Hoffman due diligence team members use a qualitative scorecard with more than 30 key questions that helps them rate the answers they heard and the impressions they got on a five-point modified Likert Scale. The results are scored, tabulated, and evaluated. We believe it is a good idea that all team members who have had significant contact with a manager prepare a scorecard. Dramatic differences in how team members rank a manager generate our best internal discussions. Before you move to the next section, flip to Appendix B and review the items presented in the Qualitative Scorecard.

Evaluating Managers and Their Teams

You want to get a feel for the managers, their leadership capabilities, and their passion. In essence, you're getting to know them, the investment team, and other principals as real people. Observe how well the investment team works together in building the portfolio. Whenever possible we try to invest with funds where the investment team has worked together in the past. In addition to asking questions that elicit factual answers, ask questions that elicit opinion and feeling, such as:

- What do you love about what you do?
- How do you delegate within your firm?
- To what degree are others in your firm responsible and empowered?
- What do you think your team members would say about working at your firm?
- How are the members of the investment team compensated?
- Do managers seem so arrogant that they might create a culture of frequent staff turnover?
- Are they good listeners?

---

*While we are presenting the process in a linear and structured manner, in reality, the qualitatively focused meetings are semistructured, guided by lists of questions on key topics but always ready to veer off into spirited and hopefully enlightening conversations.

The Strategy, Investment Process, and Portfolio Review

This component of the Qualitative Analysis is at the heart of proper due diligence. Understanding the fund's investment strategy and how it is implemented in buy–sell decisions, its strengths and weaknesses, when it's likely to do well and when it's not, is a sine qua non of investing. If the manager can't clearly articulate the answers to these questions or you and/or your consultant can't understand him, *don't invest*. It's that simple.

There are many reasons for this caution but we'll cite two. First, a clear articulation of strategy and process suggests that the manager understands where his returns come from and therefore might be able to replicate them in the future. His clarity also suggests that he understands the limitations of his approach and that he has instituted rigorous risk management procedures, including sell disciplines, into the investment process.

Second, if you don't understand how the manager makes money, what will happen when the market goes against him? Will you panic and redeem precisely at the wrong time because you didn't understand, for example, that in a low volatility environment, his strategy lags behind? Or that his trading strategy while enjoying significant upside volatility can also suffer from punishing drawdowns? Later in this chapter we critically examine the latter type of manager.

The manager's investment philosophy can be discerned by asking questions like:

- What leads you to buy?
- Under what conditions do you sell?
- What do you do when an investment appreciates substantially?
- Do you ride your winners or do you take chips off the table?
- How do you size your positions?
- Are your historical returns repeatable? Why?
- How do you hedge?
- Do you profit on both the long and short side?
- How do you generate your investment ideas?
- Are they proprietary?
- If appropriate to the strategy, do you have proprietary deal flow and how?

These very same questions will be asked again by the due diligence team when it examines the manager's portfolio. Team members will be looking for two attributes as they determine how the manager's philosophy and process are implemented in the portfolio. These attributes are conviction and consistency.

Reviewing the portfolio of the fund is the next step of this evaluation. First, you want to determine the exact sources of the fund's return history. To accomplish this goal you will want to know the answers to the following questions:

- Did the manager make money on the short book?
- How did he make his money when he had a big year?
- Was it one big play that made the year? Is that bet repeatable or was it a fluke?
- What have been his worst trades?
- What have been his worst drawdowns?
- What went wrong?
- Are they likely to happen again? If so, how is the manager likely to handle them differently?
- What changed in his sell discipline or his risk management procedures as a result of these failure experiences?
- What have the manager and his team learned from these setbacks?

The answers to the last seven questions will tell you a lot about the manager and the team. "Everybody makes mistakes," says Ron Panzier. "I actually prefer to see a manager who has gone through a tough period in their past performance. That manager went through hell during that time and he suffered. He's likely to take more risks than similar managers in his space who *have not* experienced losses. The manager who frightens me is the one who has no fear and therefore believes that he has suspended the basic investment paradigm of risk and return. So seeing a manager with a terrible down month or a bad drawdown in itself can actually be a good thing because if he survives that, that's when he grows as an investor and as a person."

Reviewing the manager's top 10 positions in the portfolio is the granular way of evaluating the manager's conviction and consistency of approach. Those attributes should be evident as the manager discusses each of his holdings and why he put them into the portfolio. Remember the questions we listed earlier on sizing positions, sell disciplines, and taking chips off the table? Here is where you will see if the manager has implemented what he truly believes in. Any disconnect or misalignment between the portfolio holdings and the manager's articulation of strategy and process is cause for grave concern.

The due diligence team should be able to come away from these discussions with the answers to the following questions: "Does the manager have conviction?" and "Does he have consistency of approach?" Anything less than an unequivocal yes to both questions should be cause for rejection.

A final type of question put to potential managers falls under the heading Event Risk. You want to get a sense of how they and their portfolios will react to major world/market events by asking questions such as:

- What if there is another large-scale terrorist attack?
- What if there is an equity market panic or a bond collapse?
- What if there is a currency crisis or sudden drying up of liquidity?
- What if there is a sudden superspike in commodity or energy prices?

If they seem unconcerned about these types of exogenous events, then you ought to worry. Remember that in Chapter 6 we interviewed Marc Lasry, the great Distressed securities investor, and he told us that his greatest fear is of exogenous events and that they seem to be occurring with greater frequency.

References and Background Checks

The manager's reference list is a starting point but with limited utility. As we said in Chapter 11, reference checking must encompass the professional life of the manager. Across this spectrum, a truer picture of the manager will emerge. Therefore, speak to colleagues, former colleagues, employees, clients, other traders, and service providers. Ask them open-ended questions such as:

- How does this person handle tough times?
- If you were going to be critical of this person, what would you say?
- Did you (or do you) enjoy doing business with this person?
- Does this person seem like a good decision maker to you? Why?
- Does he play well in the sandbox? (Matthew Hoffman's favorite question for traders).

Equally important are background checks on the principals. Some investors hire specialty service providers to provide these checks, some hire due diligence specialists who include background checks as part of their package,[3] and some do it themselves. Bankruptcies, lawsuits, criminal records, or NASD problems can show up in the principals' records. Amazingly, some investors skip over this critical step. In the interview with Terry Bilkey you will hear how a seasoned consultant underscores the importance of reference and background checks, especially in the context of Bayou's shutdown.

Ron Panzier sums up the bottom line of this phase. "The general impression we get from the qualitative phase," says Panzier, "gets a very, very high weighting in our decision process. What tends to happen is that if you really like and really believe in the manager, you've sort of made your decision: 'This is somebody we want.' The subsequent steps in due diligence are basically looking for reasons why we should not select this manager. Nonetheless, you have to steel yourself for the inevitable disappointments that may result from performing these additional steps."

Of course, the majority of potential managers do not make it past this phase, but those who do can be escalated to step three.

STEP THREE: QUANTITATIVE ANALYSIS

When it comes to examining past performance many academics believe it is a meaningless exercise, that mean reversion is inevitable, and that investors who make decisions solely based on a manager's past results will find themselves endlessly chasing performance resulting in mediocre returns (see our full discussion in Chapter 11).* Obviously, a degree of quantitative analysis has already been done in step one particularly if the sourcing of a manager is a result of running a quantitative screen, but the real number crunching takes place after the qualitative analysis.

Remember the hypothetical ELS emerging markets manager we found who was up 209 percent from 1/1/2003–10/31/2005? Clearly this manager has produced extraordinarily high returns and it is easy to be seduced by such results, as the mind naturally extrapolates continued outsized performance into the future. Now let's take a look at Table 13.1, which contains the fund's monthly numbers since inception.

This manager has a relatively short track record so there aren't many data points. Nevertheless, in the format that Table 13.1 presents it is virtually impossible to ascertain anything meaningful no matter how many data points would have been given. Monthly numbers without additional analysis don't by themselves tell us much. Additionally, even when managers do present performance analytics, they tend to include only those analytics that cast their past performance in a favorable light. Sometimes their performance summaries even contain calculation errors. Equally bad is the manager who is proud of the fact that the fund is uncorrelated to a particular index (say the S&P 500) and then prepares analytics comparing the fund's risk-adjusted

---

*While we generally agree with many of those sentiments, examining a manager's past returns can still be valuable, if done properly. Intuitively it is a bad idea to ignore any piece of information that is available that might be useful in making a good decision. At the end of the day, the due diligence professional has at least (1) performed comprehensive interviews, (2) reviewed reams of documents, (3) done extensive background checks, and (4) made judgments based on the preceding. Now how has the manager actually performed? Perhaps a reality check is in order. Given that we know how the markets as well as other managers have performed in the past, an examination of a manager's past performance in comparison to his peers and benchmarks seems prudent.

TABLE 13.1			
ELS Emerging Market Fund Monthly Returns			
	2003	**2004**	**2005**
January	5.59%	10.18%	2.22%
February	1.15%	3.24%	8.20%
March	−6.12%	3.05%	−4.57%
April	6.45%	−9.57%	−1.44%
May	20.06%	−3.70%	−1.88%
June	11.15%	−0.67%	2.32%
July	2.26%	−4.39%	4.81%
August	21.53%	−1.30%	0.77%
September	21.62%	4.37%	5.54%
October	8.54%	−1.21%	−5.09%
November	5.32%	9.91%	
December	3.94%	0.71%	

returns to the S&P 500! What's wrong with that? Simply that unless the fund is highly correlated to a particular index, alpha and/or beta scores using that index as the independent variable are absolutely meaningless.

Therefore, the first step when doing quantitative analysis is taking the raw numbers given to you and standardizing them by inputting them into your model. You will then be able to examine meaningful and correctly calculated analytics. Do not confuse the need to standardize the data to mean that one size fits all. Rather, looking at data in a comfortable, familiar manner allows you to be more efficient with your time and helps eliminate background noise. Depending on a particular manager's strategy, you will hone in on particular areas and pay less attention to others.

The first thing that you might ask yourself is: How consistent have the returns been over time? In this case, as Table 13.1 clearly shows, the manager's returns are trending lower.

Next, let's calculate the fund's risk-adjusted returns. For that we'll use the Sharpe ratio and another measure called the Sortino ratio.[4] For this fund, the Sharpe ratio is *1.84.* The manager's Sharpe ratio is very high, despite the outsized standard deviation of 25.6 percent because the annualized performance is nearly 49 percent. But what about the downside risk?

To measure downside risk, statisticians use the Sortino ratio. The Sortino is similar to the Sharpe ratio except that unlike the Sharpe it does not penalize a fund for upside volatility and therefore uses only the downside deviation for the denominator. The Sortino ratio is calculated by:

(annualized return of fund – risk-free rate)/downside deviation)

In this case the Sortino ratio is

$$(48.9\% - 1.7\%)/8.8\% = 5.38$$

The Sharpe ratio, of course, uses the standard deviation (both upside and downside) of performance. Both utilize the fund's performance minus the risk-free rate as the numerator.* If we say that the standard deviation is analogous to the total cholesterol score, then the Sortino ratio tells us only about the "LDL" score, that is, the bad cholesterol. A high Sortino means little downside volatility. For this particular manager even though they had a very high "total cholesterol score" (standard deviation equal to 25.6 percent), it is clear that their HDL (upside volatility) was a significant component of that overall number. The higher the Sortino is relative to the Sharpe, the more one can put the volatility in perspective. The fact that our ELS fund's Sortino is three times higher than the Sharpe tells us that most of the volatility of performance has been to the upside.

---

*Instead of the risk-free rate, some analysts will use zero or some other defined return bogey.

A third component of the analysis is looking at the fund's worst months. Here we find that the:

- Worst month was –9.6 percent.
- Maximum drawdown, a measurement of the largest peak to valley performance period, was from April 2004–August 2004 when the fund went down 18.4 percent.
- Number of months to recover from the maximum drawdown was from September 2004–February 2005 (six months).

We understand that it is human nature to look back on past performance records and mentally discount rough patches that occur within a record of fantastic performance. However, by systematically examining drawdowns, you are forced to confront these poor periods. Prospective investors need to accept that in the absence of a change in risk management procedures (which can be difficult to verify), a manager's risk tolerance is reflected in such drawdowns. Therefore, investors need to be honest with themselves about whether they are emotionally prepared to handle these types of drawdowns, especially if they occur soon after investment.

A fourth part of the analysis involves two important comparisons to the fund's benchmark. We now examine *Up Capture* and *Down Capture* relative to the HFRI Emerging Markets Index, a benchmark to which the fund is highly correlated.

- *Up Capture* versus benchmark (HFRI Emerging Markets Index) is calculated by the total return of fund when benchmark is positive/total return of benchmark when positive, which in this case is equal to 315.3 percent/107.8 percent = *2.93*.
- *Down Capture* versus benchmark is calculated by the total return of fund when benchmark is negative/total return of benchmark when negative, which in this case is equal to – 25.7 percent/–10.2 percent = *2.53*.

When the HFRI Emerging Markets Index went up, this fund really went up. In fact, it went up almost three times the Index. Likewise, when the Index went down, this fund went down at a rate 2.5 times that of the

Index. This is consistent with the results from the regression analysis of the returns versus the Index. This fund has a beta to the HFRI Index of 2.5 and an annualized alpha of –10 percent. What these numbers imply is that over the life of the fund, manager skill has not added value, and returns are merely a reflection of significant leverage. An argument could be made, though, that this manager displays modest timing skill.

Our final set of analyses will require some additional explanation. Research into the distribution of hedge fund returns has revealed that they are not normally distributed like IQ or SAT scores (the bell-shaped curve).[5] The reason for this abnormal distribution, commonly referred to as the "optionality of hedge fund returns," stems primarily from the fact that hedge fund managers use leverage, derivatives, and short positions that distort their returns relative to the underlying asset class returns (like stocks) both to the upside and to the downside. As a result, many researchers[6] have concluded that traditional measures such as standard deviation and Sharpe and Sortino ratios that assume a normal distribution of returns are not entirely appropriate when evaluating hedge fund performance.

Other statistical measures are therefore being used to analyze the asymmetric patterns of hedge fund performance. The first of these tools is *skewness*. Positive skewness indicates a distribution with an asymmetric tail reaching out toward the right; that is, there are more frequent positive values than there are negative values.* Negative skewness means a distribution with an asymmetric tail extending toward the left, that is, more frequent negative values than positive ones. You can guess which type of hedge fund return pattern you would prefer. Let's examine our fund's degree of skewness: The degree of asymmetry of the fund's monthly returns around the mean is equal to *0.9*, a very positive outcome.

A second measure called *kurtosis*, refers to the probability of extreme returns in either direction sometimes called "fat tails." A positive kurtosis indicates that the return distribution of a fund has greater

---

*Another way of thinking about this is when the mean value of a data set is greater than its median value, then the data set is positively skewed.

likelihood to be in the tails of the distribution than would be expected by a normal distribution. A hedge fund with positive kurtosis in its return pattern would indicate that it is likely to have outlier events either positive and/or negative. A negative kurtosis would indicate that the probability of outlier events is even less than in a normal distribution. If you're looking for a manager (such as this one) that can put up big numbers but may experience a painful drawdown on the way to more big numbers, find a distribution pattern of returns skewed to the right (positive) with a positive kurtosis. Let's examine our fund's degree of kurtosis. Kurtosis, sometimes referred to as excess kurtosis, is a measure of the "fatness" of tails in the fund's distribution pattern of monthly returns and in this case is equal to 1.0, also a very favorable number.

They say a picture is worth a thousand words. Figure 13.1 illustrates the fund's monthly return distribution. You can see the positive skewness and kurtosis that we've been talking about. If you find a manager with a return pattern that looks like the one shown in Figure 13.1, be prepared for a wild ride.

In response to the problems posed by the nonnormal distributions of hedge funds, analysts have turned to value at risk (VaR) as a way of

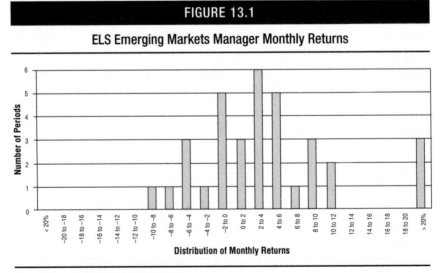

FIGURE 13.1

ELS Emerging Markets Manager Monthly Returns

Source: Mayer & Hoffman Capital Advisors.

quantifying risk exposures in portfolios. VaR, for our hypothetical ELS fund, is:

30 day VaR of 8% at the 95% confidence level

This means that the model is stating there is a 95 percent probability that over the next 30 days the value of our manager's portfolio will not go down by more than 8 percent. Or stated another way, there is only a 5 percent chance that the portfolio will lose more than 8 percent in the next 30 days. While it is beyond the scope of this book to discuss in detail how VaR is calculated, when examining hedge fund returns there are two primary calculation methods. The first, as espoused by Riskmetrics, is referred to as position-based risk management. It requires the user to have access to all the underlying positions of the particular hedge fund (full transparency). Assuming that the information is available, Riskmetrics' proprietary model will calculate the VaR of the hedge fund based on an analysis of each position held by the fund.

As one would expect, Riskmetrics posits that their method is the most accurate way of measuring risk. Intuitively, this makes sense. Nonetheless, an intriguing alternative to position-based analysis is performance-based analysis utilized by Riskdata. The inputs to their model are a hedge fund's historical performance. This can be in the form of daily, weekly, or even monthly returns. Using a sophisticated factor model, Riskdata provides the analyst with estimates of a fund's risk. Riskdata contends that by analyzing past performance you are able to capture the behavioral aspects of the hedge fund manager, which can't be done by looking at a static portfolio. We believe both methods are excellent ways of properly managing the risk of investing in hedge funds.

An even newer measure of performance is the Omega ratio.[7] Omega has been introduced as a way of addressing the shortcomings of traditional mean/variance analysis. Omega is intended to calculate the probability of returns being above a defined threshold. Although this analytic has potentially interesting applications, it is currently not being widely used in practice.

Before we conclude the topic of examining past performance, we need to look at one more variable and that is determining which measurement period is the appropriate one for review. The time frame selected can alter the outcome of your analysis. It may seem obvious that for this ELS emerging manager you'd want to review the fund's entire history since it consists of only 34 months. However, this manager claims to have completely revamped his risk management procedures after suffering losses during the summer of 2004. The result of these changes is that the fund on a going forward basis should be less risky. Since there is no such thing as a free lunch, one would expect returns to come down due to the risk controls having been tightened. Examining Figure 13.2 may help in testing whether this assertion appears valid.

The results depicted in Figure 13.2 are consistent with the manager's assertion. Volatility in the fund dramatically decreased during the fall of 2004 and has been relatively stable thereafter. Likewise, performance came down to earth but is still running at a very respectable rate of +20 percent. It is therefore safe to assume that although you wouldn't necessarily throw out the earlier performance as useless, the more recent returns are probably more indicative of the risk/return profile that you should expect in the future.

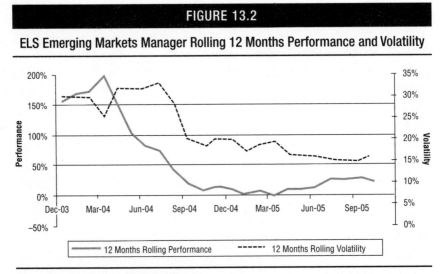

FIGURE 13.2

ELS Emerging Markets Manager Rolling 12 Months Performance and Volatility

Source: Mayer & Hoffman Capital Advisors.

An effective way of summarizing an evaluation of a manager's performance is through a quantitative scorecard. The Quantitative Scorecard used at Mayer & Hoffman rates funds in comparison to their peer group (using different measurement periods), and several measures including the Sharpe and Sortino ratios. As you look at the scorecard in Appendix C, note that two items rate a fund on the direction of skewness and kurtosis of its distribution of returns. That's because when you're looking for potential top performers you're looking for positive skewness and kurtosis in their pattern of returns. Conversely, you will eliminate those with negative skewness and positive kurtosis.

The quantitative stage of due diligence also requires more than simply analyzing the numbers. The investor needs to read between, or behind, the lines. Ron Panzier gives an example. "I can't tell you how often I see managers who present their past performance, and then you look at their current fee structure. You look at a past audit, and the fees were different then. You can bet that they were lower in the past than they are today. So you have to haircut the fund's prior performance to reflect the fact that it benefited from a lower fee structure." If the fund's quantitative assessment meets your minimum threshold for investment for that particular strategy, move ahead to step four.

STEP FOUR: OPERATIONAL ANALYSIS, RISK MANAGEMENT, AND DOCUMENT REVIEW

Step four is multilayered because it contains three discrete activities: taking a hard look into the back office of a potential manager, including infrastructure and contingency plans; the risk management procedures; and, last but not least, the final document review. If a firm comes through all these substeps with passing grades, you'll want to consider it for investment. "Maybe this part of the process isn't sexy," says Ron Panzier, "but it's really critical. A recent study shows that the largest causes for hedge fund closures are operational and business-related matters, not the fact that they underperform.[8] You know, you never make a decision to invest in a manager because of the operational due diligence. You make a decision not to invest in a manager only when you look at their operation, review their risk procedures, and check their ADV and audits." This work will likely involve interviewing a number of noninvestment professionals at the fund who aren't often subjected to outside scrutiny. Due diligence could cause their routines to be disrupted. Therefore to help ensure the necessary cooperation from the manager, it makes sense to do these steps toward the end of the due diligence process, when it is clear that there is genuine interest in making an investment.

Operational Analysis

Information gathered in this step includes a review of the answers given on this section in the DDQ and additional questions on:

- Organizational structure.
- Performance reporting structure.
- Compliance and regulatory procedures.
- Audit and tax procedures.
- Third-party service providers.
- Business continuity and disaster recovery.

Let's look more closely at business continuity. In an age when hedge funds are completely reliant on technology for every facet of their business, knowing what contingency plans they have in place is very important. We ask managers to tell us what contingency plans they have in case of:

- Computer system failure.
- Incapacitated investment decision makers.
- Inaccessibility to office due to fire or other exogenous event.

We also want to know if they have back-up systems in place, where these are located, and if the managers have written business continuity procedures.

There are many ways to capture the operations information that a fund will give you. At Mayer & Hoffman we use an Operations Scorecard that, like the other scorecards presented here, evaluates answers

TABLE 13.2

Operations Scorecard (Extract)

Fund Name: XXXXXXXX

Each statement should be scored on a 1–5 scale
Weight key = * = double weight, ** = triple weight

		Score		
	Weight	**1**	**3**	**5**

Does the fund utilize a 3rd party administrator? ** ✔ (at 3)

1	No
5	Yes

Does the firm have a dedicated financial officer? * ✔ (at 3)

1	No in house accountant
3	Weak CFO or non officer accountant
5	Strong CFO

Is the firm a Registered Investment Advisor or registered in its home country? ✔ (at 3)

1	No
5	Yes

Review two recent audits ✔ (at 4)

1	Not made available or no audit in the past
3	Qualified or new fund with no history
5	Unqualified

Verifiable historical performance ✔ (at 1.5)

1	We cannot verify
3	Less than 100% certainty
5	Yes

Source of portfolio pricing ✔ (at 4)

1	Fair value calculated by Manager
3	3rd party marks
5	Pricing service

Segregation of duties ✔ (at 1.5)

1	No segregation
3	Investment and trading segregated from operations
5	Investment, trading and operations segregated

Monthly capital balance availability ✔ (at 4)

1	Quarterly balances only
3	After 30 days of month end
5	Within 30 days of month end

The manager has adequate infrastructure ✔ (at 1.5)

1	Poor
3	Acceptable
5	Substantial

The manager has adequate contingency plans ✔ (at 3.5)

1	Poor
3	Acceptable
5	Substantial

Operations Score Results

		As a % of max
Total raw score	44	88%
Adjusted raw score	59	91%
Raw score average	4.4	
Adjusted raw score average	4.5	

Raw score key	
Minimum	10
Mid	30
Maximum	50

Adjusted raw score key	
Minimum	13
Mid	39
Maximum	65

	Scale			
	1	**3**	**5**	
Count	0	3	7	10
%	0%	30%	70%	100%

Source: Mayer & Hoffman Capital Advisors.

to the questions on a five-point modified Likert Scale. Table 13.2 shows an extract from Mayer & Hoffman's Operations Scorecard.

Note that two questions are asterisked and are given greater weight:

1. Having an administrator—No administrator means no outside third party reviewing the NAV. Where pricing is an issue such as with illiquid positions, this could be a problem.
2. Does the firm have a dedicated financial officer?

Let's look at the second question "Does the firm have a dedicated financial officer?" One might think that all hedge funds or FOFs have dedicated CFOs or financial officers. But they don't. Ron Panzier relates a pertinent experience: "I was talking to a CFO at a fund. Meeting the CFO is very important. With this particular guy, I just got a sense that I was talking to someone who wasn't strong enough to be in that position. So, I said, 'Excuse me, what's your job title here?' He said, 'Well, they call me the CFO but I kind of think of myself as a controller.' That says a lot about the organization. Basically, I look at the chief financial officer as the individual who keeps honest people honest. He's got to, in my judgment, be a person of strong character."

Risk Management

An established firm that has suffered through tough times is more likely to have a systematic way of controlling risk, and indeed may even employ a chief risk officer who is devoted solely to risk management. A new firm might be more inclined to wing it. However, even established firms bear scrutiny.

Risk management professionals consider six critical variables when looking at a manager's portfolio:

1. *Downside risk management:* assessed by knowing internal procedures that are implemented to prevent large or even catastrophic losses, stop-loss procedures if any, and the limit sizes of individual positions.

2. *Liquidity risk:* assessed by knowing the ratio of liquid to illiquid positions in the portfolio, how long it would take to liquidate the portfolio in an orderly fashion, what impact that liquidation might have on prices, and understanding the impact of a worst-case scenario global liquidity crisis on the fund's ability to raise cash through sales or borrowing power to meet margin calls.

3. *Operational risk:* assessed by evaluating the infrastructure, business acumen, and business continuity procedures that we reviewed earlier.

4. *Leverage:* evaluated as being appropriate or inappropriate for the strategy.

5. *Portfolio accounting risk:* assessed by understanding if the manager has a reliable way to determine his cost in the securities and therefore would later be able to determine his profits or losses.

6. *Valuation risk:* evaluated by determining if there is independent and reliable pricing of securities at month-end or if it's based solely on the manager's best efforts.

We have detailed these risks in great detail as they pertain to each of the strategies, so let's focus here on downside risk management and portfolio accounting risk. "Some firms," says Panzier, "claim to have a hard stop-loss at, say, 15 percent. If a security loses 15 percent of the cost, they just sell it. Now I'm not dogmatic when it comes to stop-losses. On the one hand, I recognize that it is an effective tool for limiting downside risk, but on the other hand I understand the argument that stop-losses can force a manager to sell at the worst possible time."

Panzier further explains how portfolio accounting risk is related to downside risk management. "Many managers are stock jockeys by nature. They'll buy stock on day one, more on day five, then they'll sell a little bit when the market's down, then they'll buy some again the next day when the market is up. This is euphemistically referred to as 'trading around core positions.' Now a particular manager may or may not be able to reduce risk by trading around core positions, but that's beside the point. What I'm concerned about is the unspoken truth that hedge fund managers engaging in this trading behavior have a difficult task of actually knowing the cost of their securities. So when they say they have a hard stop at 15 percent, 15 percent of what? Is it their original cost when they first built a position? Is it the adjusted cost reflecting trading around their positions? Are realized gains or losses resulting from trading activity factored into their cost calculation? What I want to know is, do they have a viable and consistent methodology for determining when to trigger a stop-loss trade?"

In addition to the elements of risk just listed, a new factor, headline risk, is discussed by Terry Bilkey in the interview at the end of this chapter. *Headline risk*, or the fear of being embarrassed by investing in a fund that blows up, is yet another reason to practice careful due diligence.

Final Document Review

This last part of step four is for reviewing the fund's ADV, audits, or any other relevant documents that you haven't had a chance to study. You will want a final look at the subscription and offering documents to ensure that nothing was missed. You may want to look at the banking procedures of the fund, especially their signatory process to take money out of the fund. For example, do they need an outside administrator to review and approve large withdrawals? You really want someone else outside the firm to act as a stopgap in case of fraud. If everything checks out to your satisfaction, you are ready to invest.

STEP FIVE: POSTSELECTION MONITORING

Mayer & Hoffman, like other FOFs, consultants, and investment teams, practice the final step in their due diligence on an ongoing basis. Once a manager receives your money, it is hopefully the beginning of a long and productive relationship. Regular postselection monitoring ensures that a manager is behaving as advertised, is exercising proper trading discipline, and is responding to changing markets in an appropriate manner. While even more essential when investing in newer managers, we find this process is nevertheless valuable even when dealing with established firms.

FOFs often make binding agreements with hedge funds that allow them access to all portfolio and transaction information on a timely basis. The underlying individual hedge fund portfolios can then be rolled up and quantitative risk assessment conducted using software programs like Riskmetrics' Hedge Fund Platform. In many other instances less formal arrangements are undertaken that still allow FOFs regular look-throughs to their managers' positions. Generally speaking, only large institutional investors and FOFs with separately managed accounts get complete transparency. Individual hedge fund investors rarely receive this sort of information.

Transparency affords the diligent investor the opportunity, on a day-to-day basis if desired, to observe and analyze everything that is occurring in the manager's portfolio. This process is time-consuming and expensive, and is rarely done thoroughly.

Postselection monitoring also includes watching for:

- Large asset inflows/outflows.
- Management and key personnel changes.
- Legal/compliance issues.
- Position and portfolio risk.
- Performance anomalies.
- Business continuity risk.

Follow-up communications can also detect early signs of style drift or other performance anomalies. As Terry Bilkey notes in the following interview, something can occur that changes a manager's "financial position materially, literally over night," causing him to change his behavior, and not for the better. "It can happen," he adds philosophically.

INTERVIEW

Terry Bilkey

CFA, Co-Founder
BilkeyKatz Investment Consultants

SINCE OUR PRIMARY FOCUS IS ON SELECTING HEDGE FUND MANAGERS, WE chose to interview Terry Bilkey, CFA, a seasoned and respected consultant who evaluates and helps select hedge funds and funds of funds for institutional clients. His clients' assets generally range from $100 million to $1 billion. Terry co-founded Yanni-Bilkey Investment Consulting, the institutional consulting firm based in Pittsburgh, Pennsylvania. After 20 years, he sold his partnership equity in 1999 and a few years later in 2002 started BilkeyKatz Investment Consultants, an investment consulting firm also based in Pittsburgh. Terry has been published numerous times in various industry publications. In this enlightening discussion with Sam Kirschner, Bilkey refers to the collapse of the $440 million Bayou Capital as a cautionary tale of due diligence pitfalls.

SK: *Terry, tell me how you got started advising institutional clients.*

TB: I got started in the business in 1979 with Yanni-Bilkey, which I co-founded. We principally dealt with sponsors that had assets of $50 million to $500 million dollars. That's where we were most comfortable. Clients ran the gamut from endowments to foundations, corporations, hospitals, and so on. About 50 percent of our current investment consulting business is not-for-profit and about 50 percent for-profit companies.

SK: *When did you start with hedge funds?*

TB: I guess we first got started with hedge funds in 1993 or 1994, thinking that the equity markets were somewhat overvalued. And our clients have been investors in hedge funds ever since.

We wanted to expose our clients to some alternatives. But when you start as a small consulting firm dealing in that $50 million to $500 million range of asset size and you make your first foray into hedge funds, you clearly think long and hard about the fund of funds side. Because it just is really problematic to choose a single hedge fund as your first allocation, and with a client that is maybe not comfortable in that arena to begin with. So for us that was the way to go and our clients were early investors in fund of funds. I think the first fund of funds investment we made was with Grosvenor Capital Management, the group out of Chicago. Anyway, once clients had core positions in a fund of funds, they also invested in some individual hedge fund partnerships.

SK: *How do your clients view hedge fund investing today?*

TB: There's a lot of similarity in terms of what their interests are and what their perceptions of risk are. We have corporations that we work for today that wouldn't have a hedge fund allocation if it was the last thing in America. They just would not do it. Some of that comes from the short side of the market. They're just uncomfortable with hedge fund managers who short stocks, potentially in their own companies. They're very uncomfortable with that element of it. But we have other corporate clients that are perfectly comfortable. They may have exposures of 10 or 15 percent in hedge funds. And then the other part of our business, the not-for-profit, has always been comfortable with hedge funds. The main risk for some of them is headline risk.

SK: *Headline risk?*

TB: Yeah. Bad publicity if an investment fails. For example, I think this Bayou Capital situation has lost money for a number of accounts in Pittsburgh. So you get the headline risk from something like that.

SK: *Has headline risk ever affected you?*

TB: Sure. I remember when one of our Los Angeles clients had Grosvenor exposure at the time Grosvenor had a 1 to 2 percent position with David Askin. And Askin blew up in 1994. [See Chapter 9 for a description of this Fixed Income Arb blowup.] And when his funds went belly-up, the vast majority of that money was lost. The *L.A. Times* got wind of the fact that Grosvenor had exposure to Askin and had lost $40 or $50 million of their clients' money.

So we got calls from our client in L.A. saying, "What's our exposure? What have we lost?" We did the calculations. The client had a total of about $10 million committed to Grosvenor and for the month, the loss came out to be about $30,000. It equated to what the client would have lost had one of our traditional equity managers sold a stock at a loss after the share price had dropped $10 from his cost. But it was still that headline risk that you had to overcome with clients in the hedge fund arena. That's another reason why we've been very careful when we have gone outside of fund of funds. Because you get a lot of protection through fund of funds diversification that you just can't get through an individual fund.

SK: *Let's step back to your comments about Bayou. A lot of people ask how professional consultants could miss the basic background checks and any number of other red flags that should have been raised about Bayou Capital and its principals.*

TB: Look, it's easy to be a Monday morning quarterback, but if we go through a partial due diligence checklist on Bayou, it could be instructive. Our checklist would start with who's doing the auditing of the financials. If you don't have a reputable audit firm behind it, you've got strike one to begin with. Then you go through the background checks on the principals. It is important to verify that the CIO or portfolio manager had similar responsibilities in their previous jobs. So if that doesn't check out,* that's strike two. And the list goes on from there.

---

*As it did not with Bayou's manager.

Additionally, I think one of the big issues from our perspective, one that we spend a lot of time thinking about, is a soft issue, and that is understanding how a fund got its performance numbers. I don't mean simply absolute performance. I'm saying that the performance of the fund and the overall performance of the strategy should be consistent. I remember when Orange County blew up back in the 1990s. Here you are in about a six percent interest rate environment for Treasuries and somebody's earning nine. Well, the first thing you have to understand is that you're obviously not operating in the Treasury market if you're earning nine because the Treasury market's only earning six. So either you're levering up sixes to get nines or you're using other instruments that don't look like sixes. But you don't get nines out of sixes.

So those are some of the things that we spend a lot of time on. Looking back, I think Bayou had some red flags. Finding them sometimes can be difficult, though. Most FOFs will admit that a perfect due diligence record is hard to achieve.

SK: *The pattern of returns, how important is that to you?*

TB: Well it's very important to us because when we're looking for a match with a client's goal, that pattern of returns is essentially what the client is buying, if you think about it. We're positioning a portfolio on the risk spectrum. We're looking at volatility and drawdown, as well as expected rate of return. So we spend a lot of time trying to understand those issues. Remember, the client is putting this fund into their portfolio for a reason.

SK: *Some of that is quantitative. What about the qualitative aspects?*

TB: You get a clue of how they invest if you go through the trading history and the portfolio with the investment team. You ask them, what can go right that will help performance? What can go wrong? When does this strategy work? When does it not work? If you go through all of that with specific examples and you get an understanding of how these people are going to react to events, I think you've got a better shot. You have to ask yourself: How far reaching are they in what they're trying to do? Do they reach beyond where their capabilities are?

Many asset classes or sectors in the marketplace can go through

rough periods of time like for two or three years. And if that's all these managers trade, and you're going to invest with them, you need the patience to stay with that or don't go in there in the first place. But you need to understand those things before you make the investments, it seems to me.

SK: *Take convertible arb, for instance.*

TB: That's a good example. We've got it in some of the fund of funds, but our clients have no dedicated convertible arb hedge funds. We've never been comfortable with the small size of that market and the nature of the securities that are in there, especially given the asset flows into convertible arb through 2003. To us, though, if it's in a fund of funds or in a multistrategy fund where the investment manager who is on the ground is making the decision to include it, that's more comfortable for us. They may see opportunity where that's a very difficult determination for us or the client to make.

SK: *But maybe not for a fund of funds manager.*

TB: But not for a fund of funds manager. I think it's a comfort zone for them to say, for example, "A lot of the convertible market is washed out. We think we've got a reasonable opportunity." But let them make that decision, not the client or us.

SK: *What else are you looking for in the qualitative due diligence?*

TB: We start with what our clients are looking for. They have major input in this. On the qualitative side, they are looking for established firms that have at least a couple of hundred million under management. So many are not interested in those that are starting out, even if they have great backgrounds. Our clients tend to be conservative, so they're going to want to know philosophically where these managers are coming from. What kinds of portfolios are they trying to build from a risk perspective? And what types of investments are they willing to make?

Clients want to know that we have vetted these managers to the nth degree. Do the managers have an investment process that they can put down on five sheets of paper, or whatever, that says "This is how we do it"? For example, if you're looking to invest in a fund of funds the CIO might say, "We have several stages in our investment process before we invest. In the first stage we have people looking at these types of managers or strategies. If they pass that screen, say, performance in a bad market, then they're going to the next level. There are six or eight factors at that next stage that are much more critical to us. "Now," he says, "we're spending our senior professional time, senior analyst, risk officer, whatever, at this juncture. If the hedge fund's principals pass that analysis, then this fund goes to the next level of what we would call a reasonable investment. And then they go through the final due diligence steps, background checks, references, reviewing all the documents, just to make sure that all the *is* are dotted and the *t*s are crossed. That's a manager or fund that knows how to conduct due diligence."

If you look at all of the investment mistakes that have been made in selecting funds that blew up or where there was fraud, you have a pretty good pattern in this country for the past 15 years. I mean you've got the back office mistakes. That's maybe 40 percent of the problems right there.

SK: *Right, at least that much.*

TB: You ought to be able to figure that out if you spend the time with the people in the back office. You have to be able to get that one behind you. Then you've got the leverage factor. That comes out in spades in this business over time. But you ought to be able to see that if you're mentoring the fund on a regular basis. Then you've got fraud. That's a tough one. Because you can have honest people wake up tomorrow and do something crazy.

SK: *That is a tough one.*

TB: Because you don't know where it comes from, initially. It may be a guy who has financial resources today, but something happens tomorrow. He gets divorced or whatever. Something occurs that changes his financial position materially, literally overnight. It can happen. And all of a sudden he may do things that he wouldn't have done yesterday. I mean, you would hope you're dealing with people who would never change their financial morals, if you will. But you don't know what pushes people to do things that they wouldn't normally do.

SK: *You mentioned earlier that your clients are generally not receptive to new managers.*

TB: Well, let's take that in context because we love newer managers. Love them, because the potential return is enhanced. We don't love all the negatives that go with that. Obviously there's more risk with newer managers.

SK: *Sure.*

TB: The easiest thing to do is to hire the guy with $5 billion. First of all, you know that the back office is pretty well intact. They've had enough time to iron out all the problems. You know that they're going to be around for the next year. I mean how can you lose $5 billion? Well, it's happened before, but the odds are against it. So you get that comfort level.

But what you miss, though, is the incentive and the motivation oftentimes, because with the bigger managers, they've made their money already. It's the emerging manager who gives you all those positives that you really like to have. So that's where the fund of funds' manager is invaluable.

SK: *So you're using the fund of funds to do the heavy lifting of finding those managers?*

TB: Absolutely. We can't directly hire the 10 or 15 emerging managers to fill up a portfolio. We need the heavy lifting to be done by specialists.

SK: *Would your clients want something like that?*

TB: Some would and some wouldn't. It always comes down to the individual risk profile of the client. If I sat in front of some of our sophisticated clients and said, "We think there is a better opportunity for performance from emerging managers," they would tend to agree with that and consider investing. And so that's what we're after, obviously, in this time of difficult returns.

SK: *How would you advise a client who cites the Bayou Capital blow-up as a sign of the danger of hedge funds?*

TB: I advise our clients that this whole alternatives area is here to stay. It's not going to go away as an asset class in spite of Bayou or whoever else falls apart next week.

And the reason is because there are more investment tools at work in alternatives' portfolios than could ever be applied in traditional portfolios. Traditional portfolios win only when stocks and bonds both go up [laughing]. I mean, that's the only time they win. So we need more going on, more alpha, in our portfolios. And we just can't get it other than through the alternative side.

We all need to accept the fact that the Bayous of this world will happen on the alternative side. But if you're diversified, you're going to take the kind of hits I mentioned earlier where our client lost $30,000 in a $10 million portfolio with David Askin. Look, Askin's company was a $600 million asset blown to the winds. But it cost our client only $30,000, which you should be willing to take as an acceptable risk in this business. And it all comes back to simple diversification.

There's going to be a fraud case somewhere. There's going to be a credit derivatives problem or whatever it is. It's going to occur somewhere. It always will. But there will always be things on the traditional side that go wrong, too. And those losses are even bigger when you look at the Enrons and other stocks. Every once in a while we're all going to lose.

What's Ahead
for Hedge Funds?

HEDGE FUNDS ARE WITHOUT DOUBT THE MOST CONTROVERSIAL SECTOR of the worldwide investment industry. Hardly a day goes by without a hedge fund article appearing in some prominent publication, usually slanted negatively in one way or another. Topics have included fraud, disappointing returns, high fees, problems with hedge fund indices, alleged overblown returns, overcrowding of capital into the space, and more. Yet it is clear, when opinions are separated from facts as we have endeavored to do throughout this book, hedge funds have continued to be superior risk-adjusted investment vehicles, and that when they are added to a portfolio of traditional assets, they have lowered overall volatility and improved performance.

We are proud to have been part of the hedge fund industry for a collective half century. Over the past 50-plus years, we have seen it go through three broad phases as it evolved from childhood through adolescence into what we now see as a critical part of early adulthood. In this Epilogue we first examine the growth of the hedge fund industry as it has moved through these phases of development, and in the process we assess the impact of SEC regulation and institutional investment on hedge funds. Then, we look at performance and make some predictions about alternative investment returns. Finally, we consider whether the industry has entered a bubble phase and, as has been suggested by several observers, is destined to blow up.

THE GROWTH AND DEVELOPMENT
OF THE HEDGE FUND INDUSTRY

Childhood and Adolescence

The first phase of development, from inception by Alfred W. Jones in 1949 through the beginnings of the FOF business by the Rothschilds in 1969 and on through the 1980s, might be called the childhood phase of hedge funds. For half of this era most managers followed various iterations of the ELS strategy including the first FOF. Money came exclusively from wealthy individuals and families. Good data was impossible to collect as funds kept their performance secret and there were no indices or databases.

Gradually, as the number of hedge funds grew, the industry entered into adolescence. Led by global macro legend George Soros, hedge funds expanded beyond the limits of ELS and began taking positions in everything from currencies to commodities. These managers cared less about being hedged than about maximizing profit either through the use of leverage or through aggressive directional bets. On the other hand, relative value arbitrage strategies also developed in this era as managers looked for more conservative ways to make money by remaining market neutral. These trading strategies also began to attract assets and the number of hedge funds grew to about 200.[1] By the time this era ended, global macro had captured about 70 percent of total industry assets, estimated to be about $20 billion.[2] While the childhood and adolescence of hedge funds may stir feelings of nostalgia and remembrances of novelty and excitement, it was also a chaotic period of tremendous experimentation that lacked rules or structure.

Early Adulthood

Continuing with our metaphor, we characterize the second phase of the industry's growth as the transition phase into early adulthood.[3] Three transformative changes occurred between 1990 and 2000 that fostered the further maturation and independence of hedge funds as a distinct asset class separate from the (adult and more mature) traditional asset classes of equities and fixed-income securities: the expansion of hedge funds into every conceivable strategy and into every corner of the globe, the rise of institutional hedge fund investing, and the appearance of global hedge fund database, indices, and large volumes of academic research.

As the industry transitioned into early adulthood, funds began to explore every possible strategy in every conceivable asset type. In particular, venturesome ELS funds in the developed nations started investing in specific ranges of companies selected by market capitalization as well as specific industry sectors such as healthcare, real estate, precious metals, technology, energy, and biotech. Around the same time that sector funds emerged, ELS and other strategies found opportunities in emerging markets in Asia, Latin America, and, later, Eastern Europe. The globalization of the industry was complete by the time the decade ended. Hedge funds had successfully followed mutual funds by investing in these new areas but, of course, they put their own indelible identity on them.

A second major change that occurred was that forward-thinking institutions, in particular university endowments, joined wealthy individuals and families as large hedge fund investors. Their investments further legitimized the industry's identity as a separate asset class to be treated with respect. Hedge funds and FOFs proliferated as their numbers grew to more than 3,000.

But there were also growing pains consistent with young adulthood. Funds like Askin and Long Term Capital blew up while others were discovered to be frauds. Despite these setbacks and despite the fact that the majority of institutional investors saw no need to invest beyond traditional investments as their stock and bond portfolios were producing outstanding returns, massive amounts of capital flowed into the industry as it flourished around the globe. Assets under management enjoyed a twentyfold increase to about $400 billion.[4]

The third change that facilitated the industry's successful entry into early adulthood was the development of global databases and indices for every conceivable strategy. Along with the proliferation of data and benchmarks came a flurry of academic research. Studies were aimed at understanding the role of hedge funds in MPT and the EMH, uncovering the performance drivers of hedge fund returns, measuring hedge fund returns relative to traditional assets, and even debating whether the performance was real. Through this process of self-reflection the industry began to take itself more seriously and made the choices that are consistent with this phase of development. Hedge funds acted more like adults (traditional assets) by being more structured, more dependable, and less secretive and rebellious. By the time the secular bull market ended in early 2000, hedge funds were ready to transition into the next stage of adulthood.

Early Adulthood: Transitioning and Settling Down

The onset of the bear market of 2000–2002 provided hedge funds and FOFs the momentum they needed to move into their current phase of early adulthood that psychologists have divided into two parts: The Age 30 Transition followed by the Settling Down phase. In the first part of this phase, young adults face a crisis around age 30 or so as they examine the choices they've made in the previous phase of early adulthood: career choices, lovers, friends, religion, and so on. Perhaps the structures they have established are not the right ones for them. Perhaps they are inconsistent with their dreams and aspirations. But whatever the case, navigating through this transition is a necessary step on the way to the next phase, that of settling down and becoming a full-fledged adult with a seat at the table.[5]

In our view, the hedge fund industry is facing its own transition phase of early adulthood. Let's examine the evidence for this opinion based on what's happened over the past five years. Having established their own separate identities and performance records, FOFs and hedge funds continued attracting capital from institutions. The biggest beneficiaries of this inflow have been the giant FOFs whose businesses have grown dramatically. FOF assets climbed from about $500 billion to $700 billion during 2004 and 2005. At year-end 2005 global hedge fund AUM totaled more than $1.2 trillion with more than half of the assets being managed through FOFs.[6] And the multitrillion dollar pension industry is poised to invest hundreds of billions more in the decade ahead.[7]

What's the crisis then, you ask? To answer that let's examine the impact of institutionalization on the industry, first by looking at the new regulations imposed by the SEC and then by understanding how institutions are shaping performance.

THE INSTITUTIONALIZATION OF HEDGE FUNDS

The Impact of SEC Oversight

By the time you read this book, the new SEC regulations governing hedge funds will have gone into effect (February 1, 2006). As we see it, SEC oversight will impact the development of the industry in three major ways: increased staffing and other costs, time and energy expenditures, and increased barriers to entry. These factors will further the maturation of the industry as it transitions from early adulthood into midlife.

Increased Costs.   Many hedge fund and FOF managers have found it necessary to hire a dedicated chief compliance officer (CCO) in addition to a chief financial officer to head up those areas that fall under the regulator's purview. This could be a substantial extra expense given the short supply of qualified candidates with SEC-related experience. Other firms are paying their CFOs extra compensation to wear both hats or outsourcing the position to service providers at considerable cost.

Related to the CCO role are the legal expenses associated with compliance. Offering documents need to be amended and all marketing materials and Web sites have to be reviewed both by the CCO and the firm's attorneys. In addition, the CCO and the lawyers must draft the formal compliance policies and procedures that funds must now adopt.

Finally, hedge fund managers face substantial increased costs associated with information technology. First, there are SEC requirements regarding archiving e-mails. These new regulations force managers to upgrade existing servers and networks. Depending on the number of employees, these costs can be substantial. Second, there may be additional costs associated with disaster recovery contingencies. An off-site location that houses the trading and investor records with duplicate or back-up servers and software may cost a firm located in a major urban area an additional $50,000–$100,000 per year or more. In the end, these additional costs will be borne either by the firm, the investors, or, more likely, a combination of both.

Time and Energy Expenditures.   As you can already surmise, the requirements imposed by the SEC will result not only in cost increases but in substantial expenditures of time and energy by the managers and their staffs. The paperwork burden will be overwhelming to some firms. For example, senior personnel will be distracted from doing their primary functions with issues ranging from document reviews, e-mail violations and what to do about them, endless rewrites of monthly letters to investors, and reviews of marketing materials where they must provide some of the content. A hidden cost resulting from these distractions could be lower investment returns. While it is certainly difficult to quantify the costs associated with these expenditures, one thing is certain: Funds will have to add staff and their employees might be expected to work longer hours. None of those consequences will be free.

Increased Barriers to Entry and Other Implications.   Faced with ever-increasing costs and demands on their time, managers who want to start new hedge funds may find themselves unable to do so. The SEC may have inadvertently, then, set up barriers to entry into the hedge fund industry. In the years ahead, we will see if there is continuity to the recent trend of 900 to 1,000 new hedge funds emerging per year. Bear in mind, however, that the majority of hedge funds and FOFs are smaller than $30 million AUM (about 60 percent) and are therefore not required to register with the SEC. These managers might decide to stay small to avoid scrutiny but, of course, that would also increase the likelihood of failure since at less than $30 million most are not at critical mass. Furthermore, they may be the very funds that need the most oversight.

Another consequence of the requirements is that some established domestic and offshore managers have changed the terms and conditions of their funds. As we write this, we know of numerous managers who have extended lock-up provisions to two years and a day in order to avoid registering with the SEC. Offshore managers have started to expel their U.S. investors or have decided not to create a U.S. feeder fund to avoid SEC registration. As a consequence, U.S. investors have already been faced with several unappetizing consequences of the new regulations: extended lock-ups by top-performing U.S. funds, expulsion, and the inability to invest in certain excellent offshore funds.[8]

While many have railed against the new regulations as being dictatorial and harmful, we doubt if the SEC's oversight will kill the hedge fund industry. In general, we are happy to see it. SEC registration will be viewed by many as an imprimatur of sorts, which will help institutions feel better about investing in hedge funds. It will force funds to tighten operational and business practices. While the changes that the SEC will bring about can only help speed up the maturation process of the industry's transition into adulthood, in the end self-regulation by managers of high integrity coupled with good performance will be the foundations on which the hedge fund industry will continue to build.

The Impact of Institutional Investors

The impact of large institutional money on the hedge fund world has already been profound. Many institutional investors gave marching orders to the hedge funds they invested in, or they invested in very large and more conservative FOFs. They didn't want volatility; they didn't want large drawdowns. In fact, zero drawdowns would get very high marks. The hedge funds, for their part, naturally became more conservative. As it is said on Wall Street, "Follow the Golden Rule; he who has the gold makes the rules."

Lower Volatility and Lower Performance.   When managers were accustomed to managing, say, $500 million and covering their overhead and salaries with their management fees, they looked to the incentive fees to make real money. And that meant as much performance as they could prudently accomplish. When suddenly they were inundated with conservative capital and were managing billions (you don't have to be a mathematician to figure out that you can get quite rich on the management fees alone), these managers were earning more money than they ever could when they were much smaller and targeting returns of 20 percent or more. Furthermore, their institutional investors seemed happy.

As hedge fund volatility was engineered lower and lower and as sophisticated risk managers played an increasing role in how portfolios were managed, they were indeed very successful in lowering risk and minimizing drawdowns. The only problem was that, in the process, returns came down, also. Over the past five years, the average hedge fund has returned only about 8 percent per annum and the average FOF only 6 percent.[9] To a degree, then, institutions may be killing, or at least reducing the fecundity of, the geese that heretofore had been laying the golden eggs.

To be fair, institutional pressure is undoubtedly improving the risk controls and risk management procedures of many funds in which they invest. By demanding more transparency, documentation, and rigor, institutions have helped the industry settle down and take a seat at the adult table of traditional assets.

By accepting the assets and constraints of their largest investors, hedge funds have, ironically, sown the seeds of the current predicament: disenchantment with performance. What has happened with the performance of some behemoth hedge funds and FOFs in the past two years shows that when an investment organization becomes very large, its value proposition can significantly deteriorate.

Not only do we see this phenomenon with asset management firms but as we've observed throughout this book when too much capital floods a particular investment space, the performance of that strategy, like Convertible Arb over the past two years, is negatively impacted. In the long-only world we've also seen the impact of too much capital flowing into an asset category, be it growth, value, or technology. The stocks in question become increasingly overpriced until finally the bubble bursts, capital begins to withdraw, and large capital losses result.

One of the outcomes of these trends has been that investors, even institutional ones, are making such comments as, "We're looking for more juice." Translated, they wish they hadn't been so conservative, are disappointed with their returns, and realize that more risk must be taken if higher returns are desired. Will the industry continue down the road of conformity, achieving indexlike or even subindex returns, or will it bifurcate as some funds veer off pushing for the performance that defined the character of the industry's youth?

We believe the latter. While some funds will cater to institutions that want low risk and low performance, others will aim higher and still be able to gather assets. As that trend develops, many institutions that wanted low volatility will reverse themselves as increased sophistication in portfolio management allows them to take advantage of the alpha-generating potential of hedge funds. When that bridge is crossed, hedge funds will have come of age: being adults without compromising the essential values that define who they are.

HEDGE FUND PERFORMANCE

Let us leave our developmental analysis behind and turn to the question of future hedge fund performance. As we've discussed throughout, hedge funds and FOFs have demonstrated that they are excellent risk-adjusted investment vehicles and portfolio diversifiers. Over the five years ending 12/31/05, the average hedge fund has outperformed traditional assets on an absolute and risk-adjusted basis, while the average FOF has also outperformed equities on both counts and bonds on a risk-adjusted basis. In 2005, the HFRI FOF Composite Index was up 7.4 percent net of fees while bonds returned about 2 percent and the S&P 500 about 3 percent. While hedge fund returns have trended lower since 2000, remember that equities have been underwater for most of the past five plus years and have yet to return to their all-time highs. Meanwhile, most hedge fund and FOF indices set new highs nearly every month.

We realize that some investors are disappointed with recent hedge fund and FOF performance. On an overall basis, we are hard pressed to see a strong case for hedge fund performance to be labeled as disappointing. We think the disappointment in hedge funds has more to do with expectations than anything else. People have expected more from hedge funds and therefore they don't appreciate the fact that they have performed so much better than the stock market in recent years. From 2000–2005, the major market indices lost money and the tech-heavy NASDAQ Index became a shadow of its former self. Yet we do not see articles bewailing the poor returns of mutual funds or other long-only managers in this context when such articles about hedge funds, which have widely outperformed them, are so commonplace.

As to future performance, we expect fees to come down in certain areas of the industry to allow for better returns to investors. We also expect that hedge funds and FOFs will continue to add value with superior Sharpe ratios in comparison with stocks and bonds. While some strategies will be unable to return to their glory days, we still believe that profitable new hedge fund strategies like Direct Financing will continue to evolve. We also confidently expect newer hedge funds to continue outperforming their bigger and older peers.

As has been the case in the past, we expect most hedge funds to outperform the stock market in sideways and down years, and to underperform in the big up years. If prominent bulls like Jeremy Siegel believe that the stock market at best produces mid-single digit returns for the rest of the decade,[10] we expect hedge funds and many FOFs to do modestly better, with lower volatility. Results for the various asset classes in 2005 may preview the coming attractions.

IS IT A BUBBLE?

Finally, let's consider whether the flood of money that has helped moderate returns and perhaps future expectations is really a disastrous bubble in the making. If we define a bubble as an asset being priced irrationally high like tulip bulbs or the Internet stocks once were, then we cannot put hedge funds in that category. We agree with Asness who argues that the influx of capital may reduce alpha but not move returns into negative territory for very long.[11] As we've pointed out throughout, as long as hedge funds continue to earn risk premiums for dealing with liquidity, credit, and other market risks, they will likely continue to sustain an edge over their traditional counterparts.

That's not to say that there won't be any blow-ups or frauds. Of course there will be some. But they will not prevent the industry from growing. There are several factors at work that will foster continued expansion:

1. There will be greater penetration of the institutional marketplace. Given all the trends and the solid performance of hedge funds, we believe that virtually all institutions will ultimately invest in hedge funds. There will also be greater allocations from those institutions that have only recently begun their investments in the space. Of the ones we have surveyed, nearly all are planning to continue increasing their hedge fund allocations in the years ahead.
2. Hedge fund returns themselves will continue to drive the growth of the asset base. For example, should the industry generate 8 percent returns and receive no net investment inflows (which we consider highly unlikely), it will double in the coming nine years to reach approximately $2.5 trillion.
3. Wall Street is a powerful distributor of financial asset products and it ultimately will get around to delivering hedge fund products to the retail investor, in particular to the mass affluent. Why should hedge funds, which have been outperforming stocks and bonds for more than 12 years, be available only to institutions and the very wealthy?

Our best estimate, therefore, is that aggregate hedge fund assets will continue to grow dynamically for the rest of the decade. This view is supported by the results of three recent independent surveys of global institutional investors. Strategic allocations are expected to increase dramatically over the next three years[12] with the result that hedge fund assets under management are forecast to exceed $2 trillion by as early as 2009.[13]

What impact will this torrent of capital have on hedge fund returns? We believe that under most equity market scenarios hedge funds will continue to do well. If there is a sideways equity market, hedge funds will continue to outperform and attract capital. If there is another bear market, hedge funds will outperform equities by at least preserving capital and therefore should attract an accelerated flow of assets. In a bullish environment, hedge funds should underperform equities, which could result in diminished asset flows or even net withdrawals. In that event, the stage would possibly be set for a resurgence in hedge fund performance.

The forecasts we have just made are intended to serve as a roadmap for future hedge fund investing. As the epistemologists are fond of saying, "The map is not the territory." Therefore, while we believe that under most scenarios hedge funds will continue to outperform on a risk-adjusted basis, there is always the possibility that unforeseeable geopolitical and/or macroeconomic changes will moderate their future profitability.

The most important megatrend that we see is that many of the best returns will continue to derive from strategies now emerging or yet to emerge. This pattern is a natural and healthy evolutionary development that provides a clear path for solid returns in the near and distant future.

APPENDIX A

Directory of Interviewees

Terry Bilkey, CFA
Co-Founder and Principal
BilkeyKatz Investment Consultants, Inc.

Craig F. Colberg
Co-Portfolio Manager and Partner
Rivanna Capital, LLC

Peter deLisser
Founder and President
Sage Capital, LP

Michael P. Dever
Chairman and Director of Research
Brandywine Asset Management

Bill Dunn, Ph.D.
Founder and Chairman
Dunn Capital Management

Mickey Harley
CEO and President
Mellon HBV Alternative Strategies, LLC

Renee Haugerud
Founder and CIO
Galtere International Fund

Matthew Hoffman
CIO
Mayer & Hoffman Capital Advisors, LLC

Marc Lasry
Founder and Managing Partner
Avenue Capital Group

Ron Panzier
CFO and CRO
Mayer & Hoffman Capital Advisors, LLC

Michael L. Pasternak
Co-Founder and CIO
Pinewood Credit Markets, LP

Robert D. Petty
Founder and Managing Partner
Clearwater Capital Partners, LLC

Peter Thiel
Founder and Portfolio Manager
Clarium Capital Management, LLC

John J. Schmitz
Founder and CIO
SciVest Capital Management, Inc.

Qualitative Due Diligence Scorecard

Extract

Fund Name: XXXXXXXX
Completed by: YYYYYYYY

To be completed after Due Diligence questionnaire is completed and manager is viable
Each statement should be scored on a 1–5 scale
Weight key = * = double weight, ** = triple weight

Statement	Weight	Scale (1–5)
We thoroughly understand the strategy		✔ at 5
1 — We do not have substantial understanding		
3 — We substantially understand it		
5 — Excellent understanding		
Manager has a believable "edge" of some kind	*	✔ at 4
1 — No convincing edge		
3 — Likely		
5 — Yes		
The manager is highly motivated		✔ at 3
1 — Not necessarily motivated		
3 — Substantially motivated		
5 — Highly motivated		
Manager demonstrates that they have a strong ability to understand the macro environment	*	✔ at 4
1 — Not a macro thinker		
3 — Pretty good macro thinker		
5 — Excellent macro thinker		
Flexible thinker	*	✔ at 3
1 — Rigid		
3 — Probably flexible		
5 — Flexible and nimble investor		
The managers have demonstrated the ability to generate short profits	*	✔ at 4
1 — Inexperienced		
3 — Fairly experienced		
5 — Ample experience and successful		
Risk controls are impressive and we have confidence in the rigor with which they will be enforced		✔ at 1
1 — Unimpressive		
3 — Fairly impressive		
5 — Very impressive on both counts		
Likely performance in extreme negative macro environment	*	✔ at 3
1 — Substantial drawdown or unknown		
3 — Assets substantially preserved		
5 — Assets likely preserved		
Manager passes the hypothetical acid test of our willingness to invest in him personally	**	✔ at 3
1 — Uncertain		
3 — Would probably invest		
5 — Definitely		
Ethical evaluation	**	✔ at 4
1 — Unsure		
3 — Probably ethical		
5 — Highly ethical		

Qualitative Score Results

		As a % of max
Total raw score	38	76%
Adjusted raw score	75	79%
Raw score average	3.8	
Adjusted raw score average	3.9	

Raw score key	
Minimum	10
Mid	30
Maximum	50

Adjusted raw score key	
Minimum	19
Mid	57
Maximum	95

Scale	1	2	3	4	5	
Count	1	0	4	0	5	10
%	10%	0%	40%	0%	50%	10%

Source: Mayer & Hoffman Capital Advisors.

Quantitative Due Diligence Scorecard

Extract

Fund Name: **XXXXXXXX**

Each statement should be scored on a 1–5 scale

		Score		
	Weight	1	3	5

The investment returns were in the top quartile vs. the peer group for the last 24 months (or fund life)   *

1	3rd and 4th quartile or limited performance history
3	2nd quartile
5	Top quartile

The investment returns were in the top quartile vs. the peer group for the last 60 months (or fund life)

1	3rd and 4th quartile or limited performance history
3	2nd quartile
5	Top quartile

The sharpe ratio was in the top quartile vs. the peer group for the last 24 months

1	3rd and 4th quartile or limited performance history
3	2nd quartile
5	Top quartile

The sharpe ratio was in the top quartile vs. the peer group for the last 60 months (or fund life)

1	3rd and 4th quartile or limited performance history
3	2nd quartile
5	Top quartile

The sortino ratio was in the top quartile vs. the peer group for the last 24 months

1	3rd and 4th quartile or limited performance history
3	2nd quartile
5	Top quartile

The sortino ratio was in the top quartile vs. the peer group for the last 60 months (or fund life)

1	3rd and 4th quartile or limited performance history
3	2nd quartile
5	Top quartile

Drawdowns have not exceeded 10% in the last 60 months (or fund life)   *

1	No
3	Yes, but new risk controls in place or extra high returns
5	Yes

The manager has done well in difficult market environments, in terms of minimizing or avoiding losses

1	Losses
3	Positive returns in bad markets
5	Good returns in bad markets

% profitable months for the trailing 24 month period

1	Less than 60%
3	Btw 60% and 75%
5	75% or greater

% profitable months for the trailing 60 month period (or fund life)   *

1	Less than 60%
3	Btw 60% and 75%
5	75% or greater

Positive skewness and positive kurtosis for 60 month period (or fund life)

| 1 | No |
| 5 | Yes to both |

Quantitative Score Results

		As a % of max
Total raw score	43	78%
Adjusted raw score	54	77%
Raw score average		3.9
Adjusted raw score average		3.9

Raw score key	
Minimum	11
Mid	33
Maximum	55

Adjusted raw score key	
Minimum	14
Mid	42
Maximum	70

		Scale		
	1	3	5	
Count	1	4	6	11
%	9%	36%	55%	100%

Source: Mayer & Hoffman Capital Advisors.

Major Hedge Fund Databases and Indices

Alternative Asset Center
Fund of hedge funds database and index
www.aa-center.net

Altvest
Hedge fund database
www.investorforce.com

The Barclay Group, Ltd.
Hedge fund, funds of hedge fund, and managed futures databases and
indices
www.barclaygrp.com

Center for International Securities and Derivatives Markets (CISDM)
Nonprofit academic research center, hedge fund, and managed futures
databases and indices
http://cisdm.som.umass.edu

CogentHedge.com
Hedge fund database
www.cogenthedge.com

Eurekahedge
North American, Asian, European, and Latin American hedge fund and
    FOF databases and indices
www.eurekahedge.com

Greenwich-Van
Hedge fund database and indices
www.vanhedge.com

Hennessee Group
Hedge fund database and indices
www.hennessee.com

Hedge Fund Intelligence
Hedge fund and fund of funds databases and indices
www.hedgefundintelligence.com

HedgeFund.net
Hedge fund database, hedge fund, and fund of hedge funds indices
www.hedgefund.net

Hedge Fund Research, Inc.
Hedge fund database, hedge fund, and fund of hedge funds indices
www.hedgefundresearch.com

HedgeIndex.com
CSFB/Tremont hedge fund indices
www.hedgeindex.com

HedgeWorld
Hedge fund database
www.hedgeworld.com

MarHedge
Hedge fund and managed futures indices
www.marhedge.com

MSCI
Investable and noninvestable hedge fund indices
www.msci.com/hedge

Standard & Poor's
Hedge fund and managed futures indices
www.standardandpoors.com

Strategic Financial Solutions, LLC
Makers of PerTrac, a leading asset allocation and investment analysis
    software program
www.pertrac.com

APPENDIX E

Hedge Fund Industry
Web Sites and Publications

Web Sites

AIMA	www.aima.org
Albourne Village	http://my.village.albourne.com
Eurekahedge	www.eurekahedge.com
Hedgefund.net	www.hedgefund.net

Publications

Magazines

Absolute Return	www.absolutereturn.net
Alpha Institutional Investor	www.institutionalinvestor.com
The Hedge Fund Journal	www.thehedgefundjournal.com
Hedge Fund Manager	www.hfmanager.com
Institutional Investor	www.institutionalinvestor.com
MAR Hedge	www.marhedge.com

Newsletters

Alternative Investment News	www.iialternatives.com
Hedge Fund Alert	www.hfalert.com
Invest Hedge	www.investhedge.com
MAR Fund of Funds Strategies	www.marhedge.com

NOTES

CHAPTER 1 The Case for Hedge Funds

1. www.hedgefundresearch.com.
2. Throughout this book we rely on three independent industry sources for our asset flow data. The first, Strategic Financial Solutions, LLC, is the maker of PerTrac, the most widely used software tool for investment analysis and portfolio construction in the hedge fund world. Most FOFs get their data feeds and run them through PerTrac. The second, Barclay Group Ltd., has one of the largest databases devoted to CTAs and Managed Futures and also tracks assets to the entire industry quarterly. The number cited of $1.14 trillion comes from the Q3 2005 survey and is available at www.barclaygrp.com. The higher number cited is from the Jones/Strategic Solutions study that follows. The third source is HFRI, which publishes a quarterly asset flow report.
3. Meredith Jones, "Strategic Financial Solutions 2005 Hedge Fund Data," Strategic Financial Solutions, December 2005, pp. 1–5.
4. Ibid., p.1.
5. Survey, 2005. Institute for Private Investors, New York, NY.
6. 2005 NACUBO Endowment Study available at www.nacubo.org.
7. External Management Development Program. Available at www .calpers.ca.gov.
8. Survey available from Greenwich Associates, February 2005.
9. Riva Atlas, "Pension Plans Pouring Billions into Hedge Funds," available at www.nytimes.com, November 27, 2005.
10. See K. Beer, "Dean of Investing," *Bloomberg Markets*, January 2006. The story includes a current asset allocation chart from Yale.
11. www.barclaygroup.com survey, op. cit.
12. Jones, op. cit., p. 2.
13. Ibid., p. 2.
14. Data from PerTrac and HFRI.

15. Our study on hedge fund performance from 1994–2005 relied on data from PerTrac and HFRI plus our internal calculations of the risk-free rate and Sharpe ratios.

16. William F. Sharpe, "Adjusting for Risk in Portfolio Performance Measurement," *Journal of Portfolio Management*, Winter 1975, pp. 29–34.

17. Harry M. Markowitz, "Portfolio Selection," *Journal of Finance* 7 (1), 1952, pp. 77–91.

18. Read the debate between Siegel and Grantham in John Mauldin, *Bull's Eye Investing* (New York: John Wiley & Sons, 2004), pp. 39–45.

19. B. Malkiel and A. Saha, "Hedge Funds: Risk and Return," Center for Economic Policy Research, Princeton University, December 1, 2004, pp. 1–49.

20. Ibid., p. 36.

21. C. Ackermann, R. McEnally, and D. Ravenscraft, "The Performance of Hedge Funds: Risk, Return, and Incentives," *Journal of Finance* 54, June 1999, pp. 833–874.

22. W. Fung and D.A. Hsieh, "Hedge Fund Benchmarks: Information Content and Biases," *Journal of Alternative Investments* 58, 2002, pp. 22–34.

23. Malkiel, op. cit., p. 44.

24. B. Liang, "Hedge Funds: The Living and the Dead," *Journal of Financial and Quantitative Analysis* 35, 2000, pp. 309–326.

25. Malkiel, op. cit., p. 44.

26. C. Brooks and H. Kat, "The Statistical Properties of Hedge Fund Index Returns and Their Implications for Investors," *Journal of Alternative Investments* 5, 2002, pp. 25–44.

27. G. Amin and H. Kat, "Welcome to the Dark Side: Hedge Fund Attrition and Survivorship Bias over the Period 1994–2001," *Journal of Alternative Investments* 6, 2003, pp. 57–73.

28. M. Getmansky, A. W. Lo, and Shauna Mei, "Sifting Through the Wreckage: Lessons from Recent Hedge Fund Liquidations," Alpha-Simplex Group, MIT, November 2004, pp. 1–40.

29. Liang, op. cit.

30. Fung and Hsieh, op. cit., p. 7.

31. T. Schneeweiss, H. Kazemi, and G. Martin, "Understanding Hedge Fund Performance: Research Issues Revisited—Part I," *Journal of Alternative Investments* Winter 2002, pp. 6–22.

32. T. Schneeweiss, H. Kazemi, and G. Martin, "Understanding Hedge Fund Performance: Research Issues Revisited—Part II," *Journal of Alternative Investments* Spring 2003, pp. 8–30.

33. S. Mackey, "Expanding the Hedge Fund Universe: Statistical Properties and Survivorship Bias," Ph.D. Dissertation, University of Massachusetts, 2003.

34. Extrapolated from Malkiel, op. cit., p. 44.

35. Fung and Hsieh, op. cit., p. 8.

36. N. Weinberg and B. Condon, "The Sleaziest Show on Earth," available at www.Forbes.com (May 24, 2004).

37. N. Posthuma and P. J. Van der Sluis, "A Reality Check on Hedge Fund Returns," July 8, 2003, pp. 1–38. Available at www.gloriamundi.org.

38. Hedge Fund-Weighted Composite Index. Data available at www.hedgefundresearch.com.

39. T. Schneeweiss and H. Kazemi, "A Check on 'A Check on Hedge Fund Returns,'" in *CISDM Monthly Review*, May 2005, p. 12.

40. Jones, op. cit., p. 3.

41. Markowitz, op. cit., p. 77.

42. T. Schneeweis, R. Gupta, and E. Mustafokulov, "The Benefits of Hedge Funds: 2005 Update," June 2005, pp. 3–4. Available at www.cisdm.org.

43. William F. Sharpe, "Capital Asset Prices: A Theory of Market Equilibrium under Conditions of Risk," *Journal of Finance* 19 (3), 1964, pp. 425–442.

44. HFRI FOF Composite Index. Data available at www.hedgefundresearch.com.

45. Our study on hedge fund performance from 2001 to 2005 relied on data from HFRI and CISDM.

46. Schneeweis, Gupta, and Mustafokulov, op. cit., pp. 1–19.

47. Ibid., p. 11.

48. See Chapter 9 for more.

49. Erin E. Arvedlund, "Spotting a Bayou Before You Step into It: A Checklist for Investors," *Wall Street Journal*, August 31, 2005, p. D1.

50. Amy Borrus, "A Guide to the Hedge Fund Maze," available at www.Businessweek.com, October 19, 2005.

51. C. Johnson, "Appeals Judges Question SEC's Hedge Fund Rule," available at www.washingtonpost.com, December 10, 2005.

52. "Scandals from Afar: Bayou Case and Others Won't Hurt," *Wall Street Journal*, August 31, 2005, p. C1.

53. www.standardandpoors.com/Indices.

CHAPTER 2   The Directional Strategies: Equity Long/Short

1. See Table 2 in B. Malkiel, "Passive Investment Strategies and Inefficient Markets," *European Financial Management* 9, no. 1, 2003, pp. 1–10.

2. Adam Smith, *Supermoney* (New York: Random House, 1972).

3. See www.fraternity-fund.com.

4. Performance or any other data from any funds mentioned in this book are sourced by senior authors as part of Mayer and Hoffman's ongoing selection and due diligence activities and are directly from the funds' own materials.

5. Many newswires, including http://biz.yahoo.com/pz/050518.html.

6. Q3 2005 survey. Available at www.barclaygrp.com.

7. Ibid.

8. Ibid.

9. Meredith Jones, "Strategic Financial Solutions 2005 Hedge Fund Data," Strategic Financial Solutions, December 2005, pp. 1–5.

10. All data from PerTrac and HFRI.

11. www.cisdm.org.

12. www.hedgefundresearch.com.

CHAPTER 3   The Directional Strategies: Managed Futures

1. As of Q3 2005. See www.barclaygrp.com.

2. CISDM Research Department, "The Benefits of Managed Futures: 2005 Update," June 2005. Available at www.cisdm.org.

3. Table 2.1.

4. John Lintner, "The Potential Role of Managed Commodity Financial Futures Accounts in Portfolios of Stocks and Bonds," *Annual Conference of Financial Analysts Federation*, May 1983.

5. H. Kat, "Managed Futures and Hedge Funds: A Match Made in Heaven," Working Paper #14, London: Alternative Investment Research Centre, November 1, 2002, pp. 1–23.

6. CISDM Research Department, "The Benefits of Managed Futures: 2005 Update," June 2005, pp. 1–13. Available at www.cisdm.org.

7. Ibid.

8. Ibid., p. 4.

9. Kat, op. cit., p. 8.

10. All quotes from Bill Dunn are from an interview with Sam Kirschner on 9/14/2005.

11. Table 2.1.

12. All CISDM CTA Indices available at www.cisdm.org.

13. CISDM, op. cit., p. 9.

14. Ibid.

15. Ibid., p. 7.

CHAPTER 4   The Directional Strategies: Global Macro

1. Q3 2005 survey. Available at www.barclaygrp.com.

2. Felix Zulauf, available at www.eubfn.com.

3. All quotes from interview with Renee Haugerud on 4/19/2005 and subsequent dialogue.

4. Peter Ahl, "Global Macro Funds: What Lies Ahead," *AIMA Newsletter*, April 2001, pp. 1–6.

5. R. Warsager, R. Duncan, and K. Wilkens, "A Comparison of Two Hedge Fund Strategies: CTA and Global Macro," *AIMA Journal*, June 2004, pp. 1–5.

6. See Table 2.1.

7. T. Schneeweis, R. Gupta, and E. Mustafokulov, "The Benefits of Hedge Funds: 2005 Update," p. 10. Available at www.cisdm.org.

8. Schneeweiss et al., op. cit., p. 12.

9. See Table 2.2.

10. HFRI, www.hedgefundresearch.com.

CHAPTER 5 The Event-Driven Strategies: Merger Arbitrage, Special Situations

1. Q3 2005 survey. Available at www.barclaygrp.com.
2. In fund materials.
3. Mickey Harley quotes from an interview with Sam Kirschner on 4/18/2005.
4. Andrew Sorkin and Barry Meier, "Rethinking the Cost of a Deal," available at www.nytimes.com/2005/10/19/business.
5. www.hedgefundresearch.com.
6. R. Berner and S. Rutledge, "The Next Warren Buffett," available at www.businessweekonline.com, November 22, 2004.
7. All newswires.
8. G. Zuckerman, "Hedge Funds Stick with Lampert," *Wall Street Journal*, November 15, 2005, pp. C1, C4.
9. See Table 2.1.
10. See Table 12.1 for HFRI rankings.
11. *AP*, reported on www.kansascity.com as "Carl Icahn Drops Suit against Mylan, Hedge Fund," May 31, 2005.
12. For an interesting perspective on these events, see the company's Web site at www.kerr-mcgee.com.
13. Personal communication.

CHAPTER 6 The Event-Driven Strategies: Distressed Securities

1. Interview with Sam Kirschner on 4/15/2005.
2. Interview with Sam Kirschner on 4/18/2005.
3. See Table 2.1.
4. See Table 2.2.
5. See Table 1.3.
6. Ibid.
7. Personal communication with senior authors. Name withheld due to confidentiality.
8. Eldon Mayer.

9. See Lars Jaeger, *Managing Risk in Alternative Investment Strategies* (London: Prentice Hall/*Financial Times*, 2002), pp. 72–73.
10. See Chapter 13 for a more complete analysis of these risks.
11. Personal communication from C. G. E. Manolovici, former director of emerging markets investing at Soros Capital Management.

CHAPTER 7 The Relative Value Arbitrage Strategies: Equity Market Neutral

1. Q3 2005 survey is available at www.barclaygrp.com.
2. For an excellent discussion of the risks in Equity Market Neutral, see Lars Jaeger, *Managing Risk in Alternative Investment Strategies* (London: Prentice Hall/*Financial Times*, 2002), pp. 53–60.
3. See Table 2.1.
4. Ibid.
5. See Table 2.2.
6. In "Stable Value and Market Neutral Funds," *Strategic Insight Overview* 13, 2002, p. 5. Available at www.stablevalue.org.

CHAPTER 8 Convertible Arbitrage

1. Q3 2005 survey is available at www.barclaygrp.com.
2. Eldon Mayer's story is from his days at his predecessor firm, Lynch & Mayer in New York.
3. Nick Calamos, *Convertible Arbitrage: Insights and Techniques for Investing* (New York: John Wiley & Sons, 2003).
4. J. McWhinney, "Headline Grabbing Hedge Fund Failure," available at www.investopedia.com.
5. Lars Jaeger, *Managing Risk in Alternative Investment Strategies* (London: Prentice Hall/*Financial Times*, 2002), pp. 42–44.
6. Thomas Schneeweis, Raj Gupta, and Erkin Mustafokulov, "The Benefits of Hedge Funds: 2005 Update," June 2005, pp. 1–19. Available at www.CISDM.org.
7. See Table 2.1.
8. See Table 2.2.

9. Mickey Harley, "Views on the Future of the Event Driven Hedge Fund Market." Available at www.eubfn.com/arts/hedge_harley.

10. All CBOE VIX data from 1990–present is available at www.cboe.com.

11. Scott Lange, Adrianna Roitstein, and Dan Sommers, "What Is Ailing the US Convertible Market, Part II?" Goldman Sachs Research Paper, June 2004, p. 21.

12. Dane Hamilton, "Goldman to Drop Convert Arb Hedge Fund Index," available at www.reuters.com, December 19, 2005.

13. Greg Jensen, Noah Yechiely, and Jason Rotenberg, "Hedge Funds Selling Beta as Alpha," *Bridgewater Daily Observations*, May 24, 2005, pp. 2–3.

14. For an excellent discussion of risks read, Lars Jaeger, *Managing Risk in Alternative Investment Strategies* (London: Prentice Hall/*Financial Times*, 2002), pp. 44–48.

CHAPTER 9   Fixed Income Arbitrage

1. Quotes and other source material taken from Roger Lowenstein, *When Genius Failed* (New York: Random House, 2001).

2. www.hedgefund.net.

3. See HFRI rankings in Table 12.1.

4. *HFRI Industry Report*, 2005.

5. Ibid.

6. *The European Banking and Finance News Network*, cited in "Observations on the Rapid Growth of the Hedge Fund Industry," p. 6. Available at www.barcap.com/hedgefunds.

7. J. Liu, op. cit., pp. 3–13.

8. Eugene Fama, "Efficient Capital Markets II," *Journal of Finance* 46, December 1991, p. 1575.

9. Lars Jaeger, *Managing Risk in Alternative Investment Strategies* (London: Prentice Hall/*Financial Times*, 2002), pp. 51–53.

10. See Table 2.1.

11. See Table 2.2.

12. Jun Liu and Francis A. Longstaff, op. cit.

13. Roger Lowenstein, op. cit.

14. http://www.erisk.com/Learning/CaseStudies/ref_case_ltcm.asp.
15. Much has been written about LTCM. In particular, we also drew from Thayer Watkins, *Summary of the Nature of LTCM*, San Jose State University. Available at http://www2.sjsu.edu/faculty/watkins/ltcm.htm.
16. HFRI Fixed Income Arb Index was down 10.3 percent in 1998, its worst showing since inception in 1990.
17. See EIRNS Press Release on Freddie Mac and David Askin, June 11, 2003. Available at www.larouchepub.com/pr/2003.
18. Vinod Kothari, "The Securitization Hall of Shame." Available at www.vinodkothari.com/sadepisodes.
19. For an analysis of this and other risks faced by MBS traders, see the Web site of the large MBS Arb hedge fund Ellington Management Group at www.ellington.com/mbs.
20. Fed fund rate increases and decreases available at http://library.hsh.com/?row_id=88.

CHAPTER 10   The Newer Strategies

1. Pete Gallo, "New Alternatives Emerge, but Are They Hedge Funds?" *Absolute Return* magazine, June 2005, p. 32.
2. Personal communication with senior authors.
3. Gallo, op. cit., p. 32.
4. Information on the EU plan is available at www.umwelt-schweiz.ch.
5. For more information on this area go to www.hedgeworld.com.
6. Quoted in Jessica Holzer, "Hedges Jump into Oil Company Lending," *Houston Chronicle*, December 22, 2005.
7. Ibid.
8. See www.sagientresearch.com for placement tracker stats.
9. Ibid.
10. Ibid.
11. Some direct financing funds do not fit under the Reg D banner and therefore Hennessee Group has launched a new Index to better cover the space. Available at www.hennesseegroup.com.
12. In *SBBI 2005 Yearbook* (New York: Ibbotson Associates, 2005), Table 8-7, p. 156.

13. Matthew Goldstein, "SEC Short Sale Probe Turns to Gryphon Partners," available at www.TheStreet.com, November 3, 2005.

14. See www.sagientresearch.com.

15. Matthew Goldstein, "Hedge Fund Feasts on Famine," available at www.TheStreet.com, January 3, 2006.

CHAPTER 11   The Search for Alpha

1. William F. Sharpe, "Capital Asset Prices: A Theory of Market Equilibrium under Conditions of Risk," *Journal of Finance* 19 (3), 1964, pp. 425–442.

2. Thomas Schneeweiss, "Alpha, Alpha, Whose [*sic*] Got the Alpha?" October 5, 1999, pp. 1–4. Paper is available at www.cisdm.org.

3. Eugene Fama, "Efficient Capital Markets II," *Journal of Finance, 46*, December 1991, p. 1575.

4. For example, Schneeweiss, op. cit., and Lars Jaeger, *Managing Risk in Alternative Investment Strategies* (London: Prentice Hall/*Financial Times*, 2002), pp. 24–31.

5. Jaeger, op. cit., p. 24.

6. Stephen A. Ross, "The Arbitrage Theory of Capital Asset Pricing," *Journal of Economic Theory*, December 1976, pp. 341–360.

7. G. Huberman, "A Simple Approach to Arbitrage Pricing Theory," *Journal of Economic Theory*, October 1982, pp. 183–191; R. Roll and S. A. Ross, "An Empirical Investigation of the Arbitrage Pricing Theory," *Journal of Finance* 5, 1980, pp. 1073–1103; Richard Roll and Stephen A. Ross, "The Arbitrage Pricing Theory Approach to Strategic Portfolio Planning," *Financial Analysts Journal*, May/June 1984, pp. 14–26.

8. Ross, 1976, op. cit.

9. T. Schneeweiss, H. Kazemi, and G. Martin, "Understanding Hedge Fund Performance," November 2001. Available at www.cisdm.org.

10. Ibid and in CISDM Working Paper on Persistence, 2003. Available at www.cisdm.org.

11. C. Asness, R. Krail, and J. Liew, "Do Hedge Funds Hedge?" *Journal of Portfolio Management* 28, 2001, pp. 6–19.

12. Clifford Asness, "An Alternative Future: Part II," *Journal of Portfolio Management, Thirtieth Anniversary Issue*, 2004, pp. 94–103; *Journal of Portfolio Management*, Fall 2004, pp. 8–23.

13. W. Fung and David A. Hsieh, "Hedge Fund Benchmarks: A Risk Based Approach," *Financial Analysts Journal* 60, September/October 2004, pp. 65–80.

14. Robert Kosowski, Narayan Naik, and Melvyn Teo, "Is Stellar Hedge Fund Performance for Real?" February 2005, pp. 1–37. Available at www.ssrn.com.

15. Roger Ibbotson and Peng Chen, "Sources of Hedge Fund Returns: Alphas, Betas and Costs," Working Paper, Yale International Center for Finance, August 2005, pp. 1–22. Available at www.ssrn.com.

16. P. Jen, C. Heasman, and K. Boyatt, "Alternative Asset Strategies: Early Performance in Hedge Fund Managers." New York: Lazard, November 2001, pp. 1–10; Tremont Partners, Inc. and Tass Investment Research, Ltd., "Case for Hedge Funds," New York: September 2000; www.hedgefundresearch.com.

17. T. Schneeweiss, H. Kazemi, and G. Martin, "Understanding Hedge Fund Performance: Research Issues Revisited—Part I," *Journal of Alternative Investments*, Winter 2002, pp. 6–22; T. Schneeweiss, H. Kazemi, and G. Martin, "Understanding Hedge Fund Performance: Research Issues Revisited—Part II," *Journal of Alternative Investments*, Spring 2003, pp. 8–30.

18. M. Lamm, "Why Not 100% Hedge Funds? Still a Viable Approach," *Journal of Investing* 13, 2004, p. 12; CrossBorder Capital. "The Young Ones," *Absolute Return Fund Research*, London, April 2001, pp. 1–7; B. Liang, "Hedge Funds Performance: 1990 to 1999." *Financial Analysts Journal* 57, January/February 2001, pp. 11–18.; Jen, Heasman, and Boyatt, op. cit.; W. Fung and D. Hsieh, "Performance Characteristics of Hedge Funds and Commodity Funds: Natural vs. Spurious Bases," *Journal of Financial & Quantitative Analysis* 35, 2000, pp. 291–307.

19. Fung and Hsieh, op. cit.

20. Schneeweiss, op. cit.

21. Kosowski, op. cit.

22. Meredith Jones, "Strategic Financial Solutions 2005 Hedge Fund Data," Strategic Financial Solutions, December 2005, pp. 1–5.

23. S. Kirschner and R. Panzier, "The Class of 2003 Revisited," Unpublished Mayer & Hoffman Capital Advisors White Paper, February 2006; S. Kirschner, M. Hoffman, and R. Panzier, "The Search for Alpha: Investing in Newer Hedge Funds," *MFA Reporter*, November 2005.

24. Infovest21, LLC. "Due Diligence Suggestions on Managers without Track Records," New York: Infovest 21 White Paper, April 2005, pp. 1–2.

25. In *Alternative Investment News*, January 9, 2006, p. 2.

26. M. Getmansky, A. W. Lo, and Shauna Mei, "Sifting through the Wreckage: Lessons from Recent Hedge Fund Liquidations," Alpha-Simplex Group, MIT, November 2004, pp. 14–16.

27. M. J. Howell, "Fund Age and Performance," *Journal of Alternative Investments* 4, 2001, pp. 57–60.

28. Ibid.

29. C. Brooks and H. Kat, "The Statistical Properties of Hedge Fund Index Returns and Their Implications for Investors," *Journal of Alternative Investments* 5, 2002, pp. 25–44.

30. Jen, Heasman, and Boyatt, op. cit.

31. C. Ackermann, R. McEnally, and D. Ravenscraft, "The Performance of Hedge Funds: Risk, Return, and Incentives," *Journal of Finance* 54, June 1999, pp. 833–874.

32. Hedge Fund Research, "Emerging Manager Out-performance: Alpha Opportunities from the Industry's Newest Hedge Fund Managers," Chicago: HFR White Paper, July 2005, pp. 1–8.

33. S. Feffer and C. Kundro, "Understanding and Mitigating Operational Risk in Hedge Fund Investment," The Capital Markets Company Ltd. White Paper, 2003.

CHAPTER 12 Funds of Hedge Funds

1. Fund details and monthly reports available at www.meespierson.com.

2. Losses do occur, however, when an FOF invests in a blow-up as we detailed in Chapter 7.

3. See note 22 below for studies.

4. Meredith Jones, "Strategic Financial Solutions 2005 Hedge Fund Database Study," December 2005. Also Barclay Group Q3, 2005 survey. Available at www.barclaygrp.com.

5. Jones, ibid.

6. Ibid.

7. Permal was acquired by Legg Mason on November 3, 2005.

8. See www.epn-magazine.com, June 2004.

9. Various databases including hedgefund.net and eurekahedge.net.

10. Survey conducted by Greenwich Associates, February 2005.

11. See Table 9.1.

12. HFRI FOF Composite Index. Data available at www.hedgefund research.com.

13. Table 9.1.

14. See Table 2.1.

15. W. Fung and D. A. Hsieh, "Hedge Fund Benchmarks: Information Content and Biases," *Journal of Alternative Investments* 58, 2002, pp. 22–34.

16. Op. cit. and in citation immediately following.

17. W. Fung and D. A. Hsieh, "Performance Characteristics of Hedge Funds and Commodity Funds: Natural vs. Spurious Biases," *Journal of Financial & Quantitative Analysis* 35, 2000, pp. 291–307.

18. See Table 2 in B. Malkiel, "Passive Investment Strategies and Inefficient Markets," *European Financial Management* 9, no. 1, 2003, pp. 1–10.

19. T. Schneeweis, R. Gupta, and E. Mustafokulov, "The Benefits of Hedge Funds: 2005 Update." Available at www.cisdm.org.

20. B. Wintner, "How Many Hedge Funds Are Needed to Create a Diversified Fund of Funds?" Asset Alliance Corporation, March 2001, pp. 1–9.

21. Ibid.

22. Thomas Henker, "Naïve Diversification for Hedge Funds," *Journal of Alternative Assets*, Winter 1998, pp. 33–38. J. Park and J. Staum, "Fund of Funds Diversification: How Much Is Enough?" *Journal of Alternative Investments*, Winter 1998, pp. 39–42.

23. Meredith Jones, op. cit., p. 3.

24. As of June 30, 2005. See K. Beer, "Dean of Investing," *Bloomberg Markets*, January 2006. The story includes asset allocation chart from Yale.
25. HFRI.
26. See studies cited in Chapter 11.

CHAPTER 13   Due Diligence Best Practices

1. The Alternative Investment Management Association (AIMA), "AIMA's Illustrative Questionnaire for Due Diligence of Hedge Fund Managers, pp. 1–31, January 2002. Available at www.aima.org.
2. John Mauldin, *Bull's Eye Investing* (New York: John Wiley & Sons, 2004), pp. 337–357.
3. A good firm for outsourced due diligence is Event Capital Markets. Contact Robert Krause at www.hedgefundduediligence.com.
4. F. A. Sortino and L. N. Price, "Performance Measurement in a Downside Risk Framework," *Journal of Investing* 3 (3), pp. 50–58.
5. See, for example, two comprehensive review papers on the topic, G. Amin and H. Kat, "Stocks, Bonds, and Hedge Funds: Not a Free Lunch," *Journal of Portfolio Management* 29, 2003; and B. Malkiel and A. Saha, "Hedge Funds: Risk and Return," Center for Economic Policy Research, Princeton University, 2004.
6. For a robust review of hedge fund return distributions, including skewness and kurtosis for each strategy, see Mark J. P. Anson's *Handbook for Alternative Assets* (New York: John Wiley & Sons, 2002), pp. 93–121. See also C. Keating and W. F. Shadwick, "An Introduction to Omega," The Finance Development Centre Limited, 2002.
7. Keating and Shadwick.
8. S. Feffer and C. Kundro, "Understanding and Mitigating Operational Risk in Hedge Fund Investments." Working Paper, The Capital Markets Company Limited, 2003.

EPILOGUE

1. HFRI data cited by its founder, Joseph Nicholas in *Investing in Hedge Funds* (Princeton: Bloomberg Press, 1999), pp. 2–4.
2. Ibid. and the HFRI Industry Report, Q4, 2003.

3. Here we follow the schema of the developmental psychologist, Daniel Levinson in *The Seasons of a Man's Life* (New York: Ballantine Books, 1978), pp. 71–135. Also, *The Seasons of a Woman's Life* (New York: Ballantine Books, 1996), pp. 69–116.
4. HFRI, op. cit.
5. Levinson, op. cit.
6. Meredith Jones, "Strategic Financial Solutions 2005 Hedge Fund Database Study," December 2005. Also Barclay Group Q3, 2005 survey. Available at www.barclaygrp.com.
7. Greenwich Associates 2005 survey cited in Chapter 1 and the Russell Investment Group's "The 2005–2006 Russell Survey on Alternative Investing," pp. 1–12.
8. We have been confronted by these consequences at Mayer & Hoffman Capital Advisors.
9. See Table 1.3 in Chapter 1.
10. Read the debate between Siegel and Grantham in John Mauldin *Bull's Eye Investing* (New York: John Wiley & Sons, 2004), pp. 39–45.
11. Asness, op. cit.
12. Greenwich Associates and Russell Surveys, op. cit.
13. The Tower Group report in www.fundstreet.org/2005/10/hedge_fund_asset.html.

BIBLIOGRAPHY

Ackermann, C., R. McEnally, and D. Ravenscraft. "The Performance of Hedge Funds: Risk, Return, and Incentives." *Journal of Finance* 54 (June 1999).

Ahl, Peter. "Global Macro Funds: What Lies Ahead." *AIMA Newsletter* (April 2001).

The Alternative Investment Management Association (AIMA). "AIMA's Illustrative Questionnaire for Due Diligence of Hedge Fund Managers." (January 2002). Available at www.aima.org.

Amin, G., and H. Kat. "Stocks, Bonds, and Hedge Funds: Not a Free Lunch." *Journal of Portfolio Management* 29 (2003).

Amin, G., and H. Kat. "Welcome to the Dark Side: Hedge Fund Attrition and Survivorship Bias over the Period 1994–2001." *Journal of Alternative Investments* 6 (2003).

Anson, Mark J. P. *Handbook for Alternative Assets.* New York: John Wiley & Sons, 2002.

Arvedlund, Erin E. "Spotting a Bayou Before You Step into It: A Checklist for Investors," *Wall Street Journal* (August 31, 2005).

Asness, Clifford. "An Alternative Future: Part II." *Journal of Portfolio Management, Thirtieth Anniversary Issue* (2004).

Asness, Clifford. "An Alternative Future: Part II." *Journal of Portfolio Management* (Fall 2004).

Asness, C., R. Krail, and J. Liew. "Do Hedge Funds Hedge?" *Journal of Portfolio Management* 28 (2001).

Associated Press, reported on KansasCity.com and various other newswires. "Carl Icahn Drops Suit against Mylan, Hedge Fund." (May 31, 2005).

Atlas, Riva. "Pension Plans Pouring Billion into Hedge Funds." Available at www.nytimes.com (November 27, 2003).

The Barclay Group, Ltd. "Q3 2005 Asset Flow Survey." Available at www.barclaygrp.com.

Beer, K. "Dean of Investing." *Bloomberg Markets* (January 2006).

Berner, R., and S. Rutledge. "The Next Warren Buffett." Available at www.businessweekonline.com (November 22, 2004).

Borrus, Amy. "A Guide to the Hedge Fund Maze." Available at www.Businessweek.com (October 19, 2005).

Brooks, C., and H. Kat. "The Statistical Properties of Hedge Fund Index Returns and Their Implications for Investors." *Journal of Alternative Investments* 5 (2002).

Calamos, Nick. *Convertible Arbitrage: Insights and Techniques for Investing.* New York: John Wiley & Sons, 2003.

CISDM Research Department. "The Benefits of Managed Futures: 2005 Update." (June 2005). Available at www.cisdm.org.

CrossBorder Capital. "The Young Ones." *Absolute Return Fund Research*, London (April 2001).

Fama, Eugene. "Efficient Capital Markets II." *Journal of Finance* 46 (December 1991).

Feffer, S., and C. Kundro. "Understanding and Mitigating Operational Risk in Hedge Fund Investment." The Capital Markets Company Ltd., White Paper (2003).

Fung, W., and David A. Hsieh. "Hedge Fund Benchmarks: A Risk Based Approach." *Financial Analysts Journal* 60 (September/October 2004).

Fung, W., and D. A. Hsieh. "Hedge Fund Benchmarks: Information Content and Biases." *Journal of Alternative Investments* 58 (2002).

Fung, W., and D. A. Hsieh. "Performance Characteristics of Hedge Funds and Commodity Funds: Natural vs. Spurious Biases." *Journal of Financial & Quantitative Analysis* 35 (2000).

Getmansky, M., A. W. Lo, and Shauna Mei. "Sifting Through the Wreckage: Lessons from Recent Hedge Fund Liquidations." Alpha-Simplex Group, MIT (November 2004).

Goldstein, Matthew. "SEC Short Sale Probe Turns to Gryphon Partners." Available at www.TheStreet.com (November 3, 2005).

Greenwich Associates. "Asset Allocation Strategies Target Incremental Alpha." Greenwich, CT. Survey (February 2005).

Hamilton, Dane. "Goldman to Drop Convert Arb Hedge Fund Index." Available at www.reuters.com (December 19, 2005).

Harley, Mickey. "Views on the Future of the Event Driven Hedge Fund Market." Available at www.eubfn.com/arts/hedge_harley.

Hedge Fund Research. "Emerging Manager Out-performance: Alpha Opportunities from the Industry's Newest Hedge Fund Managers." Chicago: HFR White Paper (July 2005).

Henker, Thomas. "Naïve Diversification for Hedge Funds." *Journal of Alternative Assets* (Winter 1998).

HFR Industry Report, Q4, 2005.

Holzer, Jessica. "Hedges Jump into Oil Company Lending." *Houston Chronicle* (December 22, 2005).

Huberman, G. "A Simple Approach to Arbitrage Pricing Theory." *Journal of Economic Theory* (October 1982).

Ibbotson, Roger, and Peng Chen. "Sources of Hedge Fund Returns: Alphas, Betas and Costs." Working Paper, Yale School of Management (August 2005). Available at www.ssrn.com.

Infovest21, LLC. "Due Diligence Suggestions on Managers without Track Records." New York: Infovest21 White Paper (April 2005).

Institute for Private Investors, New York, Survey, 2005.

Jaeger, Lars. *Managing Risk in Alternative Investment Strategies.* London: Prentice Hall/*Financial Times*, 2002.

Jen, P., C. Heasman, and K. Boyatt. *Alternative Asset Strategies: Early Performance in Hedge Fund Managers.* New York: Lazard, 2001.

Jensen, Greg, Noah Yechiely, and Jason Rotenberg. "Hedge Funds Selling Beta as Alpha." *Bridgewater Daily Observations* (May 24, 2005).

Johnson, C. "Appeals Judges Question SEC's Hedge Fund Rule." Available at www.washingtonpost.com (December 10, 2005).

Jones, Meredith. "Strategic Financial Solutions 2005 Hedge Fund Database." *Strategic Financial Solutions* (December 2005).

Kat, Harry. "Managed Futures and Hedge Funds: A Match Made in Heaven." Working Paper #14, London: Alternative Investment Research Centre (November 1, 2002).

Keating, Lon, and W. F. Shadwick. "An Introduction to Omega." The Finance Development Centre Limited, 2002.

Kirschner, S., and R. Panzier. "The Class of 2003 Revisited." Unpublished, Mayer & Hoffman Capital Advisors White Paper (February 2006).

Kirschner, S., M. Hoffman, and R. Panzier. "The Search for Alpha: Investing in Newer Hedge Funds." *MFA Reporter* (November 2005).

Kosowski, Robert, Narayan Naik, and Melvyn Teo. "Is Stellar Hedge Fund Performance for Real?" (February 2005). Available at www.ssrn.com.

Kothari, Vinod. "The Securitization Hall of Shame." Available at www .vinodkothari.com/sadepisodes.

Lamm, M. "Why Not 100% Hedge Funds? Still a Viable Approach." *Journal of Investing* 13 (2004).

Lange, Scott, Adrianna Roitstein, and Dan Sommers. "What Is Ailing the US Convertible Market, Part II?" Goldman Sachs Research Paper (June 2004).

Levinson, Daniel. *The Seasons of a Man's Life*. New York: Ballantine Books, 1978.

Levinson, Daniel. *The Seasons of a Woman's Life*. New York: Ballantine Books, 1996.

Liang, B. "Hedge Funds Performance: 1990 to 1999." *Financial Analysts Journal* (January/February 2001).

Liang, B. "Hedge Funds: The Living and the Dead." *Journal of Financial and Quantitative Analysis* 35 (2000).

Lintner, John. "The Potential Role of Managed Commodity Financial Futures Accounts in Portfolios of Stocks and Bonds." *Annual Conference of Financial Analysts Federation* (May 1983).

Lowenstein, Roger. *When Genius Failed*. New York: Random House, 2001.

Mackey, S. "Expanding the Hedge Fund Universe: Statistical Properties and Survivorship Bias." Ph.D. dissertation, University of Massachusetts (2003).

Malkiel, B. "Passive Investment Strategies and Inefficient Markets." *European Financial Management* (2003).

Malkiel, B., and A. Saha. "Hedge Funds: Risk and Return." Center for Economic Policy Research, Princeton University (December 1, 2004).

Markowitz, Harry M. "Portfolio Selections." *Journal of Finance* (July 1, 1952).

Mauldin, John. *Bull's Eye Investing*. New York: John Wiley & Sons, 2004.

McWhinney, J. "Headline Grabbing Hedge Fund Failures." Available at www.investopedia.com.

NACUBO. "2005 NACUBO Endowment Study." (February 2006).

Nicholas, Joseph. *Investing in Hedge Funds.* Princeton, NJ: Bloomberg Press, 1999.

Park, J., and J. Staum. "Fund of Funds Diversification: How Much Is Enough?" *Journal of Alternative Investments* (Winter 1998).

Posthuma, N., and P. J. Van der Sluis. "A Reality Check on Hedge Fund Returns." (July 8, 2003). Available at www.gloriamundi.org.

Roll, R., and S. A. Ross. "An Empirical Investigation of the Arbitrage Pricing Theory." *Journal of Finance* 5 (1980).

Roll, Richard, and Stephen A. Ross. "The Arbitrage Pricing Theory Approach to Strategic Portfolio Planning." *Financial Analysts Journal* (May/June 1984).

Ross, Stephen A. "The Arbitrage Theory of Capital Asset Pricing." *Journal of Economic Theory* (December 1976).

Russell Investment Group. "The 2005–2006 Russell Survey on Alternative Investing." The Tower Group Report. Reported in www.undstreet.org/2005/10/hedge_fund_asset.html.

SBBI 2005 Yearbook. New York: Ibbotson Associates, 2005.

Schneeweiss, Thomas. "Alpha, Alpha, Whose [*sic*] Got the Alpha?" (October 5, 1999). Available at www.cisdm.org.

Schneeweiss, T., and H. Kazemi. "A Check on Hedge Fund Returns." *CISDM Monthly Review* (May 2005).

Schneeweis, T., R. Gupta, and E. Mustafokulov. "The Benefits of Hedge Funds: 2005 Update." (June 2005). Available at www.cisdm.org.

Schneeweiss, T., H. Kazemi, and G. Martin. "Understanding Hedge Fund Performance." (November 2001). Available at www.cisdm.org.

Schneeweiss, T., H. Kazemi, and G. Martin. "Understanding Hedge Fund Performance: Research Issues Revisited—Part I." *Journal of Alternative Investments* (Winter 2002).

Schneeweiss, T., H. Kazemi, and G. Martin. "Understanding Hedge Fund Performance: Research Issues Revisited—Part II." *Journal of Alternative Investments* (Spring 2003).

Sharpe, William F. "Adjusting for Risk in Portfolio Performance Measurement." *Journal of Portfolio Management* (Winter 1975).

Sharpe, William F. "Capital Asset Prices: A Theory of Market Equilibrium under Conditions of Risk." *Journal of Finance* 19 (3) (1964).

Smith, Adam. *Supermoney.* New York: Random House, 1972.

Sorkin, Andrew, and Barry Meier. "Rethinking the Cost of a Deal." Available at www.nytimes.com/2005/10/19/business.

Sortino, F. A., and L. N. Price. "Performance Measurement in a Downside Risk Framework." *Journal of Investing* 3, (3) (1994).

Strategic Insight Mutual Fund Research and Consulting, LLC. "Stable Value and Market Neutral Funds." *Strategic Insight Overview* 13 (2000). Available at www.stablevalue.org.

The European Banking and Finance News Network. Cited in "Observations on the Rapid Growth of the Hedge Fund Industry." Available at www.barcap.com/hedgefunds.

Tremont Partners, Inc., and Tass Investment Research, Ltd. "Case for Hedge Funds." London and New York, September 2000.

Tremont/Tass Asset Flows Report, 2003.

Warsager, R., R. Duncan, and K. Wilkens. "A Comparison of Two Hedge Fund Strategies: CTA and Global Macro." *AIMA Journal* (June 2004).

Watkins, Thayer. "Summary of the Nature of LTCM." San Jose State University. Available at http://www2.sjsu.edu/faculty/watkins/ltcm.htm.

Weinberg, N., and B. Condon. "The Sleaziest Show on Earth." Available at www. Forbes.com (May 24, 2004).

Wintner, B. "How Many Hedge Funds Are Needed to Create a Diversified Fund of Funds?" Asset Alliance Corporation (March, 2001).

Zuckerman, G. "Hedge Funds Stick with Lampert." *Wall Street Journal* (November 15, 2005).

ABOUT THE AUTHORS

Sam Kirschner, Ph.D., is a Founder and Managing Director of Mayer & Hoffman Capital Advisors, LLC, an investment management company specializing in funds of emerging/newer hedge funds. He has co-authored six books, including *Venture Capital: The Definitive Guide for Entrepreneurs, Investors, and Professionals* (John Wiley & Sons, 2001).

Dr. Kirschner comes to the alternative investment field via a long and distinguished career as a management consultant and psychologist specializing in closely held firms. He is an adjunct faculty member at New York University, Division of Business and Legal Studies, and has also served as an adjunct faculty member at The Wharton School, Division of Family Business Studies. He has served on the boards of a number of private and publicly held companies and not-for-profit institutions. Dr. Kirschner's major areas of expertise are succession and estate planning in family firms, mergers and acquisitions, and creating family offices.

Dr. Kirschner's clients have included SunTrust Bank, Bank of Scotland, Bristol & West, Computer Science Corporation, Prudential Fox & Roach Real Estate, Focus Pointe, Schaad Family Properties, and two Forbes 400 families.

Eldon C. Mayer Jr. is a Founder and Senior Managing Member of Mayer & Hoffman Capital Advisors, LLC. He graduated from Princeton University with a degree in economics and served as an officer in the U.S. Marine Corps. After four years in sales at Kidder, Peabody & Co. he became a partner at J. M. Hartwell & Co., where he was a Senior Portfolio Manager and Director of Research. He also managed a top-performing private hedge fund, and created, arranged for the public offering of, and managed the first mutual fund to operate as a hedge fund, the Hartwell and Campbell Leverage Fund. Mr. Mayer then became Managing Partner of Winton Company, where from 1970 to 1976 he managed a private investment partnership, accomplishing high/top decile performance over this span of years.

In 1976, he founded Lynch & Mayer, Inc., an asset management firm catering to institutions as well as high-net-worth individuals. Lynch & Mayer's investment performance ranked near the top of its peer group as its assets grew to $7 billion. In addition to serving as Chairman, CEO, and CIO, he managed both institutional growth equity and hedge fund portfolios.

Lee Kessler is a business writer specializing in financial software systems. He has served on several development teams creating hedge fund accounting software and most recently participated in the development of a Web-based system for trading commercial paper and other fixed income instruments. He has also served as a consultant at MasterCard International and Reuters Analytics.

INDEX